99

PROBLEMS

AND

FREEDOM

IS ONE

GLYNIS GLASGOW-KELLY

BALBOA.PRESS
A DIVISION OF HAY HOUSE

Balboa Press books may be ordered through booksellers or by contacting:

Balboa Press
A Division of Hay House
1663 Liberty Drive
Bloomington, IN 47403
www.balboapress.co.uk
UK TFN: 0800 0148647 (Toll Free inside the UK)
UK Local: 02036 956325 (+44 20 3695 6325 from outside the UK)

Because of the dynamic nature of the Internet, any web addresses or links contained in this book may have changed since publication and may no longer be valid. The views expressed in this work are solely those of the author and do not necessarily reflect the views of the publisher, and the publisher hereby disclaims any responsibility for them.

The author of this book does not dispense medical advice or prescribe the use of any technique as a form of treatment for physical, emotional, or medical problems without the advice of a physician, either directly or indirectly. The intent of the author is only to offer information of a general nature to help you in your quest for emotional and spiritual well-being. In the event you use any of the information in this book for yourself, which is your constitutional right, the author and the publisher assume no responsibility for your actions.

Any people depicted in stock imagery provided by Getty Images are models, and such images are being used for illustrative purposes only. Certain stock imagery © Getty Images.

Print information available on the last page.

ISBN: 978-1-9822-8210-3 (sc)
ISBN: 978-1-9822-8211-0 (e)

Balboa Press rev. date: 08/20/2020

Contents

Chapter 1

FREEDOM

Individual freedom. Freedom of expression. Sexual freedom. Religious freedom. Political freedom. Media freedom. Internet freedom. Economic freedom. Freedom of speech.

Freedom is the foundation on which Western culture is built and one of its biggest problems. This bastion of western cultural ideology, championed as supreme, worshipped as a universal good also shackles its citizens to capitalism. Western culture owes its freedom to Plato whose ideas foreshadowed democracy, materialism, class, History and of course intellectual thought. This enlightenment has been the doorway to capitalist thinking labelled perfectly by the Orwellian slogan- freedom is slavery. This curious paradox of Western cultural democracy states that you are born free yet everywhere you are chained to capitalism. You must work in order to survive. You must pay taxes. You must spend money. You must also embrace the infrastructure of this slavery – ideas, values, beliefs, policies that have morphed into the capitalist system secured nationally by the mechanism of the establishment. Consequently, western cultural thought is controlled by this totalitarian ideological position with the Statue lauding over the brave worshippers in the spiritual homeland.

This way of thinking develops into the structural design which positions individuals perfectly in their respective classifications with those of inherited privilege powerfully placed at the top. Political, intellectual and financial power all divide and secure the separate substructures. Education ensures that the infrastructure is maintained with children being indoctrinated with the belief that class defines self-worth, self-esteem and self-fulfilment. People in the lower area are encouraged to be upwardly mobile because such aspirations would bring power and privilege which ultimately leads to happiness. This kind of thinking leads parents to spend absolute fortunes for private education or rather the purchase of class and others slavishly take huge financial and moral risks to move themselves and their families up the social ladder.

The problem with capitalist thinking is that implicitly and explicitly it promotes the view that money matters more than morals, more than other people and crucially more than community. Capitalist thinking has globalised the false truth that money can buy everything and anything. Essentially, to be successful as a capitalist thinker, you must be individualistic rather than altruistic; you must be egoistic to the point of being narcissistic. Not only that but you must be doggedly determined to eat other dogs in your relentless pursuit of capital in a fiercely competitive free market.

This free market ideal has been sold to the young generation who are growing up knowing the price of everything and the value of nothing. Their parents come from the generation of 'there is no such thing as society, only the individual' and this way of thinking has given birth to a rather peculiar species of self-gratification. The moral fabric of society has been destroyed and the traditional moral leaders have all been converted: politicians have been persuaded by lobbyists; bankers have risked everything for the faith and sadly religious leaders have sold their souls spreading this gospel on their mounts. How can this global crusade be stopped or even slowed down?

Historically, the crusaders have not learnt the lessons of the past and it is now a real threat to both the present and the future. The idea that money and power can secure supreme intelligence, supreme security and supreme global stability has proved to be fundamentally flawed. Many veterans have sacrificed their lives trying to defeat conflicting ideologies but there needs to be a concerted effort to win hearts and minds here. Orwell's *1984*, was meant to be a warning but has turned into a global political manifesto as we are being convinced on a daily basis that war is peace, that ignorance is strength and most of all that this slavery is freedom. The shackles must be removed from our minds and there must be an abolition of this global trade of capitalising on ignorance.

How can Western cultural thinkers address the tyranny of capitalism? How can slavery be abolished and replaced by freedom? Should western intelligence services think of an alternative to capitalism? With Chinese success on the rise, should the West consider their practices? How can Western minds be free from this form of slavery?

Freedom or Mental Slavery

The fact that the West offers no reasoning model outside capitalism is not the problem of freedom for the black community. Our problem is that we fail to acknowledge that freedom of mind is a prerequisite for any other concept of freedom. Declaring the body free is easier than having mental freedom but we have consumed the capitalist concept of freedom without filtering it first. Historically, western capitalist thinkers operate from a position of financial and political privilege that gives them the power to pass laws to forward the capitalist agenda in every field from education to politics. These have

3

given them structural advantage to declare laws to ensure the mind programming of slavery worded as freedom.

We need to free our minds so that we can think as a collective, as a community rather than as individuals because of our disadvantaged position in society. Anyone can beat Usain Bolt on his sprint race if they start 10 cm from the finish line. Western capitalist thinkers are hovering around the 10cm privileged position and they will always win from there. To avoid our children making a false start in life, we need freedom of mind to change the way we think about the race of life. Collectively, we need to think not only for individual success but also about holistic black cultural success. It is not possible for us to be quintessentially capitalist in ideology because our culture does not have the bank of capital to do so. This is why it is important to consider the rastafari rejection of Babylon (capitalist thinking) at least to some degree.

Since colonisation, we have uncritically embraced western culture and refrained from rebelling against elements of its ideology. We have not questioned the laws, the values, the policies, the very education system itself which is essentially an education of domination. No legislation has been passed to comprehensively repair the mental damage to our collective psyche left by the act of Slavery. We cannot pass laws to introduce a comprehensive supplementary education for reparation because we are not in a privileged position of power to do so. Hence, the lingering effects of mental slavery continues to affect how we think about each other, about our culture and most importantly, about ourselves. Many movements and community groups try to provide education for our people but not on the holistic scale that is required for complete reparation.

Nothing has been examined comprehensively since slavery – not the origin of our food choices, not our family practices, not our religion, not our history and not our solidarity issues. A lack of freedom to think differently has plagued our black culture and is now costing us hundreds of millions in capital. We have to start thinking clearly about family life, education, food and other life choices if we are to halt the series of interconnected problems being caused. If we look at all of the other problems that affect our community, the slavery of the mind contributes to the vast majority of them.

Let's trace the historical underpinnings of this mental slavery. Colonisation was a process that involved the systematic cultivation of the minds of the slaves. Slaves were not taught to think, not taught to reason, not taught to be rational – they were only taught to obey. For generations, this shackled thinking evolved from obedience to authority to seeing one perspective, one viewpoint – that of the authority figure, that of the oppressor. The slave culture continues as some black people still believe that being critical is being disrespectful. This thinking has been embedded as we have been conditioned to obey the one in authority – the parent, the pastor, the teacher, the authority figure without questioning what they say. The cold, cruel and clinical process of mind indiscipline lingers in our culture and we must make a sustained effort to erase the impact of this psychological assault.

Kenyan academic Ngugi Wa Thiong'o has encouraged us to "decolonise the mind" beginning by looking critically at the use of language as a vehicle of culture. Similarly, Frantz Fanon explained that "Imperialism leaves behind germs of rot which we must clinically detect and remove from our minds; Marcus Garvey referred to this condition as mental slavery and our failure to change this mentality is committing collective suicide. Our culture is being paralysed by this kind of thinking and we must now question every aspect of our culture. We need a critical cultural consciousness to be encouraged to examine our key black institutions beginning with the family.

We need freedom of mind to develop disciplined thinking as opposed to the poor thinking and planning in our community. Essentially, we must provide effective and strategic direction in every area of our lives: parenthood, diet, work life, social life and importantly our family life. Currently, poor thinking is also feeding false stereotypes. Picture an untidy black neighbourhood: rubbish everywhere. It is not that our people are untidy, but rather rubbish is dropped mindlessly and when challenged there is the view that someone will clean up the mess. This same thinking is true in different aspects of our culture: we eat unhealthy foods, become obese, get diabetes and other related illnesses and expect the doctors to clean up the mess, we have unprotected sex, knowing the risks yet we continue for social workers to clean up the mess. This poor thinking about major decisions has led to consequences that place the perception of our culture as being in a mess.

If we are to free our minds, shall we begin by questioning all of our perceptions of our customs and practices? Do we have to question the merits of our faith, the education system, the family structures that were employed for the colonisation of the mind? Should we think again about the Western cultural value system and how appropriate it is for our collective identity? Should we think of a new black identity? Should we do what Malcolm X admonished and reconstruct an Afrocentric identity? A new black consciousness? Should we study Chinese /Islamic models and extrapolate from their cultures and traditions? After all, Asian countries are on top of the world for education and literacy. Or should we recapture the strength, resilience and resolve that characterise the struggle of our African ancestors?

Chapter 2

DEMOCRACY

Pure democracy. Popular democracy. Industrial democracy. Representative democracy. Liberal democracy. Electoral democracy. Parliamentary democracy. Westminster democracy. Presidential democracy. Soviet democracy. Organic democracy. Totalitarian democracy. Authoritarian democracy.

The word democracy has Greek origins with the word demos meaning people and Kratia meaning power hence any form of democracy requires people power and assumes equality. However, the people who seem to have the power are the elite who manipulate the media, officially deceive the masses and make pacts with politicians in various lobbies. Advocates of democracy insist on promoting the democratic ideal as a principle of political liberalism and forward equality of rights and privileges whether political, social or legal on their agendas. Essentially, they fail to acknowledge the infrastructure of this system that exacerbates inequality rather than eradicates it. One of the values of the democratic systems is the electoral process which is designed to ensure fairness and equality of the political process. However, there is always the added value of gerrymandering for skewed success and of course to stamp out dissent.

Let's not forget British Parliamentary systems that use first past the post (FPTP) and the problems were highlighted in the 2015 multi-party election. Think about it, the English voted against the SNP and Labour in their attempt to lock the opposition leaders out of Downing

Street. Labour did not lose the election rather English nationalism won it. The same kind of nationalism was pandered to months later when Hilary Benn gave his Syrian war speech claiming that Islamic state fighters feel superior to everyone in the house. The irony of it all. Equality of political privilege has become yet another illusion as the right wing press seem to give unfair advantage to their political comrades. Like Saudi Arabia, power remains under the control of the privileged elite, who with careful public manipulation and secret surveillance ensure the persecution of those who threaten the party line. By allowing this official fixing of elections, those who are responsible for newspeak or propaganda ensure that true democracy prevails.

Other issues include strong leadership which cannot exist without an authoritarian stance, there is also the issue of political disengagement which can be blamed on political leaders lacking vision and simply vilify the opposition instead. Poor voter turnout also serve to plague the proponents of democracy and remind them of a clear deficit. Other problems with the infrastructure of democracy is the inevitable fat cat corruption what the Chinese refer to as black gold politics. On the subject of China, the biggest problem for democracy itself which quietly reminds the western world that equality, human rights and freedom cannot exist in a social, cultural or historical vacuum. The democratic ideal is thought of, therefore it exists fails to get to the root of the problem which can be reduced to three core elements: individual freedom, human rights and democracy. Like the three wise men they travel together far and wide bearing gifts, hoping their generous gifts will herald the birth of their god and gather more worshippers. Their gift of gold coupled with the sweet smell of solutions to social, personal and political conflict promise light to the world. Culture does not matter. History does not matter either. All that really matters is the gift of gold.

Some may argue that the three wise men, freedom, human rights and democracy are more like Shakespeare's three witches acknowledging status and making prophecies of power and security. What the advocates of democracy seem to forget is the madness, tyranny and oppression that must accompany the accumulation of these prophetic gifts. In democratic societies, laws have been passed, civil protests have occurred and fights for freedom have endured but tyranny, madness and oppression still remain. How can the West right this wrong? How can democracy cease to promote the two incompatible ideologies of equality and capitalism? Can we clearly and distinctly conceive of democracy as a solution rather than a fundamental problem for the world?

Black cultural democracy

Democracy in western cultural thought may be an illusion but from a black cultural perspective, democracy is definitely a delusion. Equality of rights and privileges after all the laws, after all the benefits and after all the civil rights protests, democracy remains for our people, a distant dream especially in the Land of dreams. However, like Barrack Obama, we must have the audacity to hope that we can construct and create a new democracy for ourselves based on fairness, hope and dignity for our people. We must fight to close the gap between our past and our present, between our dreams and our visions and most importantly between our love for ourselves individually and our people collectively. This can be achieved through comprehensive measures to close the gap between the appearance of democracy and the reality of it.

The first black president of the world's leading democracy is made to defend an indefensible ideal because as cited in his audacity of hope `a school of thought sees the Founding Fathers only as hypocrites and the Constitution only as a betrayal of the grand ideals set forth by the declaration of Independence .... Others, representing the safer, more conventional wisdom, will insist that all the constitutional compromise on slavery – the omission of abolitionist sentiments from the original draft of the Declaration, the Three-fifths Clause and the Fugitive Slave Clause and the Importation Clause, the self-imposed gag rule – which permitted the space, for abolitionists to rally...'

Later on, Barack Obama agonises over the whole experience and laments:

> How can I, an American with the blood of Africa coursing through my veins, choose sides in such a dispute? I can't. I love America too much, am too invested in what this country has become, too committed to its institutions, its beauty, and even its ugliness, to focus entirely on the circumstances of its birth. But neither can I brush aside the magnitude of the injustice done, or erase the ghosts of generations past, or ignore the open wound, the aching spirit, that ails this country still.

No matter how hard western and black cultural thinkers try to persuade themselves the uncomfortable truth will still remain that some are created more equal than others. It still rings true that power corrupts and those who move up socially, politically and economically act exactly like those who committed the original sins. Google some of our black countries in Africa and the Caribbean, who have considered themselves democracies in the world and you will see that these countries have nothing more than social inequality, educational inequality, and of course political inequality - or is corruption a better word? Our so called democracies are plagued by all sorts of interrelated problems of crime, poverty and what Cornel West refers to as nihilism in black communities in America and across the world. Our leaders lack vision to think independently like the Chinese. Instead, our leaders and their followers prefer to pursue personal ambitions over the pursuit of fairness, equal rights and of course democracy.

In Britain, one forgets that the class system exists as structured as before with an aristocracy wallowing in their inherited privilege. Those at the bottom simply grow used to their positions of poverty and concentrate on life after death instead. We must rise from this way of thinking and believing in these democratic societies and we must find a way to challenge the ideology of unfairness. We must decide to think in a radically different way that places us as the subjects rather than the objects of our construction of our reality or destiny. We have to always remember that if we are not are not sitting at the table, we are likely to be on the menu.

Chapter 3

HUMAN RIGHTS

Right to equality. Right to life. Right to freedom. Right to protection by law. Right to privacy. Freedom to move. Freedom of thought. Right to education. Right to privacy. Right to work. Right to meet. Right to democracy. Did you know that we have 30 human rights? Google the UN Universal Declaration of Human Rights.

Every human rights policy is guided by the principles enshrined in the UN Universal Declaration of Human Rights. This operates on the principle that all people are "born free and equal in dignity and rights". Human rights like democracy is now a global movement and every individual fights for dignity, freedom, justice, religion and all the other human rights. However, many blame the current crisis in Western society on 'rampant individualism' which is spiralling dangerously out of control. Human rights campaigners argue that the individual has fundamental rights as a member of the human race living in a free society. Sadly, individual freedom without boundaries, without responsibility and without empathy has produced a toxic cocktail of self-gratification, self-obsession and egoism. Many have taken human rights legislation too far so much so that this personal ambition, under the guise of individualism has inadvertently led to an unprecedented moral failure. More precisely, it has led to a massive cultural identity crisis that is inadvertently creating a false relationship between self and society. Our young people are now living in a society where the concept of community, society or collective identity has been pushed to the periphery.

Many western thinkers seem to overlook the problems created by this individualism: the destruction of any form of community cohesion. Children are telling their parents they have rights. The family right to stay together is undermined by the proliferation of women's rights, fathers' rights, children's rights, work rights and educational rights. Advocates of Western cultural rights must concede that these rights are double-edged in nature. Yet, these thinkers insist that any kind of collectivism is intrinsically Marxist, socialist, Stalinist, egalitarian, totalitarian, altruistic or even fascist. Why do western cultural thinkers believe in closing rank and standing united for national security but not promoting the principle of collectivism, unionism or social security for community cohesion? Could it be true that collective ideology is preferred over individual success in capitalist/economic terms to secure mergers, boost corporate business and feed the Cats whilst the poor are encouraged to start small businesses and set up social enterprises on their own? Is this evidence of the use of divide and rule tactics or is collectivism both a weapon and tool of the establishment?

What about the success of China, how does this fit into the notion of individualism and human rights? If the West is willing to accept China's trade why can't western cultural thinkers set up a trade in social, cultural and political ideas? Surely, one of the best exports China can send to the West is the meaning of genuine equality, freedom and of course human rights. They can teach how to capitalize on knowledge rather than adhering to the Orwellian slogan that ignorance is strength.

Why are we persuaded that individualism is more important that collectivism? Surely, there has always been safety in numbers – collectivism has always been the norm, not the exception but now western thinkers must be charged with the crime of undermining collectivism by creating this chaotic individualism? Or is there something more sinister the world is not seeing in this illusion of individualism? Is the West planting seeds of its own destruction by inadvertently leading individuals to alienation and a state of loneliness which would cause them to affiliate or gravitate towards something else - dare it be written to radicalisation? Is there some kind of innate need for collectivism that stems from fear of being totally free from friends or family like mass murderers alienated, angry and alone, desperate for company and then seek some form of affiliation? Think about it. Google the causes of radicalisation.

Black cultural rights

Respect for our freedom, dignity and equality has always been the fundamental values of the civil rights movement of the 1950s and 1960s. Our leaders fought against discrimination based on race, color, religion, sex or national origin in employment practices. The Civil rights Act of 1964 ensured that legislation was put in place to address unequal treatment of our people not just in America but in the entire diaspora. Since then individual freedom and the protection of human rights have continued to be the subject of political debates. However, problems arise when governments and policy makers overlook the unequal wealth distribution entrenched within Western societies and our black cultural access to it. Economic business and enterprise geared at the black community cannot prosper in a social and cultural vacuum. Governmental policies and the law state that all must be treated fairly or equally regardless of race, gender, religion, age and sex but this is far from the reality that we experience on a daily basis. Our rights seem to be controlled by those in authority, law, political institutions just as our right to exist has been shaped in Western school books, history, main stream media and scientists.

Through carefully designed mind programming, we are made to believe that our rights are dependent on those who have the power to mastermind our cultural identity right before our very eyes. The legacy of slavery has now morphed into global economic exploitation cleverly masterminded by corporate firms to maintain the status quo. Laws and society operate on the principle that we all have to work or rather be a slave to capitalism and anyone who dares to deviate will be punished so severely that they have no choice but to rush back to the plantations or rather the institutions.

What about our right to genuine equality to have our own cultural thoughts and ideas? What about the right to be respected for being different rather than discriminated against because we are? What about some meaningful right to life and wellbeing? What about freedom from ongoing mental and labour slavery experienced everyday through professional practice by those determined to uphold the status quo? What about the torture of Eurocentric negative thinking about us in every aspect of Western cultural thought and behaviour? What about some right to use of laws that are designed for justice rather than those to protect the privileged class? What about laws written to protect us rather than imprison us? What about designing a system of fair treatment for our young men in a fair court? What about rallying around our men who are unfairly detained because they were failed by a tortuous education system? What about their right to be innocent until proven guilty when the burden of proof rests with those who earn their wages by falsifying data? What about rights to privacy when the ministry of truth spends millions destroying cultural reputations?

What about our freedom to move freely and live where we wish being destroyed by the right to gentrification? What about the right to asylum being deceptively propagated as economic migration? What about the right to a proper nationality rather than a hyphenated one? What about our rights to marry and have a family when our rights to this are being undermined by the same movement that undermined the Civil Rights one? What about our right to own things that we do not have money to purchase? What about freedom of thought to think in an Afrocentric way about ourselves – why is this right denied? What about our right to make up our own minds, to think what we like and to share our ideas with our people? What about our boys' rights to meet up with their friends and attend functions without being told they are gang members? What about the rights of our leaders in the global world to have true democracy rather than operating on the principles of the pigs on Animal Farm?

What about our rights to a fair system of social security rather than the money being used to boost national security? What about workers' rights to have a job and a fair wage rather than the slave jobs and exploitation of workers in this global legacy? What about the right to play and have a day to relax from work when many workers have to slave on Sundays for the fat cats? What about the right to have a bed and some food when care for other people is undermined due to lack of empathy?

What about our right to a bespoke education that is designed to address our needs and the lingering effects of slavery? What about our cultural right and copyrights that have been stolen by those in the field of historical revisionism? What about our rights for a free and fair world rather than the modern world that has globalised slavery and unfairness? What about the duty to other people to share and care in our communities rather than engage in conflict after conflict? What about the right to have these rights and freedoms which as Whitney Houston sings 'no matter what you take from me, you can't take away our dignity because the greatest love of all is after all is to love ourselves as a people?'

Chapter 4

IDENTITY

Age and identity. Gender and identity. Culture and identity. Ethnicity and identity. Nationality and identity. Leisure, consumption and identity. Media-saturated identity

Social class and identity. Religion and identity. Identity politics.

According to Wikipedia, "cultural identity is the identity or feeling of belonging to a group. It is part of a person's self-conception and self-perception and is related to nationality, ethnicity, religion, social class, generation, locality or any kind of social group that has its own distinct culture. In this way, cultural identity is both characteristic of the individual but also of the culturally identical group of members sharing the same cultural identity. Cultural identity is similar to and overlaps with identity politics." The problem of conceptualizing identity in Western culture is related to separate but interrelated issues: conventional classifications (class, race, gender, religion, language), the proliferation of additional identities, time and place in the construction of identity and the location of the individual as insider or outsider in terms of identity. Let's look at each one briefly.

Conventional classifications (class, race, gender, religion, language)

Traditional cultural classifications include race, class and gender but in modern western society these categories have all been blurred. Race is no longer synonymous with a particular identity. In fact, race does more to conceal rather than reveal identity and those who have traditionally assigned this as a cultural identifier add to the confused state of affairs. Class has also been associated with inherited privilege but nowadays there are opportunities to purchase class. The same capitalist principle can be applied to the purchase of gender just ask Caitlyn Jenner to describe the transaction. Conventional classifications can no longer be static in the way they were assigned to individuals and this has led to the proliferation of additional identities.

This concept of multiple identities is now commonly accepted in western cultural circles as a form of cultural plurality which embraces political, institutional and redefinitions of conventional identities. Variety may be the spice of life but it also adds to the strife of life. Without a fixed conception of identity, the very essence of community life is undermined and community cohesion cannot be cultivated in this melee/confusion/ carnival of choice. Young people in the West are lost in this modern day tower of Babel, uncertain which elevator to take, searching for clear instructions in the corridors of power. Academics encourage them to embrace the concept of multiple identities in both theory and practice, stopping short of doing nothing more than imposing their own conventional identity classifications. No advice is offered on which identity boundaries to cross, when to cross them or with what consequences. As a result, western cultural young people end up, simply lost in translation.

Traditionally, identity has been conceptualised in cultural, historical and generational timeframes and then subdivided to consider place. However, with imperialism, colonisation and migration, identity now has to be explored over periods of time to embrace the ever increasing range and people in location from migration and dislocation (urban, rural, third world, developed world). We also have to consider exploration of identity in movement to take into the range of identity markers that are wider and more comprehensive than the conventional categories of class, race, gender and language.

Location of the individual (insider, outsider, privileged, underprivileged)

Young people now locate themselves in the plethora of identity constructs and classifications available. Everyone now sees him/ herself relative to the old or new identity categories or try to construct multiple identities. However, individual perspective in identity formation is difficult to construct within institutional structures which creates insiders and outsiders. Let's look at education. It is the institution that socialises people into western culture and its classifications and individuals are either part of the culture of domination or the culture of the dominated. Tensions between this structure and its agency are evident in exclusions for those who find it difficult to be dominated. To understand identity and location, therefore, one has to show some awareness of historical, cultural, social, political, ideological and value-centred of particular systems of knowledge and practice in education. This knowledge is generated by the need to locate oneself and make sense of frequent transitions in social contexts to new situations.

The problem of conceptualisation and classification of identity is evident because there is no longer a viable fixed essence or fixed conception of identity itself. Many speak with certainty of a mainstream cultural identity but as shown this imposes homogenising classifications of identity. Alienation, marginalisation and a massive identity crisis now looms. How do western cultural thinkers approach this crisis in a coherent way? Do thinkers explore the dynamic nature of identity classifications to open new understandings? Is there a need to re-examine the old classifications and construct renewed identities rather than additional ones?

Conceptualising cultural identity: Black Cultural thinking

From a black cultural perspective, there is a need to create identities for ourselves that transcend our disadvantaged positions in society. We cannot rediscover or romanticise the past but rather produce an identity of being as well as becoming culturally conscious of our black struggle. Black is being used in the holistic political, socio-economic rather than an ethnic sense to refer to the struggle for equality, dignity, liberty and the fight against the condition of oppression. This can be contrasted with stereotypical perceptions of being black referring to lingering elements of slave culture which have morphed into so-called ghetto attitudes, behaviour, aggression, nihilism and powerlessness. Because of the latter stereotypical position, race tends to be seen in the halo effect: the single aspect of our identity that dazzles and affects how we are seen, individually and collectively. In other words, no matter how different or atypical we are individually, we are judged by the collective stereotype of our race.

Black cultural identity as opposed to race, has to be constructed using three elements: the ethnic factor acquired by birth, the socio-cultural factor acquired by socialisation and the political factor acquired by conscious identification with the struggle against the condition of oppression. The ethnic or racial factor identifies some individuals as black but socio-economically and politically they may construct their identity as other but not necessarily western cultural `other'. This distinct `other' identity comes about because within socio-cultural identity, there are some behaviours, attitudes and attributes that are directly linked to the legacy of slave culture. Examples of this are attitudes to timekeeping, social behaviours and tone of speech. Progressive blacks tend to distance themselves from this legacy of slave culture.

However, many members of the black underclass who identify with the unfiltered slave culture refer to those who disown it as `sell outs' or refer to them as `playing white'. Such problems of identity persist because in the absence of a separate culture of black positive core values, distinct from western cultural practices, it is difficult to see where one identity begins and where the other one ends. There needs to be a black cultural identity that has filtered the negative aspects left by the legacy of slavery.

Some of our black thinkers have proposed that we make identity statements in solidarity with our African Diaspora identity. Searching for a cultural identity that reflects our common historical experiences would be a challenge because there has been too much disconnection, too much migration and too much colonisation and too much mental slavery. As Frantz Fanon puts it `the past has been distorted, disfigured and destroyed'. What emerges is the need for a conception of cultural identity that grants us power to introduce constructs to ourselves as subjects when we formerly were silent as objects and to make sense of our African traditions. Identities to explore how we challenge the traditions of western culture in which we have been RN immersed are also desirable.

Looking briefly at the historical underpinnings, slave owners tried to repress any form of cultural organisation, familial organisation and political organisation in order to prevent slave rebellions or resistance. In essence, they tried to eradicate any imprint of Africa that remained with the slaves through divide and rule methods. One strategy was through the cultivation of the house versus field slave mentality. The house slaves had more privileges and started to feel that they were of a higher class than the slaves in the field. Some historians argue that the mixed race (product of slave and master liaisons) slaves or the slaves with a lighter skin tone were chosen to work in the house and this reinforced the belief that the whiter the skin the better the person. Skin tone was one of the dividing elements in pre and post abolition societies and one of the underlying problems or rather prejudices that existed and still exist in regions like the Caribbean and inner city areas of large cities.

This created another interrelated problem of classicism within black culture. Slaves who were separated from the majority of the slaves believed that they were of a better or higher class than the field slaves. This problem has persisted in many forms: brothers and sisters who live in the West tend to have condescending attitudes to those who live in the third world countries; those who move up the social ladder to middle class and their attitudes to those of working class/ underclass and lastly those who are well educated to those who are less educated than themselves. How do we construct common cultural identities with the plethora of differences?

Do we redefine black cultural identity as distinct from both the legacy of slavery and the legacy of white supremacy? Do we appeal to politicians, preachers, teachers and the community to promote positive paradigms of black culture? Do we lead distinctive black community based education programmes to address the lingering problems of slave culture? Do we have a study of these issues and share the result of research findings? Do we propose to have a vision statement, a policy initiative or an Afrocentric perspective on black identity and consciousness and circulate it on the worldwide web?

Chapter 5

CONSUMERISM

Routine buying. Impulse buying. Excessive consumerism. Mainstream consumerism. Intellectual consumerism. Anti-consumerism. Green consumerism. Ethical consumerism.

Consumerism is not only the tool in the capitalist trade but it is also the essential part of the infrastructure of capitalist slavery. The promotion of the consumer's desires to be of greater value than his fellow men; the promotion of value-laden interests of jewellery, luxury and all forms of extravagance. Capitalist producers have even thought of ways of faking value for those who do not have enough capital. At the heart of this capitalist thinking is the notion that an increasing consumption of goods is economically desirable. Western economy thrives on this way of thinking so it is important that society has a real propensity to consume. This is ensured through clever advertising, marketing and promotion of capitalist interests with consumers believing that they have freedom to choose or rather they have consumer choice.

This freedom to consume is related to the paradox of choice. If one has too much choice then decision making becomes an additional but related problem. According to Schwartz, Autonomy and Freedom of choice are critical to our wellbeing and choice is critical to freedom and autonomy. However, he argues that we don't seem to be benefitting from it psychologically. Google Barry Schwartz for more on this. There are also those who would argue that consumerism stifles creativity as the relentless desire to consume makes us lose focus on being original in thinking and synthesising. However, the individual's preoccupation with buying goods has caused a catalogue of social problems including crime - both white collar and violent; mental health problems for those who have insufficient capital and numerous tensions caused by deepened inequality made evident by consumerism. This freedom has also made society more self-gratifying and obsessed rather than being concerned for the welfare of others and as a consequence the moral fabric of society is being torn apart.

According to advocates of this ideology, the world would be less productive, less prolific and less prosperous without consumerism. These advocates insist that if there was no need, no desire for consumer goods, then they would not be produced. The fact that people want to improve that quality of their lives by keeping up with the Jones's ensures commerce through advancements in technology. The whole process of producing and consuming in the quest to live like the rich and famous is meant to be an enjoyable occupation. An occupation that has improved and prolonged the quality of our lives and undoubtedly made the new world a peaceful paradise.

If Capitalism is the religion of freedom, then consumerism has become the new god, worshipped by millions. People have become fanatical about this new faith as they camp out waiting for their special Black Friday service. People are prepared to trample over each other and even resort to violent means to secure a bargain. Shopping stampedes. Frenzied experiences. Fanatics pray for the prices to drop, and sing praises to the gods that make them profit from these deals. If one wants to avoid congregating in this way, one can enjoy the worshipping at home privately. Opting for web worship on smartphones and tablets definitely ensures that the spirit of consumerism can be evoked anywhere and anytime.

But as the Pope warns of a world `intoxicated by consumerism, wealth and extravagance', should western cultural thinkers consider consuming Christian teachings? Should consumerism at least be regulated so that people can think about community and its benefits? Should young people be taught other values rather than being free to choose only consumerism?

Black cultural

Our problems are compounded by our consumerist mentality, another by product of dependency. Limited finances with an unlimited appetite to consume has proven to be a recipe for disaster. Contrary to popular belief, these ingredients do not blend to produce personal well-being, cultural development or economic progress. They combine to produce frustration, stress, obesity, family breakdown, alienation, marginalisation and mental ill health. Rather than a better quality of life for us, consumerism makes us poorer and unhappier.

We are effectively consuming this element of Babylon (capitalism) when it was not produced with us in mind. Let's stop slaving in jobs that we hate just to ensure that we consume the latest style, gadget or bling. Let's spend more time with family and friends rather than consuming extravagances. Let's improve our lives by freeing our minds of this consumerist way of thinking. American Author Bryant H. McGill quotes consumerism as the new slavery and insists that a day devoted to consumerism called Black Friday is not a coincidence. We must no longer bring our children up as slaves to consumption:

ordering them to get a phone, to get a bike, to get any job just so that they can consume more. This slavery is driving some members of our community to resort to robbery and lawlessness. We must abolish this slavery!

Think about the historical underpinnings for a moment. During slavery, religion was used to promote the spread of slavery and more importantly to justify it. Slaves were taught to obey their master and ended up believing that the master was right in his actions. Helplessly dependent on their masters who controlled their hearts, souls and minds, slaves were simply consumed everything thrown at them. They were taught to accept their lot, accept their situation as this was the way, the truth and their life.

Today, consumerism is to capitalism what religion was to slavery. We worship the things we consume as ceremoniously as the churchgoers do with daily doses of subscriptions, orders and admiration of the consumer goods. The dangling of the beads now called advertising and marketing has promoted the doctrine of materialism as our god and saviour. Our overconsumption of everything from fast food to new gadgets is like the overloading of the slave ship sinking under its own weight. The seas are rougher in our neo colonial islands but there is no desire to abandon ship. Instead, the captains encourage their passengers to consume transatlantic journeys in the hope of a better life.

This ongoing legacy of colonialism and slavery with its powerful control and domination over our minds will continue to oppress us until we find a way to emancipate ourselves from this consumerist stranglehold. We need to gain some access to power or preferably some access to freedom.

Should we preach the message of living within our means? Should we pread more books and consume less music? Should we begin reclaiming our minds by at least having one day of rejection of consumerism where there is a kind of rastafari type day of earth celebration and rejection of Babylonian products? Should we have some cultural engineering of a system of satisfaction rather than the current system of dissatisfaction and the pursuit of consumerism? Should we address the misapprehension of consumerism?

Chapter 6

DEPENDENCY

Economic dependency. Cultural dependency. Intellectual dependency. Causal or logical dependency. Discretionary dependency. Circular dependency.

Dependence as opposed to independence refers to the total reliance on a model, a person, an ideology, an idea. Western cultural thinkers claim to be totally free, independent and creative thinkers but there needs to be a closer examination of these claims. Does Western Culture depend on scientific, linguistic, pragmatic, economic, political, intellectual and secular models? Does Western Culture rely on experts in all fields for advice and guidance? Is Western culture stagnated by its own dependence on the ideology of capitalism? How many major political, economic and philosophical ideas have been created to address the problems in the Western world and beyond?

Is it true that in the lottery, at the casino and in theory are the only places where quintessentially independent events can exist? Is it misleading to claim that Western cultural practitioners have independent or individualistic ideas; is this a major thought crime that needs to be corrected politically?

Historically, the Western cultural thinker has cleverly used the interest gained from the original investment of ideas. Their cultural capital has purchased many assets including economic, legal and banking systems which have allowed such a thinker to be well prepared for rainy days. Instead of reinvesting new capital, the interest gained from original ideologies has been transferred to other ideas but branded as original. Banking in this way will always turn out to be a risky business; there is going to be another collapse if this is allowed to continue. There needs to be a regulated way of thinking about the risky business of distributing the wealth of ideas in this way. If not, this independent society will experience the ideological equivalent of global warming – in the short term but disastrous in the long term. Let us examine dependency, as an economic structure more closely:

> [Dependency is]...an historical condition which shapes a certain structure of the world economy such that it favors some countries to the detriment of others and limits the development possibilities of the subordinate economics...a situation in which the economy of a certain group of countries is conditioned by the development and expansion of another economy, to which their own is subjected.

> (Theotonio Dos Santos, "The Structure of Dependence," in K.T. Fann and Donald C. Hodges, eds., *Readings in U.S. Imperialism.* Boston: Porter Sargent, 1971, p. 226)

This structure which favours some countries over others must be traced to the original source of Western capital: historic exploitation of other parts of the world. Globalisation is now creating another form of dependency even more dangerous than this old model. Various euphemistic presentations of the truth abound but the fact is that poorer countries are still dependent on richer countries and richer countries are still dependent on the traditional model of capitalism. This dependency on capitalism presented as independence and the opening of markets or the free market idea has affected the thinking of many leaders of poor countries who fail to realise the wealth of the rich countries is at their expense. It has created more jealousy, more conflict and most of all more inequality.

Culture of Dependency

Our culture of dependency on Western cultural ideas is hampering our ability to make black cultural progress. We are depending on Western capitalist thinking with regards to political ideology, with regards work, family values - about everything. It is like being permanently in debt to the creditors only that the creditors have the power over us which keeps us in our place as dependents. How do we break out of this bank? Capitalist dependency has trapped generations of our people into vicious cycles; it has robbed us of our pride and dignity and continues to cultivate this dependency thinking. It demotivates, it devalues and it denies us any chance of progress. We cannot and must not depend on this capitalist way of thinking to lead our lives.

To fully understand dependency, we have to fully understand the historical underpinnings here. Slaves depended on the slave masters for everything: food, shelter, clothing, education, religion and like Pavlov's dogs, slaves simply reacted automatically. There was no thinking. Education for slaves was learning to respond or react automatically; there was no involvement or engagement of the brain. In short, slaves were trained to do things without being conscious of what they were actually doing or why. To repair this damage to our collective psyche, there needs to be a comprehensive or holistic educational programme aimed at these lingering effects.

The effects of mental slavery continue today because abolition declared physical rather than mental freedom and there has been no systematic attempt to free the dependency conditioning. We need to have a comprehensive education for reparation rather than simply depend on the education of domination to which we currently subscribe. In every area of our lives today including the inhumane structure of the benefit system seems to further enslave rather than liberate. The dependency mentality has therefore evolved from dependency on the master (slave owner) to dependency on capitalism that has produced a culture reliant on figures of authority: the teacher, the preacher, the employer, the politician, the expert. Dependency thus continues to be cultivated in our schools, our churches, our families, our music, our festivals, our food and our societies because we have not thought of a holistic approach to changing this mentality. Forget breaking out of the bank, this is more like driving through life being totally dependent on a flawed satellite navigation system.

How do we change this culture of dependency? Do we begin with inspiring our youth to challenge cultural practices rather than accept them? Do we begin by rethinking governmental policy so that we are no longer totally dependent on this body? Do we encourage the merging of entrepreneurship, entertainment and education to spark new ideas? Do we need policies that increase confidence and control of our cultural inclinations? Do we let capital work for our community rather than let our community simply work for capital?

Chapter 7

TRUTH

Platonic truth. Scientific truth. Universal truth. Absolute truth. Epistemological truth. Philosophical truth. Aesthetic truth. Historical truth. Spiritual truth. Objective truth. Relative truth. Empirical truth. Pragmatic truth. Metaphysical truth. Mathematical truth. Statistical truth. Gospel truth. Divine truth.

Truth is formulated in the minds of millions of western cultural thinkers as a concept which is objective, scientific and universal to the point of being sacred as the highest standard of morality. Another curious paradox is that all western concepts of truth seem to claim the right to universal, absolute and divine truth. In the beginning, God, in everyone's mind was the way, the truth, and the light, the absolute scientific Truth of the Universe as known by God. Human beings since Adam and Eve, have existed to engage in the process of discovering this truth, through the collective and personal experiences guided by God's Universal laws. Seeds of Western cultural truth were planted in the Garden of Eden where spiritual truth was the only truth that existed: there was the divine truth and nothing but this divine truth. This concept of truth stated that God created the world, every individual was created in the image of God (The Holy Trinity -Three in one- the father, the son and the Holy Spirit) and each human being consisted of the mind (the father), the son (the body) and the Holy Spirit (the soul).

As Western cultural thinkers are aware, Plato changed what determined the essence of divine truth by presenting his abstract, mystical idealism adopted even by Christians to explain the nature of God. According to Plato, truth exists more clearly and distinctly in the mind than in the natural world: it is not solely what we perceive through the senses as they trick humans into believing false visions of the truth. Plato paved the path on which his charioteer would direct his horse to control the truth. Aristotle, then outlined the method of training the horse by using Science to globalise a concept of truth that has reined in all other definitions. This scientific world denies belief in the inner world of spirituality that was needed to live happily in the natural world and has replaced it with the material world that instead depends on the theory of Evolution to explain itself. This latter truth makes beliefs in materialism and evolution interconnected, interrelated and interdependent. These creators of truth have masterminded a concept of reality on a universal stage, cleverly manipulated, directed and controlled. This Oscar winning production of the Truman Show gives credit to Science fiction, not as a genre but as reality. Western cultural thinkers have been tricked into believing false visions of the world based on materialism over spiritualism, mind over spirit and rationality over emotion. Even more misleading is that this truth is equated with absolute truth, universal truth and of course divine truth. Having denied the existence of a spiritual being, this version of the truth reduces the self to the reality of the mind only. Like Truman, there needs to come a time when all the players on this stage discover the fact that their entrances and exits have been nothing more than a show that failed to acknowledge or even allow the truth to make a single appearance.

Plato is definitely right with his charioteer analogy of truth being all about control and conquer. This was developed by the war poets notably Tennyson who commemorates a brave but suicidal charge. He describes men's courage and unquestioning devotion to duty just as western cultural thinkers fail to even question the essence of reason itself.

Control of the true self, the emotional inner spirit causes western cultural beings to live in denial of the need for self-discovery. The Orwellian ministry of truth must consider the consequences of rejecting the truth about women's two selves, the importance of spirituality in family life and the focus of schools almost exclusively on promoting STEM above PSHE. Rather than letting rationality work in partnership with the powerful emotions, Plato has created a lifelong battle within the individual self with the mind permanently at war with the emotions. This mirrors the constant war in wider society for control of countries, control of the economy, control of children, control of different people and of course control of women. Eve is deceived by the serpent in the garden of the original truth and Plato insists that the emotional horse is to be controlled in his ideal world of truth. Two worlds of hidden truths were created with equal intent.

So what is the truth and how do Western cultural thinkers discover the truth about themselves and the world? Should each thinker deconstruct the ideologies that underpin the material world that has been created? Could it be that Plato realised that the rational horse is really less powerful than the emotional horse? Could it be that the truth about the world has been concealed rather than expressed by Plato? Are scientists discovering more and more ways to conceal the truth about quantum physics, cosmological design and human complexity? Are psychologists and psychotherapists operating on false premises about human mind and behaviour? Is it time for Western Cultural thinkers to explore the truth as presented by other powers?

Black cultural truth

The truth is that we need to fully understand the truth about our individual and collective selves, our culture, our history and most importantly our minds. Slavery was about the systematic cultivation of the minds to self-destruct individually and collectively but over the years, the resilience against this form of oppression has been admirable. However, we have to totally restructure our thoughts, channel our powerful emotions and find the inner strength to redefine our identity. This process of rediscovering, reconstructing and redefining our collective consciousness is a long-term but urgent necessity. Too long we have been told cleverly plotted narratives about our past, our present and our future but we cannot and must not believe these negative or rather false truths about ourselves. We must begin by changing the whitewashed lens through which we have been conditioned to see ourselves and be determined to harness our intellectual, physical and spiritual strength. We have been mentally and motivationally structured to believe a false truth about ourselves as a people and we have to change this misperception of reality and truth in order to be really free from mental slavery.

The platonic model has destroyed our confidence and capability to think clearly and distinctly about the concept of truth about ourselves. His use of the charioteer analogy emphasising the need to control the black horse has globalized two false truths: one about the self and the other related to the people who share the colour of the horse.

Here was the beginning of the justification of the need to control or negate the Other as since then dichotomies have dominated western cultural thinking: good and evil, right and wrong, man and woman - scientific probable and improbable. Democracy, the Class system, History, Science and Psychology are implied in this Platonic logic. Justice, or the Good, is achieved when the best controls the worst. There is war within the self until reason controls emotion, there is war until men control women – war until white controls black. Plato's rational order is therefore based on the mechanism of control. Think of every institution of power and you will find that the promotion of the self as a thinking being rather than an emotional one rings true. Think of the real motive of Western culture; the implications of this are not difficult to extrapolate.

With power comes control. The absolute truth is that the essence of truth is control. Control of the self. Control of the other. Control of the world. No other view of harmony could be generated from this model. Essentially, the platonic view sacrifices any holistic conception of personhood as it insists that one has to be a master of himself or slave to self and this viewpoint has caused a lot of solidarity issues among our people. Disconnection of the individual self also mirrors the disconnection of the collective self and we must work to change this mindset. What Plato and his subsequent followers overlooked was the African and Eastern conceptions of truth and harmony being achieved through the balance of complementary forces. Isn't it impossible to have a functioning whole without harmonious interaction and existence of balancing pairs?

Plato entered the stage as the founding father of freedom but made his exit playing the god of truth. All the world's his stage as he still creates virtual reality in the minds of many millions. Our people must no longer be players on this stage of truth nor should we subject our children to the seven stages of mind control: presentation of concepts, labelling of concepts, classification of concepts, hierarchical arrangement of concepts, conflict with concepts, control of antagonisms and finally security for these concepts. This process of Platonic truth starts with observation of concepts presented to the child in experience– light and dark, earth and sky, animals and humans. Somewhere in the child's mind these concepts are labelled and then classified. This taxonomy develops over time into a valuation, a hierarchy where in the mind's eye, one is viewed more positively than the other. Conflict creeps in, followed by antagonism. There is a need for control of one in order to convey the other. We must trample over rather than propagate this Platonic creation of truth. If one can clearly and distinctly conceive of Platonic reasoning, then why is truth itself restricted to reason? Why is it not probable to think of another way of formulating truth? Why is the mind limited by logic? Surely, we are free to feel emotionality and therefore truth can be created from this source or a combination of sources? The real questions that we need to ask as a people - do we need is a new order, a new logic, a new perception of truth about the world that places our true self within it? Do we need a truth that goes beyond reason, beyond materialism, a truth that acknowledges the need for black emotionally fuelled intelligence? Do we need a truth that embraces rather than denies emotion? Do we need to question our purpose and highest goal in life here on earth to as if there is more to life than materialism? Does morality matter more than money? Do we simply continue living in Madonna's material world or do we embrace Michael Jackson's Earth song?

Chapter 8

SUPERIORITY COMPLEX

Individualism. Class. Exclusivity. Power. Privilege. Snobbery. Wealth. Luxury. Extravagance. Self-obsession. Self-gratification. Narcissism.

The ideology of capitalism perpetuates and maintains notions of superiority. It is centred upon the belief and the promotion of the belief, that those with more money, more privilege, more class are superior to those without. This thinking breeds the superiority complex which is an intricate part of the western cultural value system: first class travel, exclusive club membership, luxury items designed to make one feel superior to the other. Let's not forget social stratification itself with classy residential areas, estates and different degrees of extravagance were all designed for the comfort of the privileged. On an individual and collective level, these feelings, values and beliefs have furnished a superiority complex which has social, political, historical and industrial roots. These are evident in the structural advantage given in capitalist societies, in the laws that maintain these feelings and professionalism which embraces the status quo. According to Wikipedia:

> The term "superiority complex", in everyday usage, refers to an overly high opinion of oneself. In psychology, it refers not to a belief, but a pattern of behaviors expressing the belief that one is superior. Those exhibiting the superiority complex have a self-image of supremacy. Those with superiority complexes

may garner a negative image in those around them, as they are not concerned with the opinions of others about themselves. This is responsible for the paradox in which those with an inferiority complex are the ones who present themselves in the best light possible; while those with a superiority complex may not attempt to make themselves look good.

Superiority complexes are nurtured from the cradle to the grave by the structures, policies and institutional systems that insist on the use of certain characteristics, attributes and cultivated qualities. Striving for success is almost synonymous with striving for superiority. Those with the superiority complex feel superior, act superior and have a self- image of superiority. Manifestations of this abound in everyday life with many professionals with influential power: lawyers and clients, journalists and interviewees; teachers and students. To be professional virtually means to exhibit behaviours expressing the belief that they are superior. If their knowledge, displayed intelligence or professionalism is challenged, they would not relent in their attempts to prove they are right until the dissenting party concedes.

Capitalist thinking fuels the engines of the brain with impulses to be in power, in authority and in control of situations and other people. There is a definite temptation and urge to control which is driven and operated by executive and instrumental power agents in government, intelligence, banking, economy, education, security, law and medicine. Think about it. Politicians disguise their intentions to control us behind convoluted phrases or as Orwell would word it 'newspeak'. Other controllers like the bankers control our thinking about their criminal mismanagement by shifting blame from the banks to the people below. Educational and legal institutions use language as a vehicle for expressing how to develop skills in control, power and domination. This impulse to control manifests itself in different ways. Financial control. Strategic control. Operational control. Mind control. Physical control. Government control. Parental control. Spiritual control. Mood control. Personality control. Global control. Political control. Cultural control.

This domination urge has developed historically in Western cultural identity and is evident on an individual and collective level. Imperialism, Empire and supremacy are terms used in the past to describe this tendency to control. Generations past and present have been socialised to pursue power relentlessly so that the impulse to control is almost inevitable. Often, this occurs in the absence of any form of regulation as they are taught to exercise authoritative or dominating influence over others through language, intelligence, class and of course capital. On a collective level, politicians form alliances to control, corporate companies merge for more control, institutions cloze rank to ensure control; bankers take huge risks for financial control and no one has addressed this problem of global control.

How can this problem be fully addressed? Should Western cultural thinkers recognise the origins of this impulse and tackle it from its root cause? Should this urge be regarded as a conduct disorder and treated as such? Should there be workshops for individuals to talk about their tendencies and how to resist temptation? Should groups come together in an attempt to right the wrongs? Should Western cultural thinkers share power and control rather than make concerted efforts to hold on to it? In this context, does the superiority complex inadvertently stifle creativity, critical consciousness and independent thinking? Does this complex prevent diplomatic negotiations because those who think they are superior have a cognitive bias not to listen? Is the superiority complex responsible for conflicts because those with the superiority complex do not care at all about the opinions of others?

SUPERIORITY OR INFERIORITY COMPLEX

Years of seeing ourselves through the lenses of white images in the church, in the media, in literature, in popular culture has led to a flaw in our thinking which is either a superiority or inferiority complex. Individually, some members of our people feel superior to other black people when they acquire wealth and display the crab in the barrel mentality. Collectively, there is a tendency to doubt ourselves and feel that we are not measuring up to the Eurocentric standards in education, professionalism and cultural practices. Our children are made to doubt their self-worth, self-esteem and self-respect because they are made to feel inferior. Let's not forget that low self-esteem tends to be rooted in early experiences our children encounter and remains in our children's subconscious. These feelings are intensified through failure at school and is compounded by added pressures and expectations of parents. Sometimes these feelings manifest themselves in strange ways: some are attention seeking because they feel inferior and not in harmony with society. This behaviour of showing off often compensates for the feeling of inferiority buried deep within.

Feelings of inferiority affect how we think about ourselves and each other. In the absence of a black model of cultural systems and values, we feel some degree of inferiority because we have no other choice but to use the western cultural model, the only one available to us.

The paradox is that the available model of culture and values is the one that is causing the complex. Feeling inferior results from the way that we are made to feel, the way we are made to think, the way we are made to define black because we are not in power, because we are not really free. Let's examine this complex in its historical context.

The dehumanising effects of slavery itself has left deep psychological and emotional scars. During slavery, there was a learned helplessness and even though there were slave rebellions, the repression by the slave owners intensified feelings of inferiority. This problem has been passed on from generation to generation and can even be perceived as almost hereditary, as toxic, as almost permanent. This colonisation of the mind cultivated a distorted view of the black race as inhumane, as unequal, as inferior.

Ridding ourselves of this mentality does not deny that we are still victims of both the legacy of slave culture and the legacy of domination; it simply explains the mentality but does not justify its continued existence which has been passed down from generation to generation and across continents in the diaspora. Life for the slaves was total reliance on the authorities for work and the occupation of their minds. Slaves were held captive to negativity and false beliefs about themselves for generations. They felt no control over themselves and learned to be helpless and incapable of changing their circumstances.

In the African diaspora, our problems are being perpetuated by the colonial paradigm and we have to do more to reverse the effects of the inferiority complex. We have to explore new cultural paradigms and free ourselves of the chains that still shackle our minds. Chains of seeing black in a negative light through the use of language and the philosophy which underpins Western culture. Our powerlessness to effect systematic change since slavery has left many feeling helpless, demoralised and distraught. The harsh treatment by the slave owners caused a subconscious inferiority complex which resulted from years of negative mental conditioning. We loathe ourselves. We hate each other. We feel inferior. How do we progress from this aspect of our thinking? Essentially, where do we go from here? Should we explore ways to rid ourselves of this complex by focusing on positive aspects of our culture with the view of boosting cultural development programmes to develop our self-esteem and that of our children? Do we design a whole new curriculum of culture to raise the profile of black cultural consciousness? Do we stage events that showcase our cultural resilience and achievements and exhibit the diverse cultural elements of our people?

Chapter 9

ENTITLEMENT MENTALITY

Entitlement to privilege. Entitlement to power. Entitlement to inherited wealth. Entitlement to ownership. Entitlement to control. Entitlement to imperialism.

The Western cultural state of mind believes not in rights but in privileges – an entitlement to privilege: they spend their lives making investments in education, in careers and in property ownership and feel that privilege over others is due to them or owed. After all, the West created the wealth and it must stay in the family. This way of thinking that privilege is deserved rests on the assumption that wealth was fairly acquired through moral economic enterprise. Entitlement to privilege mentality also assumes that everyone else started from the same position or that everyone had equal access and opportunity to gain privilege. Such entitlement tendencies fail to understand the perspective of others. They tend to forget how the money that affords the privilege was acquired and more importantly how the privilege is maintained.

Western governments are well aware of the historic problem and promise citizens to make reparations. They campaign for better services, better benefits and better education to show that they are doing something about the privilege problem. Politicians promote the privilege mentality through funding rather than initiative; they encourage enterprise without social engineering and spend millions on inadvertently promoting human privileges rather than human rights. Many people believe that those who have political power or are in a privileged position owe something to those who do not. The donor community has a moral right to give to those who do not have.

This peculiar paradox in a democratic society that some people are more entitled to privilege than others helps to underline the fact that the problems in the West are all interconnected and interrelated. Young people from less privileged positions are told that all they have to do is work hard and they too will be entitled to the same privilege. False. To maintain the belief that some are created to be more entitled to privilege than others, countries have laws in which structural bias secures the privilege for those who western cultural society deems as deserving of the entitlement. It is important to address the entitlement mentality because it is causing much conflict and tension between communities mainly because it shares attributes with a certain way of thinking. The entitlement mindset centers upon the promotion of the belief that politically, economically and socially, Western cultural thinkers are more deserving of power, privilege and wealth than others. There is also a feeling within the culture of imperialism and domination to maintain that structural advantage. This way of thinking can be traced to its historical origins and development in various political ideologies.

How can these attitudes be changed? Do western cultural thinkers need to practice cognitive restructuring? Should thinkers heed psychological advice to practice perspective taking and sensitize themselves to the plight of others?

Black cultural entitlement

Western cultural thinkers have been brought up to believe that they are entitled to privilege but our upbringing in the West seems to create a mentality of entitlement to government interventions. We feel entitled to government jobs. We feel entitled to finances for social services. We feel entitled to health care. We feel entitled to benefits. It is an acquired way of thinking akin to the tendency to regard ourselves as victims of the negative events of the past. Having this way of thinking, robs us of achieving success and personal power. Entitlement also helps to maintain the mental slavery from which we must be emancipated because we cannot and must not keep blaming or feeling grievances for our situation. Rather than investing our thinking in this way, we can invest time, thought and resources into effecting positive change in our lives to entitle our black community to a better future for ourselves and our children.

This entitlement mentality operates almost as an impulse control issue where we need to control the impulse to feel entitlement. It is true that we have endured years of conditioning which allowed us to act on our impulses rather than control them with negative emotions of stress, anger and frustration being some of the main ones. Thinking rationally even when the emotions are raging out of control must be encouraged. Yes, some may argue that the entitlement mentality is in some ways justified as there was no reparation given for slavery but controlling the anger caused by injustice must be encouraged to avoid more conflict in and between communities. This impulse control issue needs further examination here as entitlement operates on the same principles. Impulse control involves the ability to let rationality control impulses and emotions. Its extreme form, Impulse Control Disorder (ICD) according to Wikipedia, this is a class of psychiatric disorders including substance related disorders, attention deficit hyperactivity disorder and conduct disorder. It is also thought that sexual compulsion, compulsive shopping and internet addiction are ICDS. Controlling impulses involves resisting temptation and urges. Impulses include tension, pleasure on acting, relief from the urge and guilt. It is a known fact that the impulse to eat unhealthy foods is an issue in our community as well as the impulse to talk out of turn. The other urges that we need to work on are well documented as they are causing lots of problems within our community.

We have to teach our children how to refrain from certain impulses when at school or in the wider community. They have to learn from very early ages to engage the brain at every level especially when there are impulses to control. If students feel hungry in a classroom, rationality should dictate that they need to wait and not try to sneak the snack out of their bag and eat it while the teacher's back is turned. Reason should dictate that students wait until break time. If they are angry, our young people have to be taught how to control the impulse to respond in a negative way. The lack of impulse control has to be traced back to the legacy of slavery and how it developed.

During slavery, there was no impulse control training only reactions. Slaves simply did whatever they felt as they operated on instinct rather than on thought. Imagine the slaves on the plantation working tireless in the fields. When they were hungry they ate, when they were thirsty they had sugar cane. Every instinct and impulse was simply done. Picture slaves all outside in the fields when they had to urge to laugh, scream, shout, curse and be angry, they simply did what they felt like doing. There could have been no filtering of the emotions, everything thought was expressed. Everything heard was repeated. Everything felt was communicated. Nothing was contained.

Through the years, this behaviour, these reactions have continued. Shouting out to express exactly what we feel anytime, anywhere, anyhow without thinking of the consequences. The common adage of think before you speak did not apply. There must have been calling, confrontations, cussing and swearing. The slaves must have also laughed and smiled on happier occasions but the fact remains that there was no control of the impulses. Today, in many of our communities, this way of reacting to situations continues through entitlement impulses but we must act to comprehensively address these lingering effects of slavery. We must refrain from life becoming a monotonous continuity of doing work that we do not enjoy as part of what we believe that we have to do in order to survive. Generations are continuing to feel this entitlement to work just to survive but this in itself is creating another legacy, another form of slavery. Collectively, we must change this mentality to believe that we are entitled to elevating ourselves from this kind of thinking, from this kind of mentality, from this kind of mind set.

Should we make available some form of Afrocentric cognitive restructuring?

Do we need a systematic desensitization to address this? Should we do something more comprehensive to address this kind of mentality? Should we enlist the help of our professionals to study and make recommendations for our impulse control issues? Should we emphasise some form of impulse control teaching at home, at school and at all social functions? Should we compile a comprehensive culturally specific mental health plan to maintain mental fitness in our lives? Should we produce a manual outlining ways to change this entitlement mentality? Should we forge social networking partnerships to help combat these pressures together?

Chapter 10

HISTORY OF TIME

History as a dimension of time. Time as linear. History as a cultural construct. Time as an economic value. History as mythology. Time as truth. History as a narrative. History as a geometrical concept. Time as universal History. History as time. Sacred time.

Time is a concept that everyone seems to know until asked to define it. The history of time refers to attempts made by Western cultural thinkers to operationalize time. As a consequence, two schools of thought emerge from the history of defining time: it is a dimension or part of the universe that happens in sequence. According to this viewpoint, time is seen as a physical quantity that is absolute and thus employed mathematically to count repetitions in the cycle of life like hours, years, decades and used to define other entities like velocity. Google Newtonian time. The other school of thought, connected theoretically to natural philosophy, is that time cannot be measured or contained as it is an intellectual structure or thought process having a relation to space. Google Kant and Leibniz. If this perspective of time as an intellectual structure is applied to the concept of time travel, one can clearly and distinctly conceive of the possibility. This view could have inspired H G Wells to write `The Time Machine' because the human mind operates on the same principles of the narrative and other theorists support him. Google Heidegger. According to Heidegger, individually and collectively we are time. He insists on the interrelationship between the past, the present and the future and that a linear relationship with time can be broken if you choose to step out of sequential time in your mind. Think about it. Random time travelling is possible through the machine of the mind, you do not need to be stuck in the present. You have the free will to travel back in time and travel to the future by programming the machine with knowledge. Importantly, as the time traveller theorizes intelligence becomes the result of and response to danger (fight or flight) and with no real challenges facing the Eloi (Western cultural thinkers), you have lost the spirit, intelligence and the full extent of the concept of humanity. Google for a summary of the text by H G Wells.

Instead of exploring the Heidegger view of time, the West has linked time almost exclusively with economic value and globalised the view that time is money. This operational definition of time is a powerful tool as well as an important weapon employed in the infrastructure of Western cultural thinking. Excellent timekeeping is attributed to professionalism, aligned with status and paid for by the hour. Short and long term investment in business planning are operated within timeframes and it is also taken to produce valuable commodities, resources and ideas. In short, time matters.

It is interesting to note that this Western, materialistic, Newtonian view of time has blurred the lineal concept of time with the secular concept and has excluded any significant emotional and spiritual value in the time process. This creates problems for sociologists and anthropologists who study the use of time without the emotional framework individuals attach to it. They simply look at time use and how it has changed with technology without exploring the spiritual connection one must have to time. It is accepted that the television and the internet has enabled time to be used in different ways but studying time operationally as a sequence rather than using a definition with a spiritual dimension can also be problematic. Western thinkers study sequences that focus on past events in stories, history and chronology on present perspectives on processes in science, medicine, technology and in a predetermined order for future focus on plans, schedules, timetables and procedures. These sequences are then employed by those at the top and herein lies the big problem.

The big problem occurs when time is used as a weapon of mass manipulation in the Orwellian ministry of truth. In other words, when those in power use time to secure privilege hiding behind the robes of justice. Have you ever wondered why investigations, especially the historic ones, take so much time? Have you stopped to consider why `independent' investigators need so much time? Let us all think out loud. Do they need so much time to create truths or to whitewash them? Are timewasting tactics employed to earn money for those working in the ministry or for the ministry itself? Could these investigations be anything other than exercises in futility for the victims but exercises in filling purses while protecting reputations of the privileged? Forget doggy dossiers. Forget bogus battalions. The real weapon of mass destruction is the system of recording History where time is the making of History. Think about what happened to History in the Orwellian ministry of truth, it is recreated, reconstructed and revised so that the past supports the present and future western party lines. Evidence of other cultural documentation is clearly edited or skilfully revised with secret surveillance ensuring that all proof is destroyed and the truth remains a matter of national security. Questions still remain, is there a personal as well as a cultural connection to time? Can time be felt as a sensation? Was the time machine created by H G Wells, absolute truth rather than science fiction? Is the human mind really a time machine? Should the West learn lessons from *1984* concerning war, ignorance and freedom? Should H G Wells help the Western Cultural thinker travel through time to stop in the years INSERT WORLD WARS AND SLAVERY DATES and think again about what has been done to the world over time? Time will tell or rather History will.

Black History of Time

Our minds are time machines programmed with knowledge of the past, present and perspectives for the future. If we operate within our genuine black cultural frameworks of truth, we will see that African concepts of time only become meaningful when the past, present and future give meaning to time. Our true history becomes a time dimension. By extension, history structures time. If we do not know our true history, then our minds cannot function properly. It would be like having a collective case history of having a head injury where there is memory loss and we have to rely on other people to construct, define or create our past history and identity. Black history is not only desirable in construction of identity but rather quintessential to our knowledge of who we are as a people. We must reconnect with our past. This is only possible if we explore African metaphysical conceptions of time and history. All viewpoints of time in our African traditions point to a spiritual dimension. Time is sacred. Time is internal. Time is who we are. When there is no knowledge, no recollection or no memory of who we are as a cultural collective, our minds cannot operate effectively.

All African rituals, beliefs, customs and values have a sacred or spiritual element which unites our mental, physical and spiritual strength as a people. Time or History does not exist in the past as events in the present tend to activate similar experiences or feelings from the past. Grace Nichols illustrates this point beautifully in her poem `Hurricane Hits England' (Google it) where the experience triggered a spiritual cultural connection. This suggests that we are connected to our roots via experiences that cause similar sensations or emotions that our forefathers endured. Our connection to a spiritual dimension to our cultural history is evident in every major black ideology – All African metaphysical conceptions, Rastafarianism, Black religious institutions, Hip Hop and Black language and literature. On the negative side, our failure to understand the truth about the importance of our collective and individual History may also influence personality which if misinterpreted may motivate mental health issues. This has been developed at length by our brothers Amos Wilson, Franz Fanon and Sister Warrior Marimba Ani. We have to realise that we have the strength, power and resilience of our African ancestors in our DNA to travel through time and feel the strength of those who fought against oppression and those who had real peace, joy and harmony in African cultural life; we can channel the strength into our mind, body and spirit (soul or heart) because our self is more than the platonic mind and more than the linear concept of time and history. The rationalisation of slavery past and present through the use of history begins to emerge as when history is taken away, there is no true knowledge of the self or its black power. Repressing the truth about the self has served its purpose and we must now learn from the Past and reconstruct a future in which our young people can soar from within our spiritual beings.

When we have no knowledge of the true meaning of time and history we struggle with adopting the operational definitions imposed upon us. Think about it. Time has been one of the bastions of western cultural thought but the bane of our culture mainly because we have adopted a Western concept and definition of time as linear and measurable. Our collective failure to keep Western cultural time is evidence that time has become a mental distortion. In the African Diaspora, we have joked about Coloured People's Time (CPT) or black time within black culture. Many try to explain the tendency to consciously, subconsciously or unconsciously disassociate ourselves from any form of responsibility, regard or respect for the western definition of time. For many of our people there seems to be an unconscious denying, ignoring and refusing to even acknowledge time. It is either that or there is a blatant indifference to this concept of time itself or a laid back, maintenance of being seen as 'cool' stepping into functions and events as if everyone is going to sing 'here comes the bride'. Seriously, there seems to be a cognitive bias to timekeeping that exists so the mind does not insist on any kind of urgency. There seems to be no pressure of thinking driving the action. There seems to be no mental discipline to rule this unconscious rationalisation about time.

Let's travel back to slave times for a moment and see our brothers and sisters working arduously on the plantations with the slave master undoubtedly insisting on arriving to work on time, completing work within given times and finishing for the day on time. The slaves must have felt they had a right to be slow, late and indifferent to the work fields because they were not being paid. They did not enjoy the work; they were not being rewarded for being on time and so they rightfully refused to hurry up. Now, travel back to the present. Since slavery, black people in the diaspora still seem to have a rather interesting relationship with time: it has become our slave not our master. We treat time with disrespect, disregard and disdain. We refuse to let time control, dominate or harass us. We are virtually indifferent to the very existence of time. However, do we need to change our conceptualisation of time, our attitudes to time and our thinking about time in all contexts? Do we begin by exploring rather than repressing the truth about the spiritual dimension attached to time that may be causing the rejection of Western time? Should we formulate a comprehensive action plan to reassess our relationship with time? Should we take time to educate our children about the value of time and history? Should we change our tendency to start black functions later than the time advertised? Should we have some time workshops to help people improve their relationship with time? Should we evaluate ways to free our minds to think clearly and distinctly about the relationship between time and history in the reconstruction of our culture?

Chapter 11

SEXUAL PERMISSIVENESS

The Enlightenment. Surrealist movement. Sexual revolution. Sexual freedom. Sexual liberation. Premarital sex. Casual sex. Contraception. Abortion. The Pill. Public nudity. Homosexuality. Erotic fantasies. Masturbation. Pornography. Permissive society. Important influences: Rousseau. Marquis de Sade. Wilhelm Reich. D. H Lawrence. Sigmund Freud. Hugh Hefner.

Sexual freedom in the mind of the western cultural thinker is a person's human right. Everyone has the right to be unique. Everyone has the right to express their sexual individuality or uniqueness. Everyone has the right to develop their own sexuality with whoever they choose to and whenever they choose to. Everyone has the right to have as many partners as possible. Everything and anything goes. Advocates of sexual rights insist that governments, religious leaders and society should not interfere in the individual's consensual sexual activities because it is their fundamental right to enjoy sexual expression with dignity and without any kind of stigmatization or nanny state interference. D H Lawrence in `Lady Chatterley's Lover' presents the priority for women to have physical intimacy over intellectual or financial intimacy and this has helped to reshape thinking about fidelity in marriage for the Western cultural thinker. Literary works employed the thinking of other fields notably psychiatry where advocates of sexual freedom provided was a sound epistemic base from which to launch the movement. Google what the psychiatrists studied in the clinic and referred to as 'sexual perversion' and focus on how this changed the thinking about sexual freedom. In essence, the added knowledge and focus of sexual freedom gave it an elevated status from which it has grown and developed into its modern form. This modern form of sexual freedom is self-obsessing, self-defining and above all self-gratifying.

This thinking has led to a broad spectrum of reproductive, familial and sexual problems related to gender, marital and sexuality identity in religious, psychiatric, political, societal and cultural circles. Religion, which used to have the moral authority in cultures everywhere, has been undermined by this sexual freedom. Yet advocates who try to offer a hand of unity soon discover that religion and sexual freedom is a dysfunctional marriage with each party dependent on the other for survival rather than having a separate independent existence. Religion will always be seen as the problem blocking sexual freedom and gay rights and this can never ever be locked away in the closet. Gay rights is desperate for acceptance by religion but their laws just cannot allow it. Lawyers for each party have been searching for loopholes in the law but the settlement agreement is definitely one of irreconcilable differences because both parties just cannot coexist. Terms of the agreement state that both parties must appear together in public when summoned to do so by their partisan political in-laws which means that this arrangement will always be a case of sleeping with the enemy only that neither party can ever sleep.

Sexuality has now become linked to personal identity and operates on the pleasure principle more so than any period in history. It is part of the new individualism and self-gratification that defines the preferred options of the generation of today. This is another reason why sexual freedom and religion are incompatible for the western cultural thinker. Sexual freedom revolves around pleasure and self-gratification rather than developing a meaningful connection to conception, reproduction and the creation of the family and this has led to a plethora of problems made evident in the systematic breakdown of the family as a unit. How could western society promote freedom within boundaries without undermining individual human rights? How can religious advocates negotiate with the secularist society on family values? How is it possible to have a reduction in the proliferation of sexual identities without government 'interference'? How can we promote family values without undermining individual values?

Sexual freedom in the black community

The modernization of Sexual freedom has created a series of reproductive problems for the black community and we even have our own labels with 'Baby fatherhood' and 'Baby motherhood' being the most popular. 'Single parenthood' and so called 'independent womanhood' come in a close second. The fact that we do not embrace our ancestral concepts of the wholesome nature of the black family as a 'village self' rather than 'an individual self' has worsened the perception of the problem so that it is made to look like we have larger problems than Western cultural thinkers. If we trace the history of sexual liberation and its effects on our community cohesion, we will find that the heart of the problem lies in changed attitudes to the sexual union. If it is done almost exclusively for pleasure rather than for love or reproduction then pregnancies that inevitably result by accident or by design would create problems on every level: for the parents, for the children, for our community and for the wider society. Google the number of pregnancies that are unintended, unwanted or unplanned and sort by age, ethnicity and region for evidence. Find the number of sexually active teenagers in the African diaspora and find the number of our men who claim that they did not know about the pregnancies until after the birth. Do you now agree that there is definitely an issue of sexual freedom without boundaries or responsibility; a systematic failure to think thoroughly about the consequences of this sexual freedom. Google the figures on unprotected sex, teenage pregnancies, sexual transmitted diseases and they will all confirm that we have a problem that is spiralling out of control.

Let's think more critically about the root of this problem. Is it the case that our children no longer see the sexual union as sacred but rather as exclusively for pleasure? If this is indeed the case, should our young people be taught to protect themselves more? More importantly, should we address the thinking that still lingers in the community that sex without protection is more desirable? Should we comprehensively work on our cultural socialisation and all the issues related to it? Can we really address attitudes to sex and conception without looking at traces of the slave sex culture – carnivals, dances and now the rap videos? Is it not the case that these all socialise our young black girls into thinking that sexual performance is the core element of black female identity? Have our teenage girls simply internalised the ideas perpetuated by western cultural society that sexuality is an identity in and of itself?

But, is there more to this issue than sexual identity? The black female body generally matures very quickly and this definitely has an emotional and psychological effect. Could it be that our girls are having sex too early because they have not been taught their rites of passage on how to cope with the specific effects of puberty? Could it be that our physicality causes certain emotional and psychological effects that remain unexplored in `academic' circles? Let us try to trace the historical journey in the western world. Historical underpinnings suggest that the bodies of black slaves were primarily for consumption by slave owners, male and female. Slaves were used not just for work but also for the leisure and pleasure of the owners. Slaves were raped, abused and used by many men and the slaves were forced to have sex with each other while the master watched on. The female slaves were forced to pleasure their masters and thus became their sex slaves. They were also forced to have sex with other slaves as black women were mere commodities. Since then, this colonization, this commodification, this conquest of black female bodies had detrimental effects on the mind, the body and the soul of black women. Sadly, the denigration has carried on uninterrupted through the ages. Nowadays, black women are seen in the media in the same historic role but real eyes realise the lingering shadows of slavery. This slave culture comes uninvited to carnival, barges in to present day rap parties and sleeps silently in our homes. We must end it.

Living in Western societies has severely affected our understanding of what it is to be a black woman. We have been the products of a negative perception, a social construction that is rooted in purpose, performance and yes prostitution. Similarly, black male bodies have always been perceived as sexually aggressive and savage yet coerced historically by female slave owners who preyed on their physical prowess. Black male slaves were simply sex toys and consequently black masculinity became defined by sexual conquest. Put simply, our men have been subjected through the ages to a brutal manifestation of racial and gender power. The big question remains - how do we rise from this element of slave cultural history? Do we need a new Afrikan-centred understanding of black sexuality, black womanhood, black manhood so that it is not equated with the sexuality of the past? Should we consider Black development programmes to help our young people cope with thinking about sexual activity and its consequences? Is it time to build a new legacy rooted in our Afrikan-centred traditions based on our ontological values about our ancestral collectivist approach for the empowerment of our community?

Chapter 12

FINANCIAL PROVIDERS

Non-residential dads. Modern men. Absent fathers. Financial supporters. Free fathers. Step dads. Deadbeat dads. Opting out of fatherhood dads.

Sexual freedom changed the hearts and minds of men and women in an unprecedented way as it not only changed attitudes to sexuality but also to gender roles. Something deeply existential happened when both men and women began to think differently about these things almost simultaneously. The great expectations of the father as the main provider, as the head of the family, as the one who wears the trousers and most importantly as the final decision maker changed the landscape The Dickensian notion of the man trying to prove himself worthy of love no longer applies. As a consequence, the total breakdown of the great traditional expectation of staying in a family relationship for the sake of the family has lost favour and now women are left in the same emotional place as Ms Havisham. Fathers have found a new freedom to find partner after partner without feeling any obligation from society, from family members or the state to remain for the sake of the children. The family unit has now been redefined beyond recognition and fathers and their role has gone down the same path. The path has many side roads and obstacles but as Pip discovered whichever path chosen turns out to be a dangerous one.

The `freedom from fathers as providers' pathway is most dangerous for the children who have to be dragged along accompanied by their stepbrothers and sisters all struggling emotionally to make the journey civil. The kaleidoscope of emotions experienced on these journeys paint very different pictures for all in the family. There are those who spend the whole journey thinking of an escape route and find various outlets in poor displays of behaviour, truancy and poor academic performance. Social adjustment issues of this kind mask the resentments, the fears and of course the deep unhappiness and anxieties of having missed the experience of growing up with a father in the home. Others hide in relationships that then lead to promiscuity and teenage pregnancies in the need to find someone to fill the void. Additional problems then occur with sexual health and even exploitation by those who take advantage of their plight. Young girls particularly crave for fatherly figure affection and become susceptible to the wrong kind of response. Some find shelter being homeless in an attempt to run away from the emotional loss. All of the paths inevitably then lead to mental health problems, social maladjustment, physical health problems and life chances are likely to be dependent on social welfare with low mortality prospects.

To state sexual freedom as the only or major reason for father absence is oversimplifying a very complex plethora of interrelated problems which include: the feminist movement, identity proliferation, loss of religion or traditional values and not forgetting the economic crises and its effects on families. The question then becomes where does the West go from here? How is it possible to rein in this modernisation of fatherhood and its effects on the family and by extension society? How do men repossess their place in the home? How do women encourage men to stay? How do children learn the values of being a father if there is little or no exposure to a model of fatherhood?

Father freedom in the black community

Within our community, the issues with black fatherhood is much more complex than father absence in other cultures. Many sing about it, preach about it, theorise about it and even joke about it. The urban dictionary attempts to define it: a baby father/daddy is usually a broke ass black man who a black woman met through a friend and had sex with when she was upset and confused. This definition highlights economic, emotional, entitlement, environmental and educational dimensions to the problem. If we define baby fatherhood more formally, a baby father is the biological father of a woman's child; one who is not married to or in a long-term, intimate relationship with the child's mother. Of course, we must note that sometimes baby daddies are unknown.

The truth is that in our homeland our men are kings, chiefs and warriors but in the West our men are disempowered, disrespected and devalued. Surely, baby fatherhood has resulted from a toxic cocktail of miscomprehension of the black man's true self, the seduction of sexual liberation, a cultural identity crisis, a mythical egoism and a combination of other problems experienced from living in or embracing western culture without filtering it first. Whatever the origins of the problem, the fact remains that absent fatherhood is an epidemic in our community and definitely one of our greatest challenges. To tackle this astronomical problem, we need a comprehensive long term strategic vision and solution.

Fatherhood is a lifelong process and taking responsibility for the welfare of our children should be a priority from the womb to the tomb or from the cradle to the grave. As Malcolm X insists 'to understand the life of any person, his whole life, from birth, must be reviewed.

All of our experiences fuse into our personality. Everything that ever happened to us is an ingredient". Let's remember, fatherhood is a learned skill and if it is not being cultivated in the home, then it must be learnt in an institution or through an ideology. There must be some educational strategy to address the issue of how to be an effective black father. Here lies the problem in the community and the solution to the problem: good models need to be provided through a comprehensive and holistic strategy which combines education, entertainment and entrepreneurship. Fathers learn how to be fathers by following models of fatherhood but in the absence of black father role models in many homes in the community, how are young boys learning to be fathers? If some of our black men are viewed to be loitering rather than learning, cursing rather than caring, cheating rather than committing, hanging rather than helping, entertaining rather than enterprising, how are our boys going to learn how to be fathers? Baby fatherhood is not as simple as the act of sperm giving or the act of proving paternity. The Maury Show and Jerry Springer have made a fortune highlighting the problem of the plight of fathers in our community but this should not be seen as entertainment as baby fatherhood is no laughing matter. The complexities are intertwined with all of our other problems from mentality issues to education to governmental misapprehension of the problems and we must work as a community to address these problems.

Our families need fathers. If you would like the grim statistics on this problem please feel free to google the percentage of our youth growing up in fatherless homes in different regions of the African diaspora. Kindly check the figures on the number of our boys excluded from school. Check the number of our brothers diagnosed with mental health issues. Google the number of our men in prison. Feel free to find correlations between fatherlessness, exclusion, poverty and other factors. The issue is not about finding statistics to prove or disprove the problem but rather how do we stop this vicious cycle?

An understanding of the historical context of the legacy that led to life in the West is necessary here. Slavery and the transatlantic slave trade not only separated people from their families and cultures but disintegrated, disorganised and destabilised the black family structure. The dispersion of our people around the world was implicitly and explicitly part of the old divide and rule policy of the masters. Importantly, baby slaves were not born to be part of a family: they were born to be slaves. It was unlikely that the baby fathers were going to be in a relationship with the baby mothers. Their owners made sure that dividing the family enabled the dominant rule over the slaves. Any form of familial unity would have been seen as a strength. Essentially, it was not in the interest of slave owners to form family units; it was in their interest to fragment the black family. Families were not formed through any kind of planning. Children resulted from sexual activity organised directly or indirectly by the masters. Sometimes, children were the consequence of porn entertainment activities, others resulted from rape of black female slaves by masters, or from white female conquests with black male slaves. Mixed race slaves were the consequence of sexual acts with male and female white masters. Black male slaves had children they never knew and similarly female slaves would have no idea who their baby daddies were.

Colonisation brought missionary thinking stressing the family as a married unit and this worked to a large extent for years until the impact of certain revolutions and liberations of the 1960s. Paradoxically, these freedoms have served the same purpose of the abolition of slavery act: to free the slaves without unshackling their minds. To free the slaves without changing the system or the whip or the mechanism that originally enslaved them. To free the slaves without providing an education for their reparation and most of all to free the slaves without freeing their minds. Google the facts and figures related to the liberations of the 1960s.

This practice continues and will continue unless we open our real eyes to realise real lies embedded in the systems of the West that condition us, like Skinner's rat into believing that we are free when we are simply not. At present, we are sleepwalking back into the days of chattel slavery in our behaviours with baby producing practices that blow the mind. Our collective lives have deteriorated and now we have to rethink our actions and lifestyles. Life for black boys is taking a turn for the worse as poverty, family problems, and racial segregation take their toll on our boys forcing them to turn to drugs, to crime, to extremism and to hustling to combat the pain of their environment. How do we begin to tackle this huge problem? Should we have father development programmes in our communities to teach young men how to be fathers? Should we develop a 'men matter' initiative to pressure fathers to support their children financially and emotionally? Should we have a 'Dads Army' course that teaches discipline using some military, fitness and cadet type training? Should we have 'Black Fathers Award' ceremonies, dedicated to devoted dads while inspiring young fathers to do likewise? Should we start some kind of action group – a planned fatherhood initiative run by black fathers for black fathers? Should we organise father fun days with activities for fathers to shine or rap/calypso or song competitions about fatherhood to raise the profile of fatherhood in our community? Should all community groups sit together and work out a comprehensive way forward?

Chapter 13

FEMINIST FREEDOM

Single motherhood. Working mums. Married mothers. Divorced mothers. Independent mothers. Career women. Feminist females. Second wave feminism. Women's liberation. Women's rights.

Many argue that the liberation of women was the greatest freedom won for women while others argue that it has left women overworked, underpaid and unloved. Women are overworked as they have to toil full time at the workplace and full time at home; women are still underpaid yet doing equal work to men and most of all women are now too independent and too idealistic in their notions of beauty to be perceived as 'attractive' as they were in times gone by. The fact that western cultural women define this as freedom is mind boggling. Yes, challenging traditional ideas about female sexuality is admirable and choosing partners can be seen as some fundamental right without familial, religious or bstate interference can be applauded perhaps. However, the effect of this surge in priorities for women at the expense of the rest of the family has to be examined as it has made a negative contribution to the family as the stabilising force in societies everywhere.

The heart of feminist ideology was the pursuit of pleasure for women coupled with the pursuit of female independence. There was the Pill. Abortion was legalised. LGBT helps to identify women. However, this duality at the core of the movement simultaneously undermined the family unit: men's role as the prime sexual and financial provider has been affected and so too has the priority of children and their needs in the family unit. What is worthy of note is that liberation for women has not happened on the domestic level as all such duties are still essentially women's work. The reality is no matter how much women fight to smother our nature in surmise, nature still manages to make its presence felt and although women are still fighting to close the wage gap outside the home the same problem still arises. The aim here is not to blame the movement but to show how major familial problems have arisen as a consequence of women's liberation.

Women are now the breadwinners, the victims of sexist adverts, expected doers of domestic duties, victims of wage inequalities and subject to beauty objectification and now victims of a proliferation of identities from bisexual to lesbian to transgender. How do women deal with these issues? Is a strategic shift in ideology needed here? Should women explore more ontological arguments? What about shifting completely from issues of equality to issues with a complimentary core rather than antagonism? Seriously, if the feminist movement shifted to a more academic base where ontological arguments were considered particularly to challenge the male dominated platonic view of the world, then the feminist movement just may be in a better moral position than it is now. If feminist thinkers would shift their main role from the social, political and economic equality of men and women to something more substantial for the moral fabric of society, then perhaps the world would turn out to be a much better place than it is now. If there is consideration of a new intellectual base for women's essence or core nature rather than arguing for psychoanalysis or some other Freudian connection which leads the world down other paths then we can literally create another world. No, not one with an Oedipus complex. No, not one with Libido. No, not one with unconscious drives or eroticism or repression.

Glynis Glasgow-Kelly

Black cultural perspective

Feminism has affected our community quite negatively as the sheer scale of single womanhood is now at crisis point. Society tends to blame the single woman for deciding or opting to have children without the father's knowledge or in some cases, without the father's consent. The problem becomes much more complex when `baby mama drama' starts when the baby mama starts is jealous of the other woman in the father's life. Children are also born overwhelmingly in matriarchal families as the result of marriage breakdown, the result of relationship breakdown and of course the result of unintended, unplanned pregnancies and many nowadays are the results of sperm donation or informal financial arrangements. Baby mothers often choose to `bring the child' knowing that the baby father is in a relationship with someone else or some even decide that they `want a child' and decide to have sex specifically for that reason. Others are prepared to have the child and `bring them up' themselves without any fatherly involvement. These all lead to a plethora of problems within the black family unit especially for the children who are caught up in the crossfire. When our women are doing this on a large scale in the African diaspora, our culture is perceived in a rather negative way. We have to now explore ways to heal or build relationships for our children otherwise the black family as a cultural unit will denigrate beyond recognition.

Our first challenge must be to acknowledge that the image of black women needs to be redefined through socialisation and black cultural cultivation. Respect and support must then be given to those who try their best to cope with the stress of work, of life itself and of single parenthood. One tends to forget the enormous pressure of being on parental duty twenty four hours a day, with the added pressure of chasing the baby daddies to take some responsibility be it financial or emotional. Many single mothers rely on the extended family for support and some just struggle all by themselves. This way of life has detrimental effects on the children involved in these familial arrangements. It is made even worse when mothers have children at very young ages. This has traditionally been encouraged in the black community as it has historically been equated with womanhood and responsibility. Others claim that you need to have children early so that you can be energetic enough to play with them or have them `before your bones are set' and you do not have the physical strength for motherhood. Surely, with the economic climate worsening, with housing problems on the rise, shouldn't we think again about our life choices and cultural traditions?

In recent years, there has been a surge in the number of single working black women who have chosen to have children and take full responsibility for them. But are we not pursuing independence only to find ourselves more dependent on others - our mothers, our children, our jobs? Are we overworked, overstressed and crucially unloved? Are we all responsible for the next generation of fathers who do not know how to be fathers because single working mothers were too busy being independent? Are we not depriving the next generation of young black sisters of future fathers for their children as the boys that we raise do not know how to be fathers because they have had no father models? Then let us not forget those of our sisters in desperate financial circumstances who are having children for different men and relying on the monthly payments for an additional income, rather than for the exclusive benefit of the child. This becomes very problematic indeed because some of the same men have children everywhere and simply cannot afford to pay maintenance even when pursued by the authorities. We have to find ways to end this baby father and baby mama mentality. It is destroying us.

If we trace the problem back to the legacy, slave traders preferred to buy male slaves than female ones during the slave trade. What happened as a result in the Diaspora, women were disproportionally outnumbered to men. Google for confirmation. Two things could have resulted from this imbalance: women were used by even more men and they were pressured to child bear more often. Female slaves were then used for labour, used for sex, used for child bearing, used for raising children. Our female ancestors were used and abused in many ways and the post traumatic slave trauma still needs to heal. What added to the emotional problems was the fact that children born to slave women were the property of slave owners and as a consequence raising children properly was simply not possible. Poor nutrition, extreme exploitation, ill health made proper parenting impossible. As a consequence, many children died young from poor nutrition and nurturing as their slave mothers had to work arduously in the agricultural fields. Picture our women doing manual labour and running back to shelters to look after their babies. It must have been traumatic.

Could you imagine how high the infant mortality rate would be with virtually no medical care? Could you imagine the psychological impact of not being allowed to breastfeed or to care for your sick children because you were ordered back to work on the plantations? Could you imagine the traumatic loss experienced by women who would return from work to find their children dead? Could you imagine the pain of taking children from the womb to the tomb – almost literally? Could you think about the pain and severe loss experienced by black female slaves? Could you understand how female slaves suffered from delivering still births and severely underweight children? Were children weaned too early, undernourished and uncared for?

Given this context, we can see why black women developed coping mechanisms, dogged determination and strength of will. Our foremothers were resentful of their condition but were resilient in their endeavour to fight for their families. But now, we must rediscover that strength and channel it into a movement that declares 'no more dragging up of our children because that belongs in the past.' We must find ways to break the chains that link us to this past and say 'never again!'. Sisters we can do it with the help of our sister warriors who have fought for our freedom from this mentality. Should we develop a family support and mediation service to foster emotional support for baby mothers, baby fathers and of course the babies? Should we develop sisterhood serenades or ceremonies to honour black sisters? Should we have a 'Black Women United' pressure group to engage, educate and empower the next generation of black women to think differently about black womanhood and black fatherhood?

Chapter 14

TEENAGE FREEDOM

Children's rights. Teenage pregnancies. Teenage conflict. Teenage sexuality. Teenage internet freedom.

In the West, children have rights to stand up for themselves, rights to free speech, rights to free action and of course rights to do as they please, what the French term `laissez-faire'. The fundamental human right to do anything and everything whenever and wherever one pleases has led to a series of problems in the home, in the school and in wider society. Allowing such freedom without emphasising responsibility has led to an increase in indiscipline in every institution and now there must be a comprehensive effort to rein in these rights or face the dire consequences of a society without any moral direction. The internet has provided a glorified gallery for teenage freedom and thus has not helped to solve the problem. Rather than rein in the freedom, it has opened the gates for freedom to flow rampantly and take liberty to a whole new level. There is freedom to troll. Freedom to post private actions. Freedom to selfie. Freedom to bully. Freedom to commit new crimes. Freedom to have sexual adventures earlier and earlier and earlier.

It seems like abstinence and the idea of marriage is well and truly out of date in Western cultural thinking as teenagers simply embrace casual sex as a new morality. Young people seem to consume this way of thinking about sex and sexuality in their identity formation and this leads to other interrelated problems of birth control, unplanned pregnancies and of course sexually transmitted diseases. Risk-free sex no matter how it is perceived is problematic as a concept and as a way of life and teenagers must be made aware of this fact. Normalising this kind of social practice is inadvertently undermining their rights to choose from different frames of reference such as religious, cultural and other moral value systems.

Sexual issues of this nature have become a matter of politics especially in the United States where contrasting views of abortion is crucial in political discourse. The pro-life and pro-choice activists engage in wars of words, wars of values and wars of politics with young people growing up and taking sides in the conflicts. Teenagers assume their rights and sexual freedoms without questioning the philosophy which underpins the politics itself. To think differently, young people must examine the ideology that gives birth to this way of thinking and not simply assume that there is a monopoly on truth at play in the politics of sex. Is it possible that sex is overhyped, over-commercialised and overrated? Can teenagers really enjoy sex freely or are they simply experimenting to their own detriment? With the increase in child sexual exploitation, with the increase in unplanned pregnancies, with the increase in sexually transmitted diseases, is it time for the Western cultural thinker to reconsider its massive commercialisation and politicisation of sex?

Black cultural perspective

The problem of teenage pregnancy in our culture must stem from the fact that we are missing a separate cultural framework and depending on the Western cultural freedom construct for a frame of reference. As a consequence, our young people seem lost in this free world. If we google the black teenage pregnancy rates in different parts of the African Diaspora, we will see that this freedom has led to a series of problems. Some argue that it is the cause and the consequence of poverty; others argue that our children are growing up too quickly – they are exposed to sex too quickly – in the home, on the internet and at school. There are also those who insist on the moral decline in the black community which means that parents, pastors and politicians abstain from teaching teens about abstinence. On this latter point about abstinence, we now have a generation of sexually active children, some from under the age of 12. There is an urgent need for action here as the church has lost not its message but its audience – its younger audience to the extent that even church going teenagers are becoming pregnant.

Let's not forget that some of our teenage girls are being pursued by older men; in some parts of the black underclass, this is accepted as a means of financial support for families. Many young black girls and their parents do not regard this as working in the sex trade but this is technically what it really is.

There is also the indirect cultural peer pressure to have sex early as teens listen to their mothers and grandmothers talk about their experiences of being young parents. Reality TV shows like `16 and Pregnant' and `Teen Mom' have served dual purposes: it can be argued that they have helped reduce teen pregnancy rates through education but it can also be seen as inadvertently raising the profile of teenage pregnancy. Thankfully there is better sex education provision and much better access to contraceptives to help reduce the rate of teenage pregnancy. However, the problem of sexual permissiveness remains an issue of concern: a problem.

Historically, slave culture cemented the perceived role of black women as child bearers, who take up their role quite early. This distorted image has continued to develop in the African diaspora. During slavery, young female slaves were exploited by older masters and by older male slaves so much so that many young slave girls internalised their role as sexual objects. The fact that black female bodies seem to mature quite early, childbearing must have happened before adulthood. Google for evidence of the historical underpinnings.

Slavery violated not only the bodies of the female slaves but also their childhood, their womanhood and their parenthood. Sexual abuse of teenage slaves was a harsh reality. It was trauma. It was exploitation. It was torture.

Dealing with slavery's heartache, hardships and horrors will take a long term plan of action and we must invest time to address these issues but we must deal with these consequences. We have to persuade our young women to delay pregnancy and learn about themselves and their community. We have to teach them to think critically about such practices that are rooted in slavery. Should we provide culturally specific access to Sex education?

Should we discuss these issues in an attempt to raise awareness about the advantages of delaying parenthood? Should we extrapolate from the Obama administration's Teen Pregnancy Prevention Initiative that awards millions in grants to effective preventative programs that address teenage pregnancy? Should we educate our teens with the hope of using positive peer pressure methods to address the problem in our community?

Chapter 15

FAMILY SIZES

Large families. Unwanted pregnancies. Unplanned parenthood. Family traditions. Family circumstances. Freedom to overpopulate the planet.

The Chinese one child policy was enforced to curb the population and it was claimed that this policy helped to prevent some 400 million births. Ironically, many people in the West accused China of denying its citizens fundamental human rights in its implementation of the policy. Here we are nearly forty years after the imposition of the policy and China is prospering economically while the West is crumbling under the weight of its housing crisis. The right to have as many children as one wants is unsustainable in the current climate and the Western cultural thinker must concede defeat on this human right. Society needs some kind of government intervention, initiative or 'interference', not the kind proposed by Jonathan Swift but something radically different to cope with the current state of affairs.

The state of affairs is really one of overpopulation, one of our poor planet earth crumbling under the weight of billions of people. Increased lifespan, reduced mortality rates and technological advancement in fertility treatment have all contributed to the growth of the world's population. Immigration and lack of family planning have also affected figures in Western countries. The only way forward seems to be some kind of governmental intervention to persuade citizens to be more responsible and think about the planet rather than individual freedoms. The alternative is to suffer from housing crises, economic decline, family breakdown and overpopulation. Family sizes must be curbed and curbed quickly.

The growth of population is one problem but the effects on the environment and the depletion of resources is another interrelated one. Industrialisation and air pollution have led to environmental problems with the most common being global warming. This astronomical problem must be seen as intricately linked to overpopulation, overconsumption and overindulgence in rights and privileges that need to be curbed through governmental policies. Is it right for families that are struggling to cope financially, emotionally and spiritually to continue having more children? If a family is not functioning, should the State not intervene to prevent family augmentation rather than pay benefits or simply place the children into care? Is having large families that cannot be supported an immoral act in and of itself? Is it not the case that poverty and neglect lead to greater societal ills like prostitution? Does excessive childbearing have a detrimental effect on the woman's body and causes additional stress and poor health?

Black cultural perspective

Large families has been part of our cultural fabric for generations and we have been brought up to learn to help each other, to cope with life's struggles together, to be responsible from a very early age. In addition to this, children in large families tend to adapt to different roles to gain parental affection and attention. However, some of our large families have also suffered from the effects of poverty, hardship and labour of different degrees. If the cost of raising large families is higher now in terms of finances, time, resources, property, stress, is it time for us to reconsider our traditional thinking about family size? Should our people insist on having more and more children in light of the changing economic, climatic and social environment? Is it time to think differently about family planning, about free sexual activity, about the cost of the decision to go through with pregnancy after pregnancy, about the fact that someone else will have to support the children – most likely the State, our extended families or authorities chasing the baby daddies? Is this continued practice of childbearing in large proportions leading to additional problems of overcrowding, child labour where the older siblings have to take care of younger siblings and the list goes on?

Let us think about another aspect of the problem: family size is often accompanied by multiple fathers as some black women feel obliged to have a baby to cement their relationship with a new partner. When this happens multiple times, multiple problems result. These include: negative labels, poverty, desperation, stress, sibling rivalry, father-figure feuding with step children, urgency to leave home, urgency to join groups on the streets, domestic abuse and consequently the vicious cycle continues.

Discourse about large families must be considered in its historical context as childbearing was the role ascribed to female slaves who had to endure the pain of losing their children in the trade between masters. Imagine getting pregnant and toiling from morning to night in the hot fields and when you are finished and you feel exhausted there is no time to rest, no provision of medical care, no provision of a healthy diet for mother or baby. Difficult pregnancies gave birth to further difficulties as slave mothers tried to bond with their babies but then there is further loss as some experienced either premature death or loss through the trade of babies after birth. Some mothers had to give up their babies as they were simply the property of their slave owner who could sell the babies at will as part of the ongoing trade. What a life it must have been! Slave women were traumatised being at the complete mercy of slave owners.

The sale of children and the separation of families must be among the most heartless of horrors experienced during slavery, leaving permanent psychological scars on the structure of family life that still lingers into the present day. Generations have passed but the marks are still visible on our cultural body. Some of us still think that our role is simply one of childbearing through hardship and struggle but there needs to be a thorough or complete understanding of our history and how we tend to sleepwalk back into the practices of the past. We have to work on removing these scars forever. We have to educate our young people to comprehensively repair the damage done to our collective cultural psyche. How do we begin to overhaul the devastating effects rooted in the legacy of the past? Should we extrapolate from the Chinese policy on limited numbers of children per family? Should we develop a culturally sensitive focus on family planning? Should we highlight the expense and burden of maintaining large families? Should we have culturally appropriate whole family learning sessions to comprehensively eradicate the conditioned thinking about ourselves and our past? Should we encourage our young people to delay parenthood and to be more responsible in sexual activity? Do we need a holistic supplementary educational system to address the specific problems related to family planning?

Chapter 16

CHILD LABOUR

Parental pressure. Conflict at home. Children's chores. Juvenile offending. Family disrespect. Meltdown. Dysfunctional family relationships. Freedom without boundaries.

According to Wikipedia: "Child labour refers to the employment of children in any work that deprives children of their childhood, interferes with their ability to attend regular school, and that is mentally, physically, socially or morally dangerous and harmful. This practice is considered exploitative by many international organisations. Legislation across the world prohibit child labour. These laws do not consider all work by children as child labour; exceptions include work by child artists, family duties, supervised training, certain categories of work such as those by Amish children, some forms of child work common among indigenous American children, and others."

Child labour in the West starts on the implied premise that agricultural child labour is more exploitative than intellectual child labour. However, if we consider the subordinate clause in the definition of child labour – 'that is mentally, socially or morally dangerous and harmful', one may be able to interpret child labour in an entirely different way. The mental strain on young children to be tested from primary school level, the social isolation of children being forced to study almost around the clock, having private lessons to further impose intellectual labour on young minds rather than allow them to be free to enjoy the innocence of childhood must be considered as exploitation to some degree. Excessive pressure exerted by parents who are determined to live vicariously through their children must also be correctly labelled as exploitation. Children have to labour to learn a musical instrument, labour to learn a sport, labour to learn to speak with a BBC accent and of course labour to achieve top grades in all subjects. These labour practices appear under the euphemistic label of high culture or educational achievement rather than the more accurate label of child labour.

Sixteen years of child labour of this kind leads to all sorts of mental, social, emotional problems in the Western cultural home. Many children feel that their concerns and real work interests are disregarded and even disrespected by the parents in authority and this has psychological effects. Expressing any kind of disapproval can cause misunderstandings as parents simply fail to see certain practices as exploitative even as social service figures will prove otherwise. Google for statistics on the psychological and emotional problems in the home. Google the reasons why so many children in the West are placed into care. You will find that there is a systematic lack of honest communication which only serves to perpetuate further misunderstandings and lead to further problems. Promises are not kept to listen to the needs and the voices of children and as a result this creates an atmosphere of distrust in the home and leads to more conflict outside the home. The heart of the conflict is the intergenerational clash of values with the older generation assuming that child labour is a quintessential cultural value. What results is further tension, further conflict and further disruption to family life.

Another related problem is one of sibling rivalry which results when some children embrace the values of child labour more so than others. Parental approval or additional parental attention can lead to animosities which make a difficult situation worse as some siblings may feel inadequate or even angry at preferential treatment being given to members of the family who conform. Every child matters in the family as well as wider society and deserves an equal amount of parental unconditional love. How does the West begin to address the issue of child labour that is undoubtedly causing many problems within the family? Should the Western cultural thinker begin by addressing the assumption that only physical labour can be perceived as child labour? Should there be an examination of the real reasons for imposing values on the younger generation without labelling them as exploitation of the mind?

Black Perspective

Within our black community, child labour tends to be an expectation of success that is laid squarely on the shoulders of our children. We want them to get all top grades at school when we did not. We want them to learn responsibilities of parenthood quite early so we ask them to pick up their siblings from school, bathe them, iron their clothes. We expect our children to be successful in the Western world by doing exactly what the western cultural thinkers have done by putting pressure on our children without realising that we are trying to live vicariously through our children. Is this pressure overwhelming our children rather than uplifting them? Think about it from the perspective of childhood innocence, is it too much too soon?

Google the figures on the number of children who walk unaccompanied to school and are involved in accidents on their way to school? Google how many were taking younger siblings. Is it really our children's responsibility to take their siblings to school? Yes, children need to learn responsibility but there is also something called parental responsibility.

Our children need to be children. They are forced to grow up too quickly. It is reasonable to encourage children to excel at school and do some minor chores at home in order to learn familial responsibility but do we need to think about the fact that our children must learn to be children? It is not their job to get siblings dressed and take them to school. It is not their job to do all the chores that parents are too tired or sorry, too lazy to do. This is a version of child labour.

Yes, single mothers struggle to juggle parenthood and work to make ends meet. However, we have to find a better way to galvanise support in our community. Our children are under too much pressure at home, at school, at church and in society to further crumble under the weight of expectation amongst other things. Let us trace this thinking to its source in the legacy. The untold story of slavery must be that of the oppression of children. Their experience under slavery must have been one of hardship, brutality, exploitation and loss. Imagine the children being separated from their families as their fathers may have lived on different plantations, may have been sold or may have been slave owners. Imagine the loss of their mothers who had to wean them early and give them away on demand by their owners. Children had to learn to fend for themselves. If not, they would be whipped for failures, forced to have sexual liaisons, abused or neglected. It must have been horrific being robbed of any kind of childhood.

Children as young as four were given work to clean, collect rubbish and perhaps scare away birds. Older children would learn to weed and work in the fields with the adults as well as doing other domestic tasks inside the master's house. *The Interesting Narrative of the Life of Olaudah Equiano: kidnapping* provides further reading of the experiences from the perspective of a slave. It explains the horrors of the slave trade. Since slavery, many organisations have exposed child labour and the trafficking of children - both horrors of a different kind. These show us just a glimpse of what children had to endure during the experience of slavery and the transatlantic slave trade. Where do we go from here? How do we begin to address the lingering effects of the legacy of slavery? Should we organise black community buses or provide transport in our neighbourhoods to support parents to and from school? Should we have campaigns against this sort of child labour? Should we educate parents more about the dangers of excessive pressure on children? Should we set up a culturally specific child protection agency? Is the real solution, a comprehensive holistic supplementary education system to repair the lingering effects of the legacy of slavery?

Chapter 17

RELATIONSHIP BREAKDOWN

Economic hardships. Tension. Conflict. Frustration. Lack of love. Lack of commitment. External temptation. Marital Affairs. Overworking. Stress.

The number of relationships breaking down is increasing at an alarming rate and something drastic has to be done to address the plethora of problems to lead to the breakdown of relationships. Sometimes one of the partners feels shocked by a sudden decision to leave and feel hurt, betrayed and even suicidal about the loss. Many partners think that the answer is to find another relationship almost immediately while others leave time to grieve the loss. Such losses have effects on the individual's self-esteem, self-confidence and of course, one's self-respect. It also has an effect on the stability of the family and affects members in different ways. Children often think that they are to blame and that the divorce of their parents is their fault. Many need reassurance and psychological support to get through the difficult times which are often compounded when divorcing couples ask the child who they want to live with. Additional pressure, resentment and negative tensions result. The problem of relationship breakdown is as complex as the intricacies of the problems that exist in the society that created them.

With the lack of confidence in the Church as the moral compass for society, how does secular society begin to address the decline in family values and commitment in relationships? Freedom to choose another partner creates its own problems, so does the right to marry as many times as possible. Finding another sexual identity does not address the core of the problem nor does encouraging others to experiment with another identity. Blaming the breakdown of the family unit itself for injuring society is not helping to address the huge problem either. There has to be some radical way of tackling the breakdown in society and those who claim that there needs to be a return to traditions of the past may have an argument worthy of merit. Perhaps, encouraging families to try to stay together for the sake of the children or to view marriage and relationships as a long term commitment may be a path to take in this long journey to find stability for all involved. Even returning, dare it be written, to Christian values must undoubtedly be another light for the world to follow.

The key questions still remain. The problems still remain. The big issues for the Western world to address still remain: how can society help with the breakdown of the family unit without a moral compass? How does Western society address the negative impact of family breakdown on children, on adults and on wider society? How does society help to address the transitional period during divorce or separation? How does society prevent and provide adequate intervention for children suffering from physical and psychological affects? Are counselling and mediation services offering enough guidance to resolve these huge problems? How do children learn to cope when they are not being taught enough about managing emotions in mainstream educational establishments?

The Black Perspective

The decline in black marriage needs no statistics as we all know that they are grim. Black couples are less likely to marry and more likely to divorce. Fact. There are more black single women than black married women. Fact. Black people are not getting married at the rate our grand and great grandparents did. Fact. How do we begin to address this marriage failure? There are those who point the finger of blame at the modern black woman; the charge being that she is setting unrealistic standards that our men just cannot meet. She has internalised Western culture and has higher ambitions, higher education and higher wages that cause our men to be alienated from her rather than affiliated with her. As a consequence, the black woman is now part of the independent women's movement with Oprah as our ultimate symbol of success. What some of our sisters crucially forget is the fact that Oprah chose not to marry and chose not to have children. This is important in any discussion of black female success, black womanist success and black feminist success. Independent black women enter relationships and inadvertently pressurise our men in different ways and some sisters are proud to give the credit to 'me, myself and I' without acknowledging the contributions of partners, friends and family in that success. All the honeys who are making money, raise your hands because you know it is true.

But what is the price of the black woman's success? Our black children, our black men and our black marriages – all sacrificial lambs. We cannot divorce our success as independent black women from this huge cost, the huge expense and the huge loss in value to ourselves. Let's not overlook the fact that we are to some degree, indebted to the black community. Having said that, should black men shoulder some of the cost? Have our men to some degree, lacked ambition? Have they stood still and let the sisters' success speed right past them? Were they too busy cheating, hustling and hood ratting to be running partners in the success race? Why aren't our black men 'manning up'? Let's start again because we cannot afford to play the blame game. Is commitment and the institution of marriage not worth anything anymore? If it does, then we must work together to ensure a better future for our children and we can begin by enlisting the help of the Obamas whose marriage could be a model for us all. This positive model of love and marriage is definitely a starting point for motivating people in our community to tie the knot but first we must understand the historical underpinnings that still affect us.

Our past history of slavery means that the black woman has not been defined as 'wife' and has not been defined by 'marriage'. During slavery, there was no relationship for slave women; no stability; no emotional support; no certainty that she will see her sex partner or the child that she gave birth to. Essentially, slavery destroyed the black female identity and denigrated her to the role of mere sex object. Imagine a female slave developing a relationship with a male slave. She knows that she cannot get too close to him emotionally because the chances are that she could lose him any time. There was no certainty that she would see him again: he could be sold to another slave owner, he could be killed any time or he could be taken away to be used by female slave masters in the house.

As a consequence, many slave women simply survived for herself. This was the origin of the 'me, myself and I' mentality. Slavery forced female slaves to think about themselves rather that a relationship. There could be no 'we' or 'us' as there could be no certain, stable or meaningful relationship with male slaves. Over time, black women have become the bedrock our black communities and that is one reason why they are essentially matriarchal. However, we must be aware of the history that lies beneath our present day, strong black woman outer coat. It is a secret image of black woman as merely a sexual conquest for both master and fellow slave.

Over the years, this image has been demolished and the strength of our survival has been transformed into resilience, perseverance and determination. However, we must be careful not to overwork ourselves, overeducate ourselves and overstress ourselves in the process of liberation. What we need to do is allow ourselves to love and be loved. We must now prioritise relationships and break the chains that keep us locked in our misperceived role. How do we move forward? Should we take the guidance on marriage away from the traditional black church (since their marriages are failing too) and transfer it to culturally conscious groups and movements? Should we include marriage/relationship as a subject on our community education curriculum? Should we have culturally sensitive marriage advice and counselling so that prospective couples can have the support if and when needed? Should we make marriage `cool' by raising the profile in exclusive fashion shows, queen pageants etc where wedding dresses are modelled and marriage advisory speeches are given and love songs are sung? Should we consider having `Back to love' dance nights and festivals of love where such positive values are showcased?

Chapter 18

DOMESTIC ISSUES

Domestic violence. Domestic abuse. Family violence. Spousal abuse. Physical abuse. Verbal abuse. Emotional abuse. Sexual abuse. Marital rape. Battering. Acid throwing. Stalking. Intergenerational cycles of abuse. Posting sexual images on the internet.

Violence in a domestic setting takes a number of forms and is wide ranging in the spectrum of patterns of abusive behaviour. The reasons for domestic violence are also very complex and inextricably linked to many other societal problems and therefore cannot be examined in isolation. Many domestic abusers often regret their actions and beg forgiveness, others think that the violence is acceptable and in some way justified. For many families, domestic abuse is a family matter and must stay behind closed doors, never to be reported to the authorities. This thinking may lead to further abuse in children and other family members who may feel that such patterns of behaviour can be excused. Consequently, domestic violence becomes a matter of perception more than a matter of immorality. Victims are often sympathetic and willing to forgive for the sake of the family, for financial reasons and to avoid shame. Google the range of problems that victims experience and the psychological problems children in such situations have to endure.

Domestic violence does not happen in a cultural vacuum; in the absence of religious guidance, a moral framework and cultural socialisation, society seems to be descending further and further into the abyss. What is the root cause of this violence towards others? Is it related to the conflict that one has been socialised to accept? Is the war within the individual reflected in wars that are made more visible? Is there a Jekyll and Hyde in all of us? What is the source of all this inner conflict? Is Plato responsible for one's obsession with control of one of the horses? Was Orwell right in declaring that in a dystopian society there will be an acceptance that `war is peace'? Does violence really breed violence? Is it free will or determinism at play here? How does the Western cultural thinker begin to identify and solve the root causes of the problem referred to as domestic violence?

Black cultural perspective

Domestic violence has been a Western cultural label but a black cultural problem. It has not been fully named as abuse but if we examine some of our practices that we have carried on since slavery, we will see that we are inadvertently abusing our children under the guise of training, under the guise of good parenting and under the guise of firm discipline. There is much debate in our community about the physical discipline of children: we beat, bang, batter and even bruise our children and call it discipline. It is not. It is violence. It is abuse. It is the planting of the seed that germinates into domestic violence, gang violence and even violent crime. Violence towards children disguised as discipline is definitely destroying the social development of our children. This perception of violence as physical discipline can no longer be tolerated in our culture. The yells of `I got beaten and it didn't do me any harm' or `you can't spare the rod and spoil the child' should not be uttered. Nor should `if the child cannot hear, then s/he must feel'. Training up a child in this way, the way that you think it should go, when he is old he will not depart from this violent way. This way leads to bullying, exclusions, gang violence and even domestic violence. Google for evidence to challenge or accept this viewpoint. Crucially, this intergenerational cycle of violence must be broken.

The issue is not what constitutes abuse but rather what beatings constitute. Relying on religious guidance of `sparing the rod' is not helpful in this context. Nor is the cultural belief that forceful physical discipline could be seen as appropriate in some way. Continuing to endorse physical discipline of our children, especially our boys, is effectively planting the seeds of domestic violence no matter how harsh this sounds. Google for evidence of the link between beating in childhood and domestic violence in adulthood.

Domestic violence is on the increase in our community and many intricately linked problems are responsible for its continued practice. We have to explore ways to prevent this form of violence as well as seek help for the abusers. Our people can no longer remain silent on this issue out of cultural affinity, out of familial or community loyalty, out of fear of airing dirty linen in public. Yes, we all hesitate to contact the police because we distrust them but domestic abuse is a serious crime. Our sisters are vulnerable victims and even though some women fight back, this should not be encouraged because again violence breeds violence. We have to think about what our children are witnessing behind closed doors and how we could break this vicious cycle.

Let us not forget that such physical violence is a direct legacy of slavery. Years of being whipped by slave masters, years of inhumane brutality, years of physical violence on the plantations have taken root and produced deadly fruits of violence. Slaves would pick the fruits off the cultural tree without realising that these are meant to be forbidden. Slave mothers would beat their children to toughen them up in preparation for the hardships to come; to teach lessons and to them, it was seen as being responsible. Slave masters whipped them as punishment for wrongdoing and the slaves did likewise to their children and fellow slaves. Think about it. Slaves were just conditioned to do what they were told and to do what they saw the slave masters do. There was no thought processing at all as they simply followed what was learnt from the only model of culture they knew: slavery.

This bitter legacy of slavery cannot carry on concealing its existence under the guises of these traditions: physical discipline is directly linked to the whippings that the slaves received. We have simply internalised the brutality that we have received since then without attempting to repair it. Over the years, it has morphed into physical bullying, physical fighting, gun violence, knife crime, and emotional abuse. Domestic violence is physically and psychologically damaging and we can no longer let this violence take its toll on our community. Collectively, we need to commit to refraining from beating or rather disciplining our children using physical force. It is not firm discipline. Let us use the right label for this cultural practice that has been passed down from generation to generation and make a comprehensive, collective and constructive commitment to address this kind of violence in domestic settings. Should we have a cultural campaign against the beating of our children? Should we explore different options for parental discipline bthat exclude physical and psychological pain? Should we have some form of culturally specific treatment for victims of domestic violence? Should we explore culturally relevant discipline options?

Chapter 19

INTERRACIAL RELATIONSHIP RIGHTS

Interracial tensions. External pressures. Clashing values. Negative societal attitudes. Rebellion. Racial offenses. Prejudiced in-laws.

The challenges faced by couples in interracial relationships are in abundance but with the increase in such unions it is evident that many couples are determined to overcome them. The problems range from stress from family members on both sides to compatibility of values which undoubtedly causes different degrees of tension. Research has been widespread in the West to indicate what exactly is causing the tension. Feel free to google why Caucasians tend to disapprove of interracial marriages more than others. Google why some researchers claim that interracial relationships operate for the same reasons of rebelliousness or self-hate as Romeo and Juliet in Shakespeare's tale and Winston and Julia in Orwell's 1984. The `self' hate refers to `the cultural social self', what Freud refers to as the superego rather than the ego itself so Romeo and Juliet both hated their familial connections, their cultural socialisation and their inherited identity which pitted them against the Other rather than their personal pursuit of passion or love for each other.

Like the famous couples from Western cultural literary heritage, reciprocating love must be very difficult to maintain interracial relationships against such huge pressures from within and without. Understanding different assumptions, different values and different cultural traditions must be an education in itself and couples who undertake this huge venture should be given credit especially when they choose to have children. Whether these differences are embraced or whether the decision is to embrace one party's culture over the other must still be a real journey for interracial couples everywhere. With the destination being reached after a successful experience together of dealing with rejection, stress and sheer ignorance of the reasons for the union. The journey must also be an interesting one where different perspectives are learnt about each other and each other's world. However, the negative experiences from racial insults, evil stares and offensive comments cannot be overlooked or even be forgotten.

The problem here is complex because it involves interrelated issues of identity, race, culture, language and History. Unless there is some kind of negotiation or mediation between different cultural value systems and the judgements which are partnered with such, there will always be tension, clashes, prejudices that lie at the heart of the problem. Traditionally, the West has seized the monopoly on truth about the world without acknowledging or rather understanding the truth from other cultural perspectives. Crucially, the Western cultural thinker must clearly and distinctly change this assumption about the rest of the world and those who want to see people differently. This will then have far-reaching implications for not only interracial unions but also for cultural relations around the world too. How can the Western cultural thinker change negative societal perspectives on interracial unions? Should the Western cultural thinker begin by revaluating its cultural systems and values? Should couples who have had successful unions form a think tank to share perspectives for progress?

Glynis Glasgow-Kelly

Black cultural perspective

Miscegenation or race- mixing is on an astronomical rise and this is creating tensions for families on both sides, for the mixed race children and for the future of the black race in the diaspora. The issue is not whether or not there should be interracial marriage but rather how to cope with the tensions in our community towards those who have chosen to marry outside the race. Charges are made against the brothers, that they are marrying other women for upward mobility, for status symbolism. The sheer number of black men marrying other women seemingly for these reasons is a real cause for concern for black women as well as for the posterity of our race. Google for exact figures in the region of your choice. Our celebrity sports stars in Europe, particularly, seem to have difficulty meeting black women.

In defence, the brothers argue that the sisters are preoccupied chasing academic success, putting fitness first and being one of the honeys making money. Even the needs of the children are considered before their needs – our black brothers argue. Consequently, they date and marry the women in their circles from other races who put them first. According to many brothers, the classy black sisters are too keen to be successful, too lean to be their ideal and too mean to be approachable. They insist that marriage is not just about love anymore; it is also about preference, power and politics. Some white women prefer darker men just as their gentlemen prefer blondes. There is no law against that. Many marry and become power couples like Kim and Kanye. Others marry for subconscious reasons: marry a black man indicates a moral and political stance. Let's not forget that we live in the liberal era when civil rights activists identify with the black cause. There is no law against that either. Other charges of self-hate, rebelliousness, sexual conquest are left for you to research yourself. Suffice it to state that the negativity within the black race towards interracial union is an issue that needs to be addressed within the community. There is still the feeling within the culture that black men belong with black women and that interracial marriage is robbing the bank of its limited resources of eligible black men.

The challenge is to resolve these conflicts for the benefit of our mixed race children caught in the clashing of cultures. Respecting both races and avoiding cultural assumptions is a starting point. Expecting the in-laws to accept the relationship needs time because those who feel that you should be with your own kind will not change their standpoint overnight. This may be perilously close to reverse racism but we need to identify the problem before we try to solve it. Let us trace the source of the tension in the African diaspora back to the legacy that brought us here. Sexual conquest during slavery with the raping of black female slaves and the brutality meted out to black male slaves who dared to even look at a white female owner will always cast a shadow over interracial unions. White female slave owners were undoubtedly the ones doing the gazing and the pursuing during slavery as black male slaves knew that even glancing could result in the violent loss of their lives.

Black bodies were property, commodity and sex toys serving the needs of everyone except themselves. White female slave owners had to avoid being disowned, disinherited and disrespected if caught pursuing an interracial sexual relationship with a slave. The physical and psychological toll must have been devastating; reduced to sexual objects for use at the beck and call of those in power. Stripped of their dignity, their humanity and their sanity, male slaves were reduced to mere sex machines. Over the years, the number of interracial unions has increased but the brutality of history still hurts, still lingers on in the minds of family, friends and fellowmen. How do we rise from the burning flame of history that engulfs these unions? Should we work on forming networks of mixed race professionals to understand the issues and agree on strategies to move forward? Should we have support of interracial unions which involve meetings for families and friends to promote understanding of the unions? Should we have 'Cultural Cohesion' networks to address the issue of clashing value systems within interracial unions? Crucially, how do we address the inner conflict experienced by children of mixed heritage?

Chapter 20

FAMILY VALUES: THE LOSS OF LOVE

Proliferation of identities. Paradox of choice. Lack of faith. Lack of cultural clarity. Lack of consensus on values. Lack of collectivist values.

> "Family values, sometimes referred to as familial values, are traditional or cultural values (that is, values passed on from generation to generation within families) that pertain to the family's structure, function, roles, beliefs, attitudes, and ideals. In the social sciences, sociologists may use the term "traditional family" in order to refer specifically to the child-rearing environment that sociologists formerly called the norm. This "traditional family" involves a middle-class family with a breadwinner father and a homemaker mother, raising their biological children. Any deviation from this family model is considered a "non-traditional family".
>
> Wikipedia.

The family was traditionally the unit that taught young people how to love. Freud and other theorists identified two main reasons for human existence here on earth: to learn to work and to learn to love. The West has invested most of its time teaching children the skills to work in a capitalist society but not the skills to learn to love. The Greeks specified seven different types of love which include Philautia (self-love), Storge (family love), Philia (empathy/ shared experiences), Agape (humanity), ludus (flirtatious love), Eros (romantic or erotic love) and pragmatic (enduring love). There seems to be the commercialisation of romantic love or Eros almost to the total exclusion of other types of love. Young people are not learning how to love and both the home and religion seem to have failed in their duty to teach adequately this core cultural value. In all of the major religions of the world, love is identified as one of the key virtues. Secular society may argue that there are self-help books and guidance online about these values and that should suffice while others insist that religion is responsible for teaching love in all its forms as it is divine and sacred. In fairness, religion has not lost its voice, but rather the voices of the secular world have drowned it out.

In the West, there seems to be a clear excess of demand over supply of love. Everyone wants to find love but the investment of time and commitment to understanding and teaching this value must be prioritised. Loss of love, in all its forms has created a web of problems in the home and for wider society. The problem arises in the home when love is not classified appropriately and expressed in ways that are unacceptable. Such expressions of affection between siblings develops as incest; between other family members as child abuse and towards partners it sometimes morphs into domestic abuse. Incest, paedophilia and other perversions that are happening in homes all point to a psychological confusion in dealing with strong positive emotions. It then becomes evident that there is a definite need to teach different forms and expressions of love and to teach how to control this powerful emotion which can morph into hate almost simultaneously. Love's hate is not simply an oxymoron expressed by

Carol Ann Duffy in her poem 'Havisham' but also a manifestation of the Jekyll and Hyde ontology of emotion being love or hate.

Family love matters and mothers as the primary model of love especially in the early years matters too. The struggle to value love in modern society is an uphill one which needs political, educational, cultural and moral investment for the improvement of the family and society as a whole. Love is meant to define us as human beings and there has to be a cultivation of self-sacrifice or altruism on an intergenerational level otherwise the care services and professions would suffer and so too would society. At present, there is a crisis in care and a crisis in love which is damaging society's mental, physical and social health. Western cultural thinkers must look in their hearts for emotional capital rather than be driven solely by economic capital. One of the key questions for educationalists and politicians, why is love not taught fully in schools and social circles? Why is the emphasis almost exclusively on the game of love (romantic love) rather than the ontological aspects of love itself? Why is there no systematic teaching of each form of this important value? Why is there not a marketplace for these values?

Black cultural perspective

Positive African cultural values have been overshadowed by the lingering negative aspects of slave culture. Our core values of strong family networks, strong spiritual and moral principles and strong pride in our achievements are all being eroded by an overemphasis on the negative aspects of our culture. These values reflect our struggle against subjugation but varies according to location within the African diaspora and within geographical location. Status and education also play a role in the adoption of cultural values. In the absence of a sound knowledge and promotion of our shared cultural values, our black culture has been presented as one which is quintessentially negative and one which depends on western cultural values for its historical, spiritual and intellectual core. In the African diaspora, we are presented as anti-institution and a people without a distinctive set of cultural values when all evidence shows that we are spiritual and emotional beings. The fact that black culture in the African diaspora has its base in slavery means that we have a huge mountain to climb in order to elevate ourselves from this foundation. Some stand at the bottom of the mountain and say mission impossible, while others concede that a real challenge exists and brace themselves for the long term challenge. There is a need to subscribe to this latter way of thinking and commit to our climb, commit to our struggle, commit to our elevation.

Slavery and its bitter legacy will always be remembered for its brutality to its victims rather than the strength and resilience of the slaves. One will recall the hardship rather than the survivorship; the slave ships rather than the friendships, the subservience rather than the resistance: the insensitivity of the oppressors rather than the integrity of the oppressed. Why do the negatives always overshadow the positives and more importantly why do we allow this perception to carry on? During slavery, strength of character was cultivated during the struggle as we learnt how to learn and how to grow spiritually and intellectually. Slaves had integrity. Slaves respected each other and instilled in their children respect for family and friends, the aunty and uncle, an African cultural practice. Why are we letting go of such family values and more importantly how to we regain our cultural core?

Slaves found faith in religion and that gave inspiration and great inner strength to struggle through circumstances. Communal worship further cultivated the positive values of black culture that are still evident today: good manners greeting one another, avoiding backchat, gaining emotional, psychological and financial support. How do we pick the good fruits from a tree with slave roots? Or, how can our cultural tree that is rooted in slavery bloom as an evergreen? Should we re-establish strong family presence by building strong community support groups? Should we have more community- based functions that educate as well as entertain about the positive values of the community? Should we popularise the quintessentially black values through music and media forms? Should we create a real marketplace to showcase our positive values of inner strength, resilience and of course love?

Chapter 21

EDUCATION AS A RIGHT

Education as cultural heritage. Education as socialisation. Education as a capitalist tool. Education as morality. Education for social change.

In Western culture, a good education has now become an official privilege rather than a human right; a privilege for those who can afford to invest in it. The perception of a good education is one that gives access to economic capital by virtue of inheritance, affiliation and appearances of class. Look at the educational backgrounds of those working in journalism, politics and economics in your geographical location and google their educational backgrounds. Western politicians, who wallow in their inherited privilege, impose a plethora of changes to the education system to present the idealistic view that every child really matters. They have the absolute freedom to mislead the underprivileged into thinking that education is improving when in fact the opposite is true. Education is now characterised by its progressiveness or its freedom to transform itself with new idea after new idea, change after change. It is a process of effecting change of curriculum, change of pedagogy, change of policy, change of disciplinary procedures, change of staff, change of students. However, real change in thinking is needed to address this key question - how can the rights of every child really matter if the individual needs of every child are overlooked?

The notion that one-size-fits-all cannot be applied in real terms to an `every child matters' policy and should not be used as a basis for educational establishments. Yet, privileged politicians continue to make changes for the underprivileged class without understanding the issues at the very core of the problems that cause the disadvantage, disaffection and disengagement with the system. Evidence of this can be found in the proposed English Baccalaureate which narrows the curriculum options for those millions of students who have a creative intellectual inclination. Google the number of petitions and challenges made here and the arguments forwarded. Will the government listen?

Western educationalists have now become preoccupied with change so much so that change has become, in and of itself, the essential core of education. This imposed one-size-fits-all thinking about change needs to be inspected, not by OFSTED, because their body requires improvement but by other educational practitioners who are opponents to the pace and the content of these changes but are classed as incapable and given a golden handshake. Without these principled practitioners of the past, the value of education will continue to diminish and society will end up with an entire generation who knows nothing, has nothing and can produce nothing but another generation where ignorance is strength.

In England, schools for the underprivileged have become academies of accountability preoccupied with performance data. This new occupation frequently fosters nepotism, minimises meritocracy and institutionalises unfairness. Capitalist masters are compelling schools to narrow their curriculum, forcing free teachers to become slaves to the system of change. These resistant teachers are whipped into submission by the threat of omission from the profession even though they are more capable than those who inspect them. In the capitalist educational system, freedom is definitely slavery as those who refuse to bow to the masterminding of the new professional development are forced out by the housekeepers. Google how many teachers have called ACAS to report such incidents. Google the number of changes to policies in education over the past ten years. Google the number of curriculum changes dictated by capitalist thinkers. Now google how much time is spent on what really matters- the education of the whole child and the whole community. You will find that like everything else, that too has changed from Personal Social and Educational development to Social, Spiritual Cultural and Moral development and given minimal time, minimal money and minimal priority. Where do western cultural thinkers go from here? Should educationalists advocate a philosophy of education that extrapolates principles from social constructionism, where students learn social skills to access the mainstream curriculum whilst shaping and elevating themselves through different cultural identities? Should education cultivate a love of learning in our young people whilst developing knowledge and skills to achieve social, cultural and professional goals? Should education focus more on students' interests and experiences that are both personal and cultural, whilst working within the framework of the mainstream curriculum? What should the main function of education be in a world that is rapidly descending into chaos?

Black education should be our right

The philosophy and function of education varies from society to society; from culture to culture but because our history is so intertwined with that of the West, it is important that we consider a different system of education for reparation and progress. Traditional western education was not designed with us in mind. This kind of education would be the key to elevating ourselves, the key to opening doors for our people and the key to our collective success. So why is education cited as one of our problems? The heart of the problem is the fact that the current system of education is quintessentially capitalist in its ideology, philosophy and spirituality. It does not function to educate the whole child about the whole curriculum and how to make a positive contribution to the whole community. Western education serves to promote the value system of capitalism - individualism over collectivism, selfishness over selflessness, superiority over equality; this system is designed for the benefit of one particular type of thinking, the thinking that promotes the concept of self over the concept of community. This philosophy of education must now be replaced, firstly in our minds. We must adopt one that challenges prejudiced views that have now become more engrained, more acceptable in the office, more evident in the playground and caused society to be even more divisive.

Protesting that the education system is quintessentially Eurocentric in content, discipline, opportunity, delivery, pedagogy and philosophy is not the answer. Demanding cosmetic change like inclusiveness, multiculturalism and tokenistic curricular insertions is not the answer either. What we have to propose is a supplementary community led system based on the philosophy of progression that serves to address the fundamental human right to an education for the whole black child, through the whole black curriculum and for their inclusion in the whole pluralistic community. Please google the grim statistics on exclusion, bullying, lateness, defiance, disruptive behaviour, examination failure if you would like evidence of the failure of the western educational system to cater for the fundamental human rights of our children.

Let's trace the problem of education to its origins in the legacy. Google what Frederick Douglass and his biography where he wrote about "slavery and education being incompatible". You will find that the right kind of knowledge means power and learning to read and write gives our people intellectual power to think of ways to change our condition. During slavery there was a conflict of interest if slaves were taught how to read and write properly and that is why slaves received biblical literacy in order to `obey their masters' as the word of God admonishes. Biblical literacy, whether we want to accept it or not, is based on the development of uncritical thinking where the mind learns how to consume knowledge rather than produce different ideas. Consequently, we learn how to simply obey without questioning the authority figures or their ideologies. This cultivation of uncritical thinking has developed from generation to generation and is evident in many aspects of our culture. Preachers continue to preach sermons and lay the foundations for oral literacy in black communities where we focus on charisma over content; on style rather than substance. We now need to focus on substance over style, on education over entertainment and on progress over protest. Google what Frederick Douglass states about the pathway from slavery to freedom and you will see that the power to read and write must be in our possession to change everyone's perspective of our people.

What is needed is a comprehensive and holistic supplementary educational system that is not perceived as Eurocentric; the curriculum of which places our people as subjects and not objects where our children are not burdened with the task of being exclusively capitalist in outlook in order to be successful in life. Google what American academic Bell Hooks advocates for education and you will see what she states about education being seen as `the practice of freedom'. Some other black educational writers from across the diaspora to research are Tony Sewell, Gus John, Rosemary Campbell (British),

Jawanza Kunjufu, Bell Hooks, Cornell West and African writers Wole Soyinka, Ngugi Wa Thiongo and Chinua Achebe. Hooks speaks directly to teachers `we cannot be teachers who invite students into radical openness if we're not willing to be radically open ourselves, if we are not willing to be a witness to our students of how ideas change and shape us how something affects us so that we think differently than we did before'.

Our children's minds need to be free from the capitalist paradigm of education which is plaguing our community. Western cultural thinkers have recognised this and that is why culturally inclusive educational initiatives were introduced over the years. However, these were met with fierce criticisms that they ignored the negative aspects of cultural histories and presented a distorted view of history. Rather than improve on this perspective of education, critics highlighted its failures in experiments, its failures in practice and its failures in resources. According to its critics, it inadvertently perpetuated negative stereotypes rather than cultivate positive conceptions about different cultures. Like many other initiatives that were designed with our culture in mind, this was another one to bite the dust.

There needs to be a philosophy that reconstructs society, a philosophy that engages our youth rather than isolates them, a different way that embraces rather than alienates; a view that really socialises rather than radicalises. An education system that elevates our young people morally, spiritually, culturally and economically – a system that simply frees their minds. We must return to the education of our children, valuing them and empowering them to be true leaders in our communities. As our African ancestors rightfully say `it takes a village to raise a child' – that village in the African diaspora is our black community.

Glynis Glasgow-Kelly

We must take charge of supplementary educational measures to address the educational needs for reparation. Should we devise a system of supplementary education with a bespoke curriculum that highlights social reconstruction as the aim of education and places it strategically as a vehicle for social change? With a particular focus on the achievement of our black boys, should we devise literacy strategies within a critical consciousness framework and evaluate actions on real problems that affect our community? Should we aim to promote wisdom, wealth and wellbeing for our children in our quest to elevate our people and move on from civil rights to civil heights?

Chapter 22

ATTITUDES TO EDUCATION

Education perceived as control. Education perceived as repressing voices. Education as an institution of oppression.

Education does not exist in a vacuum but in the cultural, social and economic infrastructure of capitalist ideology. Western societies are socially stratified with each class possessing different perspectives, and different attitudes to education. Some may classify education more as a delusion than an illusion. Others may emphasise the function of education over its innate benefits. Within either framework, attitudes to education result directly from societal conditions and experiences with those positioned at the top enjoying education as their privilege afforded and secured by status rather than a right granted and maintained by hard study. The privileged class have the freedom to board or not to board, to attend a private school or not to attend one; to go to Oxford or to attend Cambridge. The only freedom denied those at the top is the freedom to choose between education as a right and education as a privilege. As their parents would assert, "education is always a privilege, darling".

For many different reasons, those who fight for education know the simple stubborn truth: the underprivileged do not have the freedom to choose – it will always be a struggle just to secure their right to a good education. It will always be a struggle to have a relevant curriculum; it will always be a struggle to survive the avalanche of change rolled down by the imperialist government. Parents, teachers and students then bring their own values and attitudes to education based on their knowledge, perception and experience of the system. Many parents want to live vicariously through their children and this adds to the pressure on students to succeed. Attitudes to education, whether negative or positive are therefore cultivated systematically in the hearts and minds of every single child. Young minds are no longer being programmed to believe in the traditional message of `get a good education to get ahead' but rather `many have tried doing so and it has failed them'. The younger generation can now deconstruct the message that equates academic success to economic success to secure a life akin to that of those with inherited privilege. Political messengers who insist that one should get educated for its intrinsic value seem to miss the fact that educated students understand what a political message is. Paradoxically, the politicians are the ones who need to realise the value of education: it is now turning into nothing more than another democratic ideal, another evasive human right, another illusion or is delusion the right word?

Education, in capitalist societies, operates like a giant fruit machine owned by the established class and the less privileged now seem to understand how it works. No matter how clever you are, no matter how much money you put in, no matter how much time you spend studying the operation of the machine, the fact remains that the machine is rigged. Hard working families are simply wasting their time and money hoping for a lucky win. Refrain from selling your homes, abandon elocution lessons and forget the costly private tuition fees. Instead, invest your time learning the rules that govern the playing of the games. Did you know that you can beat the machine through the use of foreign influences and other radical techniques imported from China and the Far East? How about studying why such countries have the highest literacy standards in the world? Why do these countries seem to outperform Western countries in core academic subjects? Have you thought about the curious paradox of these countries not adhering to human rights with such outstanding educational and societal policies?

Black perspective on attitudes to education

There has always been a strong belief within our culture that education is the key to success in our community and we all have a right to it. We have always had faith in the education as a key element to our children's development and as a means to improve the life chances for our children. For this reason, we invest time and resources encouraging our children to work hard at school and offer parental support to educational establishments when contacted. Many questions are springing to mind here about reported failings of our children, about the achievement gap and significantly about the attitude gap. How do our children, especially our boys attend primary school bright eyed and bushy tailed but end up in exclusion in secondary school? Is there something about the school system that kills our children's spirits and their desire to learn? If learning is a personal and emotional experience, is there some disconnection with the teachers? Are there failings at home that affect our children's social, intellectual and emotional development? Is it an incompatible combination of elements within our culture and that of the mainstream educational system? Why do our figures for educational achievement consistently cluster towards the end of the academic spectrum?

The curriculum, pedagogy, policies and the culture of the practitioners in the education system cannot be divorced from attitudes developed during the process of learning. It is a fact that many of our children enjoy going to school initially but somehow and somewhere these seeds of joy germinate into hate and ultimately grow into negative attitudes to school and school life.

Negative attitudes to teachers, to the school curriculum, school policies and to their fellow pupils produce disruptive behaviour, bullying, defiance and truancy as our young people lose faith in educational system. How do we address the underlying causes of this plethora of negativity?

If we consider for a moment the history of education in the West – it was designed for the privileged class only. Google for evidence. The laws, policies and legislation passed were simply to secure the status of those in the higher strata of society. Put simply, education was not designed for the elevation of the lower classes but to function as a means of keeping us in what is perceived to be our place as workers for the elite. Any discussion of the cultural and historical context of education must take into account the legacy of slavery and how 'education' was essentially the systematic programming of the mind. Education of slaves was prohibited and met with severe punishment. Google what Frederick Douglass writes in his Narrative about slavery being a 'poor school for the human intellect' and also read other writers like Heather Andrea Williams in *Self-Taught: African American Education in Slavery and Freedom*, chronicles African Americans' quest for education and their struggle to achieve it. She outlines personal and collective fights to become literate. Becoming well educated automatically poses a threat to authority – the authority of the systems, the policies and the practices of an institution. Any attempt to challenge the status quo was and still is repressed as it triggers a fear of rebellion.

The key question becomes does rebellion share elements of critical thinking? If there is a common denominator, then what we refer to as negative attitudes to education is misleading. Could our boys be challenging or rebelling against the unfairness that covertly and overtly resides in the policies, curriculum and culture of the educational system? Are the negative attitudes really describing the tension created by the development of critical consciousness in our boys? Is this the reason why calculated attempts have been made throughout history to prevent our people from becoming educated?

The fight to reverse the process must not be through negative attitudes but through strategic action. Protesting in the traditional way is hampering our progress rather than championing it. We have to be careful with equating education with oppression as education in principle is intrinsically good. Negative attitudes to education from our children comes from the frustration of trying to engage with a system that is automatically oppressing and liberating almost simultaneously. We have to try to build bridges and be aware of different views from each bridge as engaged narrators. In other words, if we do not try to understand each other's viewpoint, we will both stand powerless as tragedy unfolds. Let us be empowered to prevent tragedies in our community. Should we develop culturally specific, school-oriented attitudes and behaviours in our boys? Should educators rid ourselves of attitudes, misconceptions, stereotypes, and inappropriate methods that undermine effective teaching? Should we train teachers how to build quality relationships with black students and their families? Should we understand and actively counter the impact of culture on a child's sense of competency and identity? Should we have more community outreach and parental engagement?

Chapter 23

MUTUAL RESPECT AND TOLERANCE

Intolerance. Misunderstanding. Unfairness. Disrespect. Defiance. Inflexibility. Rules. Status Quo values

According to Ofsted, in addition to democracy, the rule of law and individual liberty, mutual respect for and tolerance of those with different faiths and beliefs and for those without faith are the core British values.

If mutual respect/tolerance is hailed as one of the key values of having British identity, why is it cited here as an educational problem? The problem arises when the educated understand how the system of values actually work and learn how to challenge them rather than embrace them. The problem develops with the realisation that mutual respect is an ideal aspiration for students, teachers, parents and politicians but not a reality for everyone. Put another way, in the classroom, idealism and realism are not parallel in meaning as there is no mutual exploration and understanding of the values. One forgets that respect is earned rather than legislated by the educational institution. Feel free to survey as many students as possible especially those who are in charge of Student Voice initiatives and they will confirm mutual respect in schools is not a reality as nothing really happens to address the issues that students raise as real matters of concern. If leadership teams opt to make cosmetic changes, students are smart enough to realise exactly why such measures are done. Students everywhere know that there is no such thing as mutual respect; they are required to respect rules, respect policies and respect practices. The process is one way. The policies of the establishment are set in stone just like the Rhodes statue at Oxford. Everyone knows that mutual respect will forever remain nothing more than an aspirational ideal in Western cultural classrooms.

Tolerance or willingness to accept another person's viewpoint even if you do not agree with it, is another pride and joy of the West and another illusion. If the West is willing to accept Islam as a model of cohesive cultural practice that would be a nice place to start. Showcasing Islam as the religion of peace would go a long way in schools to combat the threat of extremism and will definitely prevent radicalisation. One should not forget that alienation precedes radicalisation and if Western schools are concerned about preventing radicalisation, addressing alienation and its causes may be the ideal starting point. Google the records of grievances and you will find more than a grain of truth to how alienation leads to radicalisation. If educational institutions are committed to getting young people to obey the rule of law and tolerate everyone then the existing policies and practices may be the best place to start. Learning to reflect is always an effective educational method - especially when thinking about real change.

The rules, policies and practices of educational institutions are steeped in history and the Rhodes debate in January 2016 is evidence of what they symbolise. Dethroning physical statues should not precede the dismantling of the institutionalised practices that they represent. The practice of authority figures cleverly concealing bias by effectively using language about student misdemeanours of verbal abuse, threatening behaviour, violence, harassment and other unacceptable behaviour must not be looked at more closely. How can students in 21ˢᵗ century western democracies free their hearts and minds from the shackles of historical unfairness? How can mutual respect become a cultural value that is not monomaniac, monopolistic and monotonous?

How can mutual respect become a cultural value that is not monomaniac, monopolistic and monotonous? How do policy makers right the wrongs of the past that are leading to negative attitudes and disrespect for authority? How can mutual respect and tolerance be realism rather than idealism?

Mutual disrespect and intolerance

Western cultural educational institutions may be struggling to show us respect but we have no problem showing them what disrespect means. We tell it as it is and perhaps we need to work on how we rally to be respected. The thinking that we could tell it as it is without softening the tone ever so slightly has to be revisited. In times that should have gone by, we were told 'if someone hits you, hit them back' or by extension, if they disrespect you, then disrespect them. The biblical roots of this thinking of 'an eye for an eye' must be stopped because our culture is slowly but surely losing its eyesight.

Respect should be learnt and practised at home but it should not end there. Yes, there are issues with child socialisation or how we bring up our children which are dealt with in other sections but many teachers point to a plethora of problems at school that all relate to a lack of respect for authority. Authority does have historical, cultural and political connotations but all racial authority figures are struggling to cope with back chat, rudeness, confrontation, unruliness and hostility in the education system and we have to begin by looking at ourselves in the mirror. Our children have to learn when to be quiet and how to be polite even in protest. Yes, they are misunderstood but they have to be socialised to work on their tone of voice as well as their content and mannerisms. These are not to be confused with blind obedience or acceptance without questioning which happened in the past. During slavery, respect meant wholehearted obedience to the slave masters including religious teachers. The teacher, like the master, was not to be challenged or questioned and by extension, teachings were not meant to be challenged either. Education, religion and thinking therefore combined to promote poor thinking skills of the slaves. This systematic effort failed to focus on the empowering potential of education but rather ensure the systematic development of critical unconsciousness in the minds of the slaves. Put simply, it was meant to ensure that the slaves did not learn to think of ways to rebel.

Following the abolition of slavery, provision of education particularly in the British Caribbean was seen as a perceived social need to control the freed slaves and the Church and State thus worked together in the education and shaping of emancipated slave societies. Through the decades to the present day, education cannot be divorced from its painful history to serve the needs of those in power. From slave owners to capitalists, education simply contributes to the commodification of students everywhere. The lack of respect for education and those associated with it is just the product of this uncomfortable reality. However, in fairness, many western cultural teachers work hard to earn respect but some students seem to be hell bent on waging war on all forms of authority. If we were to conduct a study of the number of our black students recorded for defiance, disruption and disrespect, we would be in a state of shock. Yes, there is institutionalised unfairness within the education system and yes, there are many instances of injustice where the voices of our youth are not heard but no one can deny the sense of disrespect for authority that exists within society and among some of our young people.

The question is not who is to blame for this lack of respect but rather how are we going to work collectively to address the breakdown of respect within and across communities? Should we have a comprehensive educational program to help students understand the need for advanced cultural literacy and critical skills in critical consciousness? Should we outline a black charter of respect for education and make young people aware of expectations in schools and communities? Should we work on a holistic comprehensive supplementary program or free school system for our children?

Chapter 24

FREEDOM TO READ

Cultural reading. Leisure reading. Analytical reading. Reciprocal reading. Wider reading. Internet reading. Accelerated reading. Shared reading. Critical reading.

Reading should inform children in a modern democracy and provide a sound academic base for educational success in the global race. However, the cultural, philosophical or social context of reading in the West is slowly becoming the Stalinist dream of production. Children are just becoming mere commodities in the spell of capitalist ideology with government policy now dictating a narrow list of writers on the curriculum under the guise of cultural heritage.

This cultural experience fails to provide a broad and rich curriculum integrating diverse cultural education into lessons. Some questions need to be posed relating to the nature of this cultural education: is it exclusively cultural heritage education or should it be more inclusive to recognise the diverse culture of those who access it? Why are children in the West denied access to reading Chinese stories, Islamic narratives and African folk tales in mainstream schools? Shakespeare and the canon writers should not be the only narratives provided in multicultural, democratic English speaking societies. Surely, children need to be offered the opportunity to read widely and allowed the freedom to think outside the western canon of writings, histories and politics to ensure a more culturally authentic measure aimed at systematically addressing any concerns about the Orwellian slogan of freedom being slavery.

The problem of Western cultural reading reflects or is parallel to the English attitude to learning foreign languages: everyone must learn English, one of the most difficult languages to learn but English people find great difficulty learning foreign languages. What tends to be overlooked is the fact that conceptually language is more than just communication, it is more than just the medium of instruction, it is more than just idiolect - language is essentially culture. Unwillingness to learn a language means unwillingness to learn a different culture. Reading cross culturally, therefore, enables children to understand the world and the perspectives of different people who live in it. Failure to acknowledge writers from different cultures reflects a failure to address the issues created historically from the navigation around the truth that all education is not quintessentially Western in origin. Children from different cultures have advantages of understanding different school cultures, different kinds of ethos, different teaching and learning styles, different codes of behaviour rather than disadvantages working against them.

If Western governments are serious about education for all then they would consider an approach to teaching English language as a foreign language. Within this framework, meticulous attention to the structure and intricacies of the English Language would be paid, instead of operating on the historical assumption that language learning would happen incidentally. Many communities in multicultural societies do not hear English language being spoken at home or in the wider community. One must remember that in London and many parts of the United States, some areas in Western countries are virtually third world enclaves where Standard English is a foreign language that is rarely spoken, heard or read. How can educationalists in the West consider different ways of thinking about reading and language learning? Should the English language curriculum focus on modernising the language rather than exclusively studying the narratives of the past? Should there be real freedom to read widely and critically in the National Curriculum?

Black cultural language

Reading is the foundation on which all academic excellence is built and laying the foundation means reading to our children from 'the cradle to the grade'. We have to promote reading above music, above sports and above smartphones. The value of reading should reflect the time and money we invest in gatherings, gifts and going out. Think about it. Instead of buying games, we could buy an interesting book about the games. Rather than gathering with friends to gossip, let us provide articles or magazines for discussion. Going out for entertainment could be literacy related, so too can going on holidays with a book or kindle to read for the duration of the plane journey. To promote good reading habits is essential to transforming our culture into a reading one.

It is a fact that traditional reading has been hijacked by the internet and there needs to be some kind of negotiation or a whole generation will be held to ransom. If the internet is occupying our young people then we need to find other reading strategies for all in the family. We have to explore key questions together as a community to build the literacy skills of our children. How do we get our boys to choose reading over rap, how do we get our boys to study alone rather than with the phone, how do we get our boys away from their toys?

Study after study, research report after research report, statistic after statistic all point to a crisis in the education of our community and we need some strategic focus and direction to tackle it from within the culture.

President Obama, a worthy role model, acknowledges the fact that black children need male role models. His 2015 father's day speech to a black audience insists that "we need to replace that video game with a book and make sure that homework gets done. We need to say to our daughters, don't let images on TV tell you what you are worth, because I expect you to dream without limit and reach for your goals. We need to tell our sons, those songs on the radio may glorify violence, but in our house, we find glory in achievement, self-respect, and hard work." Obama promotes the value of reading and of education in general.

Our boys are capable, committed and courageous but concentrating is often difficult because obstacles are in the way. Boys cannot concentrate if parents are not monitoring the content of the media that is fuelling their young minds. Our boys cannot concentrate if they are hanging, loitering or liming on the streets. Our boys cannot concentrate if they are hungry, uncomfortable or living in an abusive environment. We have to tackle these obstacles that are preventing our boys from becoming critical readers and ultimately rational human beings.

Reading in its historical context will reveal that laws existed to forbid slaves to learn to read; it was also a crime for others to teach them. Slave masters knew that "once you learn to read you will be forever free" Google Frederick Douglass. Proficiency in reading would enable the slaves to free their minds from the shackles of slavery and more importantly convince other slaves to do likewise.

The fear was that learning to read would in some way free their mind and incite rebellion was a real one for slave owners. They knew that some slaves were resilient, some were determined and some were very clever. If slaves were to combine their reading power with their physical power, they would be a force to be reckoned with. Slaves had to be stopped by whatever means possible and their owners ensured that they were doomed to a life of abysmal ignorance.

The education of the Negro took shape in one formal form: Christianity. For obvious reasons, the Church offered instruction in Christian religion and education and this kind of uncritical reading indoctrinated rather than liberated the mind. History would suggest that slaves would be encouraged to learn to read scriptures and share their knowledge with other slaves. Bible readings and memorising them would be the form that literacy would take for slaves. However, labour demands would make any sustained effort to teach others to read virtually impossible.

To address the issue of reading in our community, we need a cultural and historical shift. Essentially, a concerted effort of our entertainers, educators and evangelists need to promote positive reading challenges for the cultivation of reading within the culture. The legacy of Slavery did not produce a reading culture but rather a culture without this key foundation. As a people, we have to fight to destroy the remnants of truth that exist within the adage: If you want to hide something from a black person put it in a book'. The simple, stubborn fact is that we need to rebuild and rebrand our cultural practices so that they revolve around reading and writing not around pleasure and leisure. How do we move on from here? Should we create literacy based activities suited to kinaesthetic learners? Should we form a network or agency of black male teachers and readers to support our young boys in particular? Should we promote `positive peer pressure programmes that provide positive influence and reading out loud support where our children can read aloud to peers? Should we celebrate our boys' successes with reading challenges, awards and ceremonies? Should we create a supplementary Saturday school initiative that is a combination of spirituality, critical readings of History and entrepreneurship for empowerment?

Chapter 25

FREE SPEECH - LANGUAGE AND COMMUNICATION

Silence of the Speaking and listening lambs. Silence of the Student Voices. Silence of the excluded. Silence of the mind.

Language has become the vehicle for English culture with the beliefs, values and traditions sitting comfortably at the steering wheel. Spoken language is the mouthpiece of individual drivers enjoying the ride of free speech. Political correctness and the politics of language are welcomed on board to ensure that everything runs smoothly until everyone panics as the vehicle of free speech crashes headfirst into the Trump tower. The impact has shook the entire Western world especially those who have enlightened us. Muslims are now free to speak out against the oppression that once was the exclusive possession of people in Africa and the Diaspora. Similarly, the Scottish National Party are now free to negotiate an exit like the one being negotiated in Brussels on Britain's behalf. Let us not forget free speech in England with junior doctors enjoying their freedom of speech to negotiate deals with spin doctors who are spinning straw facts into golden promises. Fairy tales of free speech have had a great fall and now the Western cultural thinker must try to put the pieces of humpty dumpty back together again. The biggest problem for free speech is that it is Orwellian; the bastion of the official deception of democracy and all the Queen's horses and all the Queen's men can no longer put the pieces back together again.

The truth is that everyone now understands Western democracy. The truth is that everyone now understands how language and culture are inextricably linked. Everyone now understands how political correctness works and they have had enough of its essence. The absence of any clear solution has magnified the problem for politicians especially those in America whose Middle class is staring at the glaring problem and fear falling into the abyss. Western culture revolves around its use of language and the tool of the system is altered, changed or rather damaged, the Western cultural thinker is likely to be staring into an abyss which will expose the weaknesses of its key institutions: law, justice, education, politics, health, economics and media. Historically, language was the fuel that powered the engine of these vehicles and ignorant masses were the passengers. Sadly for the Western cultural thinker, everything has now changed. Ignorance is no longer a strength. Key questions have to be addressed and quickly. How can language and communication be used to build rather than topple Western cultural society? How can free speech be used to effect positive change? How can silence be perceived as no longer golden? How can the truth be told without being politically correct or rather how can the Western cultural thinker replace politically correct speech as it has effectively lost its value?

Black language

The dilemma for us living in the African Diaspora is the fact that we have adopted the language and essentially the culture of our former masters for use in our culture and this is problematic. Speaking and writing Standard English is essentially adopting implicitly and explicitly the philosophy, ideology and culture of the ones who were our former masters; shrouding ourselves in an uncomfortable, unsuitable and inappropriate identity. Google the meaning of `black' and you will understand exactly what the problem is. Many of our boys particularly, search for a way to express themselves that does not betray who they are and more importantly what they would like to be. In the Caribbean, broken/pidgin English is used by the lower classes and it has almost become an official dialect. Crucially, it helps to shape or carve an identity that is different to the language of colonisation. However, we must be made aware that in so doing it denies our children the opportunity to make progress in the capitalist world which still insists on doing things the western way or hit the highway.

Painfully aware of this fact, many of our children are cleverly code switching between Standard English at school and their dialect in their cultural and familial environments. However, for some, they find it a burden to code switch and opt for one or the other. Those who decide to adopt a Standard English idiolect are ostracised and accused of `playing white' or being a `coconut' while those who speak in the `black' way are then perceived as being `unintelligent' or `inarticulate'. Either way, our children have to struggle with issues of identity when using language and this causes additional problems related to written and oral communication.

If we trace the roots of language back to the legacy, preventing the slaves from learning to communicate with each other was one of the main aims of the slave masters. It was imperative that slaves did not learn to read or write to communicate with other slaves on the plantations as the fear was that rebellions and riots would result.

Language and communication were most effective in the church settings and emphasis was placed on teaching slaves to `obey their masters' or to 'forgive (the masters) seventy times seven.' Ever wondered why the pastors are some of the most articulate in our society? The seeds of communication were sown in the church during slavery and over the years, ministers have kept up the tradition of being charismatic to communicate about the gospel.

Language and its problems are explored in detail elsewhere in this book but the issues of communication in so called mainstream classrooms must be addressed here. How do we ensure that our children are articulate in their use of language? Should we encourage our children to learn English as a foreign language?

Should we teach skills in code switching? Should we encourage the use of Standard English to give our students more opportunities for success? Should we promote 'urban' English in cultural settings and offer a dictionary of idioms and expressions used within the black community? How do we equip our young people with the skills to exercise their right to free speech?

Chapter 26

MORAL FREEDOM - RIGHTS AND RULES/WRONGS

Listen and Learn. Hand homework in on time. Write clearly. Present work neatly. Wear the uniform. Respect the school rules. Respect your teacher. Respect your environment. Respect everyone. Do not disrupt. Do not fight. Do not swear.

War and conflict in wider society seems to be seeping into families, into societies and into school settings. Western cultural media has inadvertently desensitised the suffering of our fellowmen and women so much so that many have embraced and internalised the Orwellian slogan that `war is peace'. In addition to this, there is racism on the rise, nationalism on the rise and we are now living in a time when hate is the new zeitgeist. Against this backdrop or rather in this cultural milieu fuelled by the laissez-faire attitude, schools are trying to implement rules and maintain the status quo. The problem is that the process of osmosis cannot be stopped as the avalanche of hate in wider society is threatening to overwhelm the school systems. Politicians, Heads of schools, leadership teams and teachers are battling to implement school rules and policies but they are fighting against the tide of negativity in wider society.

Breaking rules is definitely the by-product of modern culture and this is symptomatic of the moral decline in society at large. Not only that, but there is a general breakdown in respect for authority, respect for life and respect for oneself. Without addressing the wider problems within society to offer clear guidance and leadership to the younger generation then rules cannot simply be made to exist in a vacuum. The problem with rule-breaking is a combination of many aspects that cannot be studied in isolation. Students are told to do their homework which implies that they know exactly what to do, it also implies that they have the inclination to complete it and that they are in some way scared of the punishment if they refuse to do it. Sometimes, students simply scoff at the school rules and the consequences. Many do not care if their parents are informed. Many do not care if they are excluded or expelled. Many simply do not care.

What happens when society is faced with a large percentage of the population who simply do not care? How do we motivate young people who have lost faith in the system, in society and in the self?

How can such negative attitudes to rules and regulations be prevented? How does the West cultural thinker find ways to engage young people in something that they could believe in? Should systems change to allow young people to feel a part of the process of rule-making? Should young people be allowed to have a genuine voice that is heard and acknowledged? How can society break free from itself and what it has become?

Black cultural viewpoint

Moral freedom or the freedom to choose one's own moral identity seems to be on the rise within the black community. If our young people are no longer attending church, no longer going to community events then our young people are on the road to a moral decline. More importantly, our young people are not being socialised to adhere to rules of any institution. Our young people are not learning how to be punctual for events because community functions are often started later than scheduled. As a result, our young people are having issues with lateness or rather timekeeping; this is more prevalent now than ever before. This generation of young black boys and girls are not learning how to keep rules because they are not exposed enough to organisations where challenging rules must be kept. Consequently, they are experiencing difficulty in adhering to general rules in school. Exclusions are on the rise and we have to offer clear guidance and leadership from within the culture. Rule-breaking cannot be seen in a social-cultural vacuum but as a part of the need for cultural reparation within our community.

Late to school. Late submission of homework. Habitual lateness. Failure to turn take. Failure to listen. Failure to code switch. Negative reactions when reprimanded. Issues of respect for authority. If we look at each issue that has plagued the progress of our pupils, we can trace them back to their roots in the legacy. These issues have been denied but never systematically addressed and as a consequence generation after generation has faced the same problems and been punished in mainstream school. It is now time to formulate a comprehensive plan of action to repair the issues within the culture that allow these tendencies to continue.

We have to face the simple stubborn fact that school and society cannot function without rules and regulations. Evidently, the rules were made by the capitalists who control every aspect of society and the rules, which are made by the privileged class, are unfair, unjust and unacceptable for our people but we must find ways to challenge the system so that the mechanisms for rule making acknowledge the interests of all classes in society, not just the privileged at the top.

We have to work to pressure politicians to make a fairer society but in the meantime our young people must realise that if there are no rules, there will be chaos and anarchy.

Rule breaking must be studied in its social, cultural and historical context here to gain a clearer understanding of the problem. Slave masters made rules to subjugate and oppress the slave; from the slave's perspective the rules were made to be violated because in the eyes of the slave, the slave master and his rules could not be separated. Both were part of the same oppressive system, part of the perceived sinfulness and part of the same abuse of power. Rules were seen as the slave whip, the oppressing force of keeping the slaves down and the means of preventing any kind of organised rebellion. The slaves grew to equate any kind of rule as being intrinsically negative because of its association with the slave master.

Through the years, our people within the African diaspora, still tend to equate rules with the maker of the rules without examining the rules objectively. Some rules still operate on the same principles but in fairness, some have changed to address the concerns raised by the civil rights movement and others. For generations, we have not addressed the unconscious and subconscious thinking that still lingers: we are linking the rule with the rule maker almost automatically and this is part of the problem. Rules must be examined objectively particularly the timekeeping ones. We cannot simply rebel for the sake of rebellion. Google as much as you can on the reasons for rebellions. The question for educationalists and policy makers now becomes how do we comprehensively re-evaluate the school rules so that students or all races feel less alienated from the school system? In light of the fact that black students are being expelled/excluded from school everywhere, should we devise culturally sensitive behavioural policies forwarded by cultural organisations which can then operate on the same basis as parent-teacher associations? Do we need mediation departments where students can voice their concerns, frustrations and anger with adults or senior students?

Chapter 27

EQUALITY FOR TEACHERS AND STUDENTS

Equal opportunity. Equal access. Equal rights. Every child matters. Pupil premium. Safe-guarding children. Numerous changes in pedagogy. Attempts to recruit and retain black teachers.

Many practices have been tried to achieve equality for all but still equality evades us and the slogan from Orwell's Animal Farm reminds everyone that all are created equal but some are more equal than others. Equality can never be achieved until and unless, society concedes that it is operating on idealistic rather than realistic principles for progress. Many of the problems within the classroom stem from a disconnection between the ideals of equality and the realism that teachers and students experience. Theoretically, one cannot clearly and distinctly conceive of what true equality looks like and more importantly how it will operate in practice. All government initiatives are made with a view of equality that is shaped to educate students for their place in a capitalist society that cannot exist without structures of inequality. No matter how hard one tries, no matter how well intentioned, the system is what creates the inequality and this automatically creates disconnection. The disconnection between students and teachers can be traced to a lack of empathy, a genuine lack of understanding of issues related to class and race, a lack of understanding of cultural complexities, a lack of understanding of the issues associated with the generational gap and lack of expectations for young people.

Without this understanding there would also be a lack of academic expertise, lack of adequate pedagogical training and lack of life experience to target the specific needs of the children and the issues that lead to different degrees of disconnection. Many argue that there is a need to diversify the teaching workforce or rather reflect the culturally diverse student population in the staffroom. Recruiting and retaining black teachers is necessary for our students' self-esteem and for role modelling. At present in many schools, colleges and universities in England and America, students do not have the privilege of being taught by a teacher from their cultural background. They go through their educational lives without seeing someone from their cultural background and this must be a cause for concern. Do we need a renewed effort to address the nature of the education (there was multicultural education, then there was inclusive, now we have a progressive system characterised by change itself) of our children?

Black Cultural Viewpoint

The issues of teacher-student relationship cannot simply be reduced to race or class but to the intricacies of the problems linked to different aspects of race and class within the context of multiple identities. We can have middle class black students having difficulty with middle class black teachers and lower class black students relating more to the middle class black teachers than the middle class black students.

What is important is that middle class teachers should be aware of their need to understand the intricacies of the problems associated with race and class: self-fulfilling prophecies, condescension, over-ambition, pressure from parents living vicariously through their children and the list can go on and on and on.

Teachers, white or black, in schools with majority black students also tend to have different problems than those in a school that is equally mixed. Such schools suffer from negative stereotypes on all levels: these schools are seen to have lower numbers of teachers who are certified in their degree areas; black middle class parents refrain from sending their children there because they feel the education would in some way require improvement. There are also perceived problems of behaviour management, peer pressure, drug taking and poor social skills. In short, these schools are breeding grounds for racial misconceptions.

Black teachers cannot win; they join a school with a large black student population and they are perceived as less qualified than those who teach in schools with a large white population. In the latter, black teachers have to challenge prejudiced opinions from staff and students because misconceptions and stereotypes are so engrained about race and how we achieve our positions.

As racial divisions deepen in wider society, this will undoubtedly be reflected in school appointments and school intake. Schools will become nothing more than breeding grounds for negative attitudes and behaviours on all levels – from the head teacher's office to the classroom and of course in the playground. Where do we go from here? How do we foster cultural cohesion in the classroom and the staffroom? How do we use our skills to elevate ourselves and our people? Many black people have educated themselves but historically, we have not worked together to better the race. Education has been like a rope to be used to elevate our people. Individually, black brothers and sisters use the rope to climb out of the ghetto rather than use it to help other brothers and sisters come out as well. We have to use education as a tool for the collective as well as a tool for the selective – the self. We can no longer have the crabs in the barrel mentality with regards to education. Should we work on establishing a black union of teachers to give voice to T.H.E C.A.U.S.E – Teachers Helping Everyone (teachers, students, assistants, parents) Campaign Against Unfair Systems in Education? Do we need to find ways within mainstream education to address the issues that need to be addressed within our culture operating as cultural workers in an equivalent role as social workers do?

Chapter 28

HOMEWORK RIGHTS AND WRONGS - RIGHTS TO WORK AT HOME

Homework. Private tuition. Private study time. Private study spaces. Private homework resources. Private network of support. Private boarding schools.

In Western societies, there is parental pressure put on pupils to excel at all costs and as a consequence high value is placed on homework. Parents, especially those who live vicariously through their children, insist that extra work is completed at home. Private tutors are employed, private study areas are prepared and private resources are provided for the privileged. The fact that the poor child has spent hours upon hours toiling in the various fields of study during the school day does not seem to matter, nor does the fact that family time is more important than additional time for schoolwork. Prioritising pressure on children to succeed, euphemistically termed as homework, must be labelled for what it really is – slave labour. The problem with homework is the same problem of slave labour: the lack of freedom. Young people need to be free from the shackles of labouring with money and power being the driving force. Parents, as masters, condition their children to believe that this labour will guarantee them success in the future and their young minds are programmed to obey their parent like man's best friend was taught by Pavlov or should that be the little rats programmed by Skinner.

The whole notion of homework or extra school work cannot be divorced from the ideology or value system of the western cultural thinker. Everything seems to be about gaining material success at the expense of social, cultural or spiritual investment. The time consumed doing homework could be invested in extended work at home like cooking, interior designing (after cleaning up those teenage bedrooms of course) playing games or even engaging in spiritual worship like meditation, relaxation or exercising together as a family. What about taking time to teach the family how to genuinely love other people and teach how western wealth was acquired from the rest of the world. Such discussions or rather home work will help not just the family but the wider society. There is a need in Western culture to prioritise the family unit and invest time and resources in the spiritual education of the next generation or the moral fabric of society will further disintegrate. How can Western society be reconstructed? Should homework be redefined as Social Moral Spiritual and Cultural education at home? Should parents campaign to ease the pressure of homework on young people? Should schools refrain from setting so much homework especially in light of the proposed extension to the school day?

Black Cultural Perspective

Black cultural viewpoint

Homework has been viewed as an important tool in closing three different gaps in the black community: the achievement gap, the attitude gap and the learning gap. Decreasing the gaps calls for additional educational provision that supplements what should be provided at home as well as what should be an extension of school based learning. In other words, there needs to be an effort to combine a moral, cultural and academic educational program that helps to cultivate a culture of success within our community. In middle class black families where private rooms to study are available, where private tuition is affordable and where private school is possible, homework is not an issue. However, for other working and underclass black families, such private provision is not an option. Let us not forget that our students who struggle with work at school are likely to struggle with work at home and the problems associated with the broad spectrum of issues are complex.

In America, President Obama laid out a goal to provide a complete and competitive education for every child from cradle through career and these are some of the issues his advisors must have considered in looking at education as a need within black communities. As president Obama insists "We're not going to transform the urban school system in a year...It's going to have to be a sustained effort, including a change of attitudes about education within our own communities." These attitudes include a change in extended learning or work outside the school to consolidate what has been taught within the school. Many middle class and aspiring black middle class parents insist that their children complete homework tasks and submit these on time for which they deserve merit. However, what is plaguing segments of the black community is not an unwillingness to invest time and resources in the education of their children but rather home situational factors that affect the children's ability to do homework.

Firstly, some children need additional help to do the homework and if no funds are available for private tuition and no time is available for parents to assist then problems will not be solved. Secondly, the home environment is often not conducive for concentration as many of our children do not have access to quiet study areas at home. Thirdly, children need time away from child labor tasks of caring for younger siblings, cooking and cleaning to concentrate in a private place (the local library if the home is too noisy or crowded). Fourthly, there needs to be parental pressure to insist that children focus exclusively on their work rather than be distracted by their access to social media. If parents are busy working or doing home chores, who is going to monitor the completion of homework?

Since slavery, we have always had a culture of sharing knowledge with each other as slaves would help spread literacy in their quest to be educated. Google Frederick Douglass's narrative where he insists that slaves who learnt to read and write taught others to do the same. Sharing learning became a common practice as slaves realized the power of education. Whether it was biblical literacy or not, slaves embraced the idea of learning to read. How do we build on the resilience and determination that the slaves had in their desire to be educated? How do we rebuild this shared desire to educate each other, starting in the home? Over the years, we have argued for segregation and desegregation where education is concerned. We have also looked at Afrocentric, multicultural and inclusive education as ways forward but there is still a missing element.

Essentially, the performance of black children is systematically different from other groups because of various combinations of our complex problems. We must aggressively address not only the learning, attitude and achievement gaps but also the opportunity `and relevance gaps. Students must have lessons that apply to their daily lives and our students need to learn the skills within a framework that is culturally inclusive or supports their cultural identity. In teaching these skills, resources and activities must tackle stereotypes rather than perpetuate them. The success of our students' educational provision must contribute to the success of our community. Unless our children fully understand the function of education in improving themselves and not just as a means to social mobility, or to getting a job, we will never close the relevance, achievement or opportunity gaps that exist. Should we extract elements of Afrocentric, multicultural and inclusive education to design a program of black cultural practice? Should we press for policies and legislation to promote cultural education in mainstream and supplementary schools? Should we collaborate with churches to promote an advanced literacy campaign that is linked to critical thinking and educational success?

Chapter 29

SCHOOL DISCIPLINE

Verbal reprimands. Detentions. Exclusion. Sanctions. Corporal punishment.

In different times, corporal punishment was the standard way of maintaining discipline. In different times, teachers had more respect, more authority and more status. In different times, they were valued almost as a parental figure and children expected to be disciplined if they broke the rules. Those times produced a different kind of student, a different kind of society and a different world. Sadly, those times are history. Nowadays, school discipline is characterised by systems of rules, regulations, sanctions and strategies to improve behaviour. Systematic preventative measures are missing and core values are conspicuously absent from codes of conduct that are cleverly constructed to control actions rather than for compliance. Here lies the problem of a free society: it simply undermines any concept of core values or expected standards of behaviour as a laissez-faire lifestyle is implied. If everyone is encouraged to be free to make their own rules and to live by their own standards, then any system of school discipline will be fighting against this tide. Stormy seas of sanctions are unsustainable in such a climate with teachers struggling to swim in the rough waters, sinking under the weight of their paperwork and shouted at by politicians, parents and pupils. The government persuades everyone to get on board the ship rather than change it, rather than change its captain or change its course.

Western politicians have confidence in this ship sailing students to a successful destination and encourage them to enjoy the expensive experience aboard the ship. Let's not forget the name of this ship. It is called the Titanic.

The Western World needs an entirely different ship to be built, one that will effect real climate change, allow everyone to see the sea with different eyes and one that is definitely made in China. In the People's Republic of China, school discipline is the envy of the world, in the People's Republic of China, academic success is the envy of the world and in the People's Republic of China, students are obedient and compliant with the school rules and codes of conduct. What about their record of human rights is the question undoubtedly in your mind. Yes, in the People's Republic of China, beatings by schoolteachers is still practiced even though corporal punishment is banned. Western cultural thinker do not have to use every Chinese resource in the construction of a different ship but there is no denial that some human resources are created more equal than others. How do Western politicians address the problem of indiscipline in schools? Is there a need to implement social, familial and political policies in wider society to provide consistency of expectation with home and school? Should education itself have a different philosophy and function - to equip young people with life skills, citizenship skills and emotional skills and not just work based skills for capitalism? Should there be a mutual exploration or negotiation of codes of conduct so that students share in the responsibility for creating a better environment? Should there be an emphasis on behaviour problem solving rather than producing punishment policies?

Black cultural viewpoint

Exclusion figures for our community are astronomical and they are sky rocketing to frightening heights. Statistic after statistic, report after report, study after study all suggest that there is definitely a real problem with school discipline and our children. Black parents of yesterday's generation claim children are out of control because society has abandoned the use of the cane and are sparing the rod and spoiling the child; they insist that if children cannot hear, then they must feel. Those who reject that way of thinking, lack a clear alternative as they concede that naughty steps haven't worked and now the younger generation are out of control. Some point the finger of blame at the media, others at the politically correct police and some even go as far as accuse the Church of failing to stand up to secularism.

Let us just try to imagine what life would be like if corporal punishment was reinstated in schools in the 21st century? Imagine the fights between the teachers meting out the punishment and the students being punished. We cannot forget that corporal punishment worked in times gone by when young people were more obedient, more compliant and more submissive. Today's generation would refuse to be punished in this way. Today's generation would fight back. Today's generation would be confrontational. We can no longer play the blame game so let us examine the problem of discipline and try to find ways to solve it without trying pointing the finger of blame. Whoever is responsible, the facts remain that teachers cannot cope with our children in the classrooms any more and more worryingly, parents cannot cope either. Teachers everywhere are left with no alternative but to exclude our children, especially our black boys. Consequently, our children are being criminalised (exclusion goes on their school record which is similar to a criminal record) and are losing out on their hopes and dreams of success however it is defined.

Understanding the legacy of slavery and education is crucial in moving forward and understanding the problems our young people face in an education system that was not designed with them in mind. Discipline, historically, always involved the use of force – of whipping, of beating and of brutality even of death. Tracing the problem of discipline back to Slavery and the Transatlantic Slave trade will show how family members were separated from their families and not allowed to teach about culture or anything - positive or negative. Slave children were dragged up, beaten and just taught how to be slaves to work on the plantations. There was no upbringing. No family time. No discipline. Working or rather slaving for the master was all that was considered important in the life of the slave. Unfortunately, since then, we have not comprehensively addressed this issue at all from within the culture. Fast forward to today's school discipline in some of our countries still involves caning and beating in the home, at school and within the culture. We have to address this from within because our children have to be taught discipline of a different kind to the one left by the legacy of slavery. Leaving in the There is also exclusion and leads to jail or incarceration even death.

For today's generation, the overall issue of discipline is much more complex, thanks to the internet and the globalisation of absolute freedom to choose their standards of behaviour. Our children are choosing not to respond to authority figures nor respect them and the reasons for this intricate and related to Post traumatic slave syndrome or the lingering legacy of oppression. Discipline at school is not designed to address the intricate problems but the intricate problems are causing problems of indiscipline. Addressing the problem comprehensively must be done to prevent the vicious cycle of punishment, exclusion, incarceration, crime and death. We have lost an entire generation and we cannot afford to lose another one. The question now becomes what is our community going to do about this monumental breakdown in discipline? How are we going to work with Western society to negotiate for provision within mainstream schools? How can we target parents and families? Should we give advisory services to parents and teachers on the needs of our children? Should we have model television shows that follow the format of `Super Nanny'? Should we design a Youth army course that applies the discipline and principles of military training to teach discipline to our girls and boys? Should we confiscate mobile phones and other valuables as a form of punishment so that our young people can fully focus on discipline?

Chapter 30

EDUCATIONAL VALUES

Education for domination. Education for inclusion. Education for control. Education for capitalism. Education for cultural heritage. Supplementary education. Education for socialisation. Education for cultural literacy.

Everyone's educational beliefs originate from personal experience, personal values and attitudes to knowledge about the world. These have cultural roots and unconscious motivations that undoubtedly influence practice, action and behaviour. Each educational institution should provide a professional service of high quality learning through its shared values, its policies, practices and philosophy to inspire the young people whose attitudes and behaviours should be shaped by the establishment.

Philosophies about education, cultivated during school years along with academic subject preferences, teachers and teaching all positively or negatively affect behaviour. In short, educational beliefs shape teachers' professional practice. The problem arises when these educational beliefs or values have negative consequences as they dictate decisions made, determine discrimination and impose prejudices on others.

Personal perspectives and philosophies about education in Western society are underpinned by idealism, realism, pragmatism and existentialism which apply to education on a metaphysical level. The nature of reality is perceived and explored through these four schools of thought but attempts to find unity still remains a metaphysical proposition. Idealism has found favour with many who subscribe to the view that education is about discovery and development of every child's ability and achieving moral excellence for the collective good of society. Idealism is about ideas, intuition, introspection and insight. Realism, on the other hand is about objective truth, observation, the scientific method and rational thought, standardizing and experimentation. Pragmatism or experientialism focuses on what is experienced and how students should be encouraged to apply experiences and thoughts to problems as they are encountered. For the pragmatist thinker, the world is not static and truth about the world must evolve, must progress to allow thoughts to produce action. Existentialists believe that reality lies in the soul, is subjective and is about individual standards as everyone determines who they are and make meaning of our lives. Should western cultural thinkers create a moral dimension to education based on values that link school and community values?

Should teachers systematically examine what motivates and inspires them? Should teacher professionalism be regarded both as a virtue and a commitment to competence? Does each educational establishment need a covenant of shared values?

Black cultural viewpoint

"Too many of us see education as essentially a preparation for jobs, as a preparation for moving up in social status, and as a means of securing a better lifestyle. And certainly, these are some of its major functions. However, I do not see them as the primary functions of education… I think it is vital that we understand that the major function of education is to help secure the survival of a people."- Amos Wilson

The success of our people depends on our success in educating the younger generation. Community action groups and community education seem to be declining at the same rate as the decline in church attendance, moral standards and family functioning. Yes, there are those who argue that this type of education begins in the home and nowhere else. They insist that it is the responsibility of parents to train up a child in the way that he should go but who is responsible for training the parents? Where do busy parents get time to properly parent their children? In an ideal world, in an ideal community, we expect parents to fulfil their role but there must also be community groups to support parents when they cannot. Traditionally, it has been the school, the church and government bodies but now we have to acknowledge that these institutions have not only lost the faith of the community but have also lost faith in themselves. It's not up to the teachers, the church, or even the government's responsibility to make sure our children are able to be functioning members of society, they are there to help reinforce the things that we should be teaching in the home. But what happens when the home has failed as an institution in our black community?

What has happened is many of our children have turned to role models for guidance and a sense of identity but there lies another problem: they begin to admire the rappers, basketball stars, footballers and some even look up to the drug dealers, pimps and gangsters. Our young people are bombarded with negative images on social media and beyond which only serve to teach disrespect of themselves and their communities. They teach them to have sex early, use drugs and enjoy life now because they are only young once. To reconstruct our community, we need to address the issues that are preventing the success of our young people within the community. We all agree that there is no simple solution to these complex problems. However, we must elevate ourselves through an education that addresses the 'tangle of pathologies' that are keeping us from the success that we deserve to enjoy collectively as a people.

To fully elevate in the African diaspora will require the creation of public policies and legislation that support educational establishments committed to identifying and setting high, worthwhile, and attainable goals for our students and ensuring that teachers and students are supported in these efforts. It will also require meaningful collaboration among community organizations and leaders, parents, and the school. *The success of our cultural education must become the success of the community.*

As president Obama says, "We're not going to transform the urban school system in a year," "It's going to have to be a sustained effort, including a change of attitudes about education within our own communities."

Historically then, slaves were simply being educated for individual and master gain and not for the good of the wider slave community. The house slaves did not realise that they were being manipulated for the master's benefit. They simply followed orders and got educated by the master for his benefit. The master controlled everything that the slave thought and how he learnt to think.

Here we are, over a hundred years later and this practice still continues to ring a familiar alarm bell? We must rise and devise our own cultural education for our community and not simply consume western education wholesale? Should we pressure politicians to create policies and legislation that support such education for our community? Should we produce and circulate mentorship literature for our people to access at their convenience? Should community groups and churches merge to promote moral guidelines for our community? With the global economic difficulties, what is the plan B for graduates, when there is no work available anywhere? Should we consider pooling our ideas to think of entrepreneurial enterprises to empower our people? Should we use our knowledge and expertise to build a new black education based on progressive principles?

Freedom from Faith

Chapter 31

RELIGION'S ROLE IN SOCIETY

Islam – Judaism – Christianity – Baha'i Faith-Hinduism – Taoism –Sikhism -Buddhism – Shinto - Slavic Neopaganism, Celtic polytheism, Heathenism – Semitic Neopaganism – Wicca- Kemetism (Egyptian paganism) – Hellenism

The key question for the Western cultural thinker to consider is whether or not society can function without religion. For the West, Christianity has always been the foundation on which the ethic of civilisation is built, cemented to its essential ideology but lately it has become nothing more than a precious commodity. With the exception of France, the Church and State have both benefited from their highly valued relationship and continue to work for the basic good of the economy and of course the moral fabric of society. The big problem now for the church and state of society is though the relationship may be valuable, it is far from holy. In fact, secularism, humanism and the science of the swinging sixties have led to the decline in the usefulness of this traditional bond. It is important not to overlook the enlightenment, the renaissance, the liberation movement which most definitely devalued the role of Western Christianity but sadly they did more: they undermined the stability and cohesiveness of society itself.

Another related problem for the West is the concept of religious freedom now that most western societies are diverse. The three Abrahamic faiths of Judaism, Christianity and Islam provide the monotheistic world-view that Moses, Jesus and Muhammad brought to the world. They had one mission to bring peace to the world and the problem for the West is its failure to embrace the message of peace as a way of freeing society. The virtual failure to embrace even the basic tenets of this trinity of religions is affecting the bedrock of western society: its education, its social care and crucially its politics. In terms of education, students can no longer identify and analyse religious allegory in Shakespeare and other writing from the canon nor can they genuinely care for others as they have not been taught how to. The lack of basic empathy to care for others at home, at school and in wider society has resulted from a lack of knowledge of Christianity or any other religion. Students can no longer clearly and distinctly perceive the meaning of spiritual, moral, social or cultural without basic understanding of religion. Even basic knowledge of Christian or religious festivals, cultural influences, historical criticisms of the historical use of the bible to justify oppression and colonialism is lacking in the young Western cultural minds.

This systematic failure to acknowledge the need to embrace Christianity as a religion and not as a commodity or ethic has allowed problems related to the moral decline in Western societies to incubate. How can Christianity begin to effect Western attitudes, particularly those of the younger generation, to embrace virtue over vice? How should religions promote spiritual literacy to this generation? How can the religious world persuade this society to find faith? Should a new moral movement be formed which emphasises religious principles in a youth-friendly manner? How can there be a moral transformation of modern society without religions having an impact?

Black cultural perspective

In many parts of Africa and the Diaspora, Christianity has had a strong cultural influence on education, morality and political activism. By contrast to its role in Western society, Christianity, for us has always been revered as a sacred covenant rather than a cultural commodity. However, the complexity of the problem with the role of Christianity, has to be historical, cultural, experiential and ontological. Let us start with some historical facts related to religion and the world view of civilisation. All the central figures of major world religions walked the earth in the Middle East: Moses, Jesus and Muhammad. Many followers of these prophets do not realise that throughout history they have always been in competition and conflict not considering that all three had the same mission of peace to the world. Moses, Jesus and Muhammed all called for belief and moral conduct and by doing so often conflicted with the established order based on corrupt practices and oppression.

Our knowledge of Christianity and religion must be separated from our painful history of slavery. Christianity was used by missionaries and slave owners as a tool of oppression but knowledge of religion must be perceived through different lens or we must seek religious understanding independent of its historical use and then we will discover that the underlying principles espoused by all religions are essentially based on the same message of peace for the human soul. It is a fact that our mother land is now home to many Muslims, many Christians and many others and for us this dispersion of religion across our homeland is parallel to the dispersion of our people across continents, across regions and across cultures. Historical reasons for this religious dispersion must be examined as a core aspect of the underlying problems of disunity, miseducation and family disharmony which combine to prevent the development of our collective cultural consciousness.

The problem in both Africa and the African diaspora of having our own collective religion and culture hidden from us has caused a plethora of problems for us as a people and these are well known. Not knowing who we are spiritually, culturally and intellectually presents existential and ontological problems. Rastafarianism has attempted to address the core of the problem especially for those of us born in the Diaspora. This movement emphasised the need to reject Babylon (the cultural ideology of the West which conditions us to perceive ourselves negatively). Our African essence has been defined by the West and many of us now realise that this false essence has made us misrepresent, mislead and misunderstand each other. Importantly, this conceptualisation of people of African descent reminds African Christians everywhere that it is difficult to forget the role of the Church in the conversion of slaves to Christianity when its role should have been preventing the brutality, oppression and greed of slave owners. It is difficult to forget the inhumanity of slavery and colonisation and many of us find it difficult to find one way to pardon this unforgiveable holocaust of enslavement. Yes, many may argue that Christianity was abused rather than used for its main purpose but it still remains very difficult almost impossible to forgive this uncomfortable truth about history and Christianity.

However, many may rightfully argue that God allowed slavery to show the world that after such atrocities, such oppression, such evil against our people, yet collectively, we still rise. For this reason some feel it is our spiritual obligation to forgive the past as we cannot overlook the fact that it was some of the same missionaries who were influential in ending slavery and still fight for our rights alongside us.

Despite the plethora of problems associated with the historical role or rather use of Christianity, we cannot deny the positive influence it has had on the black community. Whether we want to accept it or not, it has been the catalyst for encouraging education in our community as biblical literacy was the main education given initially to teach slaves how to accept the authority of the bible without questioning. For years and years, for generations and generations slaves were just taught to read unquestioningly rather than being taught how to read critically. Biblical literacy has sown the seeds of critical unconsciousness that have created more complex problems in education, politics and other aspects of our culture. Historically, slaves were taught incorrectly and now generations later, this practice of blind literacy must be corrected through the education system. Yes, the question whose education and for whose benefit immediately comes to mind so we must create a totally different education system designed specifically to address these issues.

The question of God's role in slavery still lingers in the mind: how could God allow this evil? God is omnipotent, omnipresent and omniscient so it would be unreasonable (using the Western definition of reason) for an all loving, all knowing God to allow the evil of slavery. There are those who would argue that God allowed it for a purpose and we will learn about the purpose when we get over on the other side (Heaven). Similar arguments claim that God allowed it because he created people with free will and if He intervened then that would be determinism. Others hold on to biblical justification of slavery. Feel free to google Ephesians Chapter 6 and verse 5. Interesting arguments abound here but the continued pain and suffering of our people around the world has far reaching religious implications.

At the heart of Christianity is forgiveness, obedience and faithfulness. These key principles were undoubtedly preached to the slaves. Picture them citing the scriptures of Jesus and his crucifixion, the ultimate forgiveness for the people who killed him. Father forgive them for they know not what they do and the ultimate forgiveness, the slave masters would insist is for the slaves to forgive their masters. Today, we still forgive those who continue to use the same system that has oppressed and continues to oppress our people. Is it time to explore ways to elevate our culture from these shackles? Should churches have bible studies to address some of the scriptures like Ephesians Chapter 6 and verse 5 that were emphasised during slavery? Should the Established Christian church publicly apologise for its role in the Slave trade? Should we rethink some of our traditional beliefs or rather should we critically assess some of the tenets of the Christian faith? Should we pray for inspiration to start a new faith for our people to believe in? Did God allow our people to show the world that after everything thrown at us, we can still rise?

Chapter 32

CHRISTIANITY AND COLOUR

Black. Sinfulness. Darkness. Evil. Hell. Damnation. White. Goodness. Light. Purity. Whitewashing. Aesthetics. Symbolism. Representation.

The influence of Christianity in Western cultural ideology cannot be divorced from religious colour imagery which radiates in the glory of God appearing as a white, shining light. Christians do not walk in darkness anymore but they walk in light or whiteness. As Isaiah 1: 18 states "come now let us reason together, says the Lord. Though your sins be as scarlet, they will be as white as snow; though they are red like crimson, they will be like wool. Throughout the bible, light, purity, goodness, perfection, glory, righteousness and whiteness have all been used interchangeably and one must question why. Revelation 19:8 cites that it was given to her to clothe herself in fine linen, bright and clean; for the fine linen is the righteous acts of the saints. What does this mean for the white race? Dare it be asked but the million dollar question becomes is this a form of justification for something that is claimed by Caucasians?

The philosophy of language proposes that the English language is based on observations, associations and representations in the natural world as shown by canon writers like William Shakespeare and John Conrad some of the founding fathers of promoting interrelated images of nature and religion in writing. According to the Bible, God created nature – the heaven and the earth, night and day, all creatures great and small. In the beginning, there was darkness upon the face of the deep and God said let there be light. - God called the light Day and the darkness he called Night. If we return to Conrad and his writing of the Heart of Darkness referring to Africa, could it be that God created Europe to be the heart of darkness on a metaphysical level referring to the Darkness of the human soul? Within this framework, Ephesians Chapter 6 and verse 12 will then have a very different meaning. This can then be contrasted with Africa's light of spirituality as an opposite to Europe in a spiritual sense. The greater light to rule the day Genesis 1:16 and the lesser light to rule the night.... And God saw that dividing the light from the darkness was good. What does this imply for segregation, apartheid and slavery? Does this imply that light (brightness, whiteness) was meant to rule over the earth, literally but not metaphorically?

Consider nature for a moment. Do you prefer day to night? Answer honestly. Why? Is it because you can see better in the brightness and light of the day and you feel better in the sunshine of the summer than the darkness of the night and the greyness of winter and of course its coldness? Do you prefer to see white clouds than black clouds? Has nature and the Bible shaped your view or rather coloured your view of light and dark? Do you think that it is almost natural to feel this way? How does this affect your view of the races – white and black and those in between? Within each race there seems to be a greater appreciation for `lighter' than `darker'. In the caste system in Asia, do the lighter castes have more status? What is the function of colour imagery in the Bible and beyond? How can Christianity change perceptions of people of colour when its scriptures have far-reaching implications?

Black cultural viewpoint

Black and white imagery in the bible makes for uncomfortable reading for black people everywhere: the association of black with darkness, with sinfulness, with evil and ultimately with the devil, the Prince of darkness cannot be denied. At the heart of the Christian religion are the polar opposites of good and evil, of God versus the Devil, of Hell and Heaven. Given that we learn through associations, representations and imagery, this stark contrast of colour symbolism creates negative impressions of our people and has far reaching implications for light and dark, for purity and impurity and crucially for black and white. Throughout the bible, this seems to be the case as people will be cast out `in the outer darkness; in that place where there will be weeping and gnashing of teeth (Matthew 8: 12). There are a plethora of scriptures which equate blackness with negativity and show how Christ himself became sin on the cross in the darkness so that sinners could know righteousness (or sins become white as snow). God turned away from Christ when he dies on the cross and remained in death and darkness in the grave. As the 2 Corinthians 5: 21 says `He made Him who knew no sin to be sin on our behalf, so that we might become the righteousness of God in Him. The scriptures show that the image of darkness and blackness seems to represent evil in the bible and in nature.

Let us explore nature and the creations that seem to feed into associations of black with negativity. Why are the big fearsome animals black? Why are doves and swans white? Why is the dirt black? Is it that we are looking at these creations with the wrong perceptive lenses – is it that dirt should be seen as the earth necessary for growth rather than something we wash away? Should the big black bears and gorillas be seen for their awesome power rather than as something to be feared? Has negativity and blackness been constructed rather than created? Is it conceivable that the bible could have been whitewashed? The big questions still linger why does nature and by extension Christianity feed people's notions and ideas about blackness and ultimately about our race? Why does the Bible use darkness, sinfulness, impurity, evil and blackness interchangeably when referring to negativity and the devil? How do we change the image of darkness and blackness to make it more positive and boost the self-esteem of our people? How can we change the perception of the imagery that serves to reinforce negative stereotypes of our people? Do you see why 'our faith' has been highlighted here as a problem and a real cause for concern?

Let us not forget that the legacy of slavery and Christianity cannot be divorced and color imagery illuminates the problems not just for the church but for everyone in our black community. The established church cannot be forgiven for its role in conditioning the slaves into thinking that God is white depicting white images in churches and schools. It is difficult to forgive missionaries for their role in the evil act of slavery where slaves were systematically taught to hate themselves through association with the Devil and sinfulness. However, the bitter irony of the legacy of slavery and the church's role is that our people developed collectively to be kind, loving and caring against all these odds.

Important Christian values lie at the heart of our practices in every area of our lives and we are always the first to forgive not just seven times but seventy times seven. As a consequence our cultural, religious, political and moral guidance are all rooted in the teachings of Christianity.

No one can deny that Christian values helped the slaves cope with the brutality of slavery. No one can deny that religion gave the slaves something to believe in: a better life in heaven. However, no one can deny the fact that slaves were implicitly and explicitly taught through biblical instruction to hate blackness/darkness and ultimately themselves. This has affected our people greatly and still continues to have a psychological, spiritual and emotional impact on black peoples' lives today. How do we begin, as a people to love ourselves, to teach our children to love themselves, to teach our people to love our blackness? Should we do something drastically positive to ensure that black symbolizes goodness – perhaps have our brides marry in a gorgeous black gown? Should different denominations of black churches get together to address the biblical symbolism and how to address it in the context of our cultural identity? Should we pray for a sign or a reason why biblical blackness is depicted as the representation of evil? Should we reexamine, redefine and repossess the definition and concept of blackness?

Chapter 33

RELIGION AND CAPITALISM

Money. Morality. Materialism. Prosperity. Greed. Spiritualism. Competitiveness. Conflict. Class. Christianity. Catholicism. Anglicanism.

Corruption of cheating, greed, theft, evil and oppression is the cancer of capitalism, destroying the cells of morality and human rights in its global spread around the global body. From West to East, religious people are deeply affected by this disease which divides their unity of purpose uncontrollably. It terminally kills many of its victims while religious leaders insist on praying for the victims rather than praying for a cure. In the West, Christian leaders will undoubtedly defend themselves by reminding the world that only those without sin can cast the first stone and continue to endorse the global gospel of greed. If one googles the history of capitalism and the history of the Church, one would find that they both have the same DNA and thus are affected in the same way by the same disease. One may also find that it was the nurture of the Church that caused the nature of capitalist cells to form in the first place and now there seems to be a desire to be fruitful, multiply and replenish the earth. The western cultural thinker tends to forget that the system of rules, regulations and rationalisation in resolving conflicts are cells of Christian ethics and values that have been influential in economic systems. Surely, church teachings should have been stopping the cells of profit over people rather than supporting the spread of this disease. In today's western society, the church is now praying for a miracle to redeem capitalism but it is difficult to hear this devil speak truth and it will take a miracle of some magnitude to save this system from its sins. The truth is that capitalism is beyond any form of redemption.

Religiously, the church continues to pray like arsonists around their fire, begging with buckets for bailouts to stop the spread of this disease. The Church still tries to reform an immoral system by preaching against unfairness in the distribution of wealth or rather the system that denies equality for all in accessing material wealth. Rather than deny the poverty in the system of thought and rather than deny the deficit in action to change it, the church politicises about the financial system being at fault. The refusal to preach against the capitalists who mastermind the infrastructure of this modern day slavery, the church chooses to convert the poor to principles of prosperity and force these poor souls to worship and obey those capitalists who rule and oppress them. Where does Christianity and capitalism go from here? Should they engage in a bitter divorce battle? How can the West think of a system other than socialism, communism or any form of collectivism to change things? How can Christianity help to save western society from the sins of its soul? With marginalisation, exploitation and alienation on the rise in western countries, how can Christians preach against additional issues of poverty and injustice working within a system that creates and perpetrates the problems? With so many western theologians, preachers and religious leaders, why is there such a desert of divine inspiration?

Black Church and Capitalism

Historically, culturally and socially, the black church used to be a haven of rest from exploitation, oppression and poverty. In times

171

gone by, the church was the place to feel part of a community, part of the choir and part of a movement. It was the place where we could realise our ambitions to be leaders, singers, teachers and entertainers. We were educated, entertained and empowered at church and we felt loved, respected and inspired. We got spiritual highs singing, dancing and being 'in the spirit' and we got praised for regular attendance and participation. In short, church offered a microcosm of life on earth in preparation for the afterlife. Fast forward to now and everything has changed as the black church has lost its sheep, has lost its sincere shepherds and crucially it has lost its soul. Even more sinful, even more sinister, and even more satanic, capitalist verses are being introduced in our churches and we are all singing from the same hymn sheet.

The church tax of 10% of income ensured the prosperity of the church and its leaders but now the latter wants more. Instead of praying for patience in wealth accumulation, pastors ask for additional taxes to pay for their prosperity. Poor members have to pay additional taxes for special occasions and funds for the fat cat ministers to prosper and function financially in the business. With fund raising events on a regular basis and encouragement to support money making measures, the church secures its place. American ministers particularly are now millionaires as their ministries spread across the world. Sometimes, perhaps inadvertently, they tend to use capitalist techniques to encourage more and more people to give financially, whilst promising blessings and miracles.

Why is this problematic? Many of our people believe in giving to receive blessings in the face of the harsh realities and our committed Christian brothers and sisters would give their last pound/dollar to the church rather than spend it on themselves. Church members financially commit to ministries without ensuring that they too are prospering as their souls prosper. Some ministries even persuade members to give more than the specified ten percent encouraging them to give up to 40% of their salaries to receive more blessings from the Lord. In addition to this, the offering plate seems to circulate multiple times in many of our black churches. Surely, the ratio of giving to receiving needs to be readdressed and so too does the uncomfortable emphasis on doing these acts in the name of God. One has to wonder, whether this giving to receive is slightly misleading members as the banks misled thousands of customers. Banks had to reimburse and perhaps, in good faith, Church bodies should consider doing likewise.

Studying such practices needs to be traced back to the legacy of slavery when Christian teachers and missionaries seemed to have a hidden agenda. It seems like through the ages, this practice of hidden agendas has continued and our leaders seem to be suffering from a version of post traumatic slave syndrome in their display of this oppressive behaviour which bears a striking resemblance to the money grabbing actions of masters with missionaries who would simply stand by and watch. How could the slaves not see the motives of their masters and the missionaries? Fast forward to the 21st century, why do we still have a problem with our perception of such fraudulent activity?

In British colonies, Christianity was used not only to indoctrinate but also to educate. When slavery was abolished, the Church played a key role in maintaining the stratification of Caribbean societies through the use of Christian education and this was maintained at all costs. The British government ensured education to be provided was to be Christian education. Accordingly, financial provision was made in the

Emancipation Act of 1833 for the "religious and moral education of the Negro population to be emancipated." Google for more information. These funds, known as the Negro Education Grant, were allocated to the missionary bodies who were already involved with the religious and moral upliftment of the slaves. The grant was 30,000 pounds per year for five years. It was then progressively reduced each year for an additional five years until it ceased completely.

In territories like Jamaica that had a strong missionary presence, the missionary societies took the lead in establishing schools in the years after emancipation. They intended to use their schools to effect conversion and cement denominational loyalties. Each missionary body struggled to establish and maintain schools in as many colonies as possible. On the other hand, in Trinidad, which was a Crown Colony with a strong Roman Catholic presence, the government established government schools and for a time excluded the church schools from the public school system. This was in a deliberate attempt to anglicize Trinidad and curb the influence of the Roman Catholic Church. Eventually in these two countries, as in the others, a dual system of church and state control of elementary schools evolved as the first Boards of Education and school inspectors were appointed and the governments began to give financial support to church schools. Google for details here.

How can the black church and capitalism cease to cohabit? Should the church confess its sins and seek forgiveness? Should church bodies use the money received from promised protection for its poor reinvest in supporting its poor members? Could there be regular tithes relief for struggling members who give their money in good faith? Should the Church contribute to the re-education of the black community with a view of paying for the sins of the past? Should the church make provision for critical thinking sessions rather than sermons from the mount of the pulpit? Should the Church refocus on preaching Godliness with contentment rather than Godliness for great financial gain?

Chapter 34

RELIGION AND MORALITY

Rights. Wrongs. Good. Evil. Good. Bad. God. Devil. Light. Darkness. Heaven. Hell. Holy books.

For many people, religion and morality have always been the perfect partners providing the model marriage for societies everywhere. For the Islamic faith, there can be no separation of morality from faith as religion informs the moral, political and cultural framework of society. Similarly, in the West, Christianity has been modelled and closely intertwined with politics, philosophy and the structure of society. Traditionally, the rules and laws of the land have been Christian principles that have been isolated to be regarded as society's commandments with the law-makers, politicians being perceived as moral authority. The problem then becomes muddled as politicians are now influenced more by ideology, linked intrinsically to value systems than by Christian morality. The traditional marriage of religion and morality has now become separable and many western cultural thinkers moan the happy marriage that has guided society to paths of rights and wrongs and the ultimate destination of community cohesion. They also moan society's love and respect for the law-givers; this used to provide spiritually high moments for society but sadly the marriage is now over as liberation is causing more and more conflict of interest.

Liberation movements destabilised, devalued and distorted the image and values on which this marriage was built and redefined morality as rational, intellectual reasoning and logic. They caused conflict in the marriage which has led to chaos in the self, chaos in society and chaos in the world at large. Unfortunately for us all, these movements destroyed the bedrock of this marriage, destroyed the sanctity of this marriage and destroyed the stability of this marriage. Secularism, liberalism and Science are now wreaking havoc everywhere presenting the world with multiple materialisms, multiple value systems and multiple rights and wrongs. What has now occurred is a total decline of this moral and religious marriage which once stabilised the world. Can the relationship survive?

Advocates for total separation or divorce now insist that the relationship is no longer based on equality and assert that moral practice is no longer reconcilable with religious tenets. They also argue that different religions pose different ethical challenges which cause conflict leading to eventual breakdown in the relationship. However, what cannot be denied by the western cultural thinker is that the marriage of morality and religion gave birth to spirituality and other such value frameworks as both values undoubtedly share the same DNA. How can western society modernise morality? How can morality be worshipped religiously by the younger generation? How can society rekindle the flame between religion and morality? Is it possible to have morality in the West without Christian Ethics? Should Western thinkers form a spirituality based on universal principles expressed in major religions?

Black cultural perspective

As a microcosm of society, as a center for education, as a force of political activism against oppression, the church across parts of Africa and the Diaspora, since slavery and colonisation has been the both our morality and our religion. It has been central to the development of community cohesion and moral principles by which we live. Historically, the black church has always provided an organizational structure for coming together, socializing and politicizing. Central to the moral principles that shaped our people, family and our community has always been Christianity; it has been the focal point of our black community. However, one now realises that having one authority on morals, one authority on structuring our society and one authority on defining how we should live is problematic. It has been the sole voice in justice, righteousness and equality for all. Not only that but it has been instrumental in providing the moral compass for family values and the family unit itself. In recent times, the church has lost its way in addressing the breakdown of black marriage. Some argue that this is just a sign of the times rather than a shift in moral values but the issue of the centrality of the Church in the moral growth of society.

In times gone by, marriage was for life not just for the good times. Women and men endured the challenges, prayed together and stayed together. Now, even church leaders seem to think that marriage is not forever as church divorces are on the rise, leaving our young people searching for examples of strong black marriage unions. Staying together and providing stability for our children must be a priority in the community. Presenting marriages like the Obamas' offer a positive model of love and family life and can have an impact on motivating more people in our community to tie the knot.

In addition to having strong bonds like that of the Obamas we also need community structures to work in addition to or in collaboration with the church to guide our young people. Traditionally it was the church that filled the void but there still needs to be some organised structures or bodies to bring our people together for a common cause. It is true that the Church has uplifted our people in times of depression and oppression. It is also true that our people have benefitted from the teachings and values of Christianity as we are more forgiving, honest and kind as a result of our religion. It is true that the faith has been a source of strength in the fight for liberty, equality and issues of civil rights.

The problem is we have never comprehensively examined the faith, never thought critically about the religion that was forced on us by our masters. Do we need to think critically about Christianity and its appropriateness for our people as the sole moral authority?

Historically, the church has been the only moral authority in the black community from inspiring black civil rights activists to guiding our daily lives. With its emphasis on evangelism, it has been used to encourage more people in the community to share the faith with others, making society a better place. The church has also been influential in fighting for justice and being a reaction to discrimination. No one can dispute that the church offers moral guidance, allowed black freedom of expression and highs of spirituality. Slaves during and after slavery saw Christianity and the church as a haven of rest, a place where they could be autonomous and escape white oppression. They affirmed their dignity as a people in their fight for freedom of mind. The question now becomes: with the church now steadily on the decline, where does the black community get its moral foundation? Should we draw from different voices speaking to establish a moral code within black communities? Should the church concede that many young people have turned to secularism and work with other agencies to try to target them there? Should we return to mother Africa to perceive the essence of our culture without romanticising the past? Should we begin an integrated, educational approach to the elevation of our people that combines education for reparation, education for entertainment and education for entrepreneurship?

Chapter 35

LACK OF FAITH IN LEADERSHIP

Pope. Priests. Preachers. Ministers. Pastors. Theologians. Teachers. Politicians. Scientists. Musicians. Celebrity role models.

In the Western world, leaders of principle over power, morality over money and integrity over greed seems to be an extinct species. World class moral leaders like Mahtma Ghandi, Martin Luther King, Winston Churchill, Abraham Lincoln and Nelson Mandela were leaders of principle who used their moral convictions to inspire and change the world. History will applaud them as men of the past who left a legacy for the present and future generations but history will also show that the present generation are growing up in a world almost devoid of moral leadership. What has happened to the present generation is that they are not presented with strong moral values and this has led to different values of consumerism and self-gratification that denies the link to the past or the future. Not only that but leadership too has changed as the triple values of honesty, morality and integrity no longer apply to current aspirations of leadership. Crucially, these have been replaced by nepotism, manipulation and dishonesty. Meritocracy is now a fact of history in the modern workplace so too is justice and ethics.

Lack of leadership reflects a lack of vision, a lack of real integrity to lead by example. Effective leaders must have a moral stance that persuades others to follow his/her course of action. Political, religious and moral leaders must be trustworthy and aim to serve rather than rule. They must develop the capacities of others and stand by their strong moral ideals with accountability and transparency being part of their leadership. With leadership comes a huge responsibility to sustain personal integrity for the benefit of all. How can the Western cultural thinker cultivate moral leadership in the minds of the young? How can modern leaders learn to leave a moral legacy? Why can modern Western leaders change this vast wasteland from its barren state?

Black Cultural Perspective

In the African Diaspora, because of the Black Church history, religious, moral and political leaders were terms used interchangeably and rightfully so. The Black church, historically, was more than a place of worship: it was a social, political and spiritual haven of rest from the outside world of oppression, racism and alienation. The church was about growth and development; it was about organising, educating and building business for the community. In America, particularly, it was a political power base for black activism from which the civil rights movement developed. In short, it was a microcosm of wider society – a spiritual homeland away from the motherland.

In these modern times, leaders of the black community are no longer synonymous with religion or morality. Religious leaders still lead but the community no longer follows. Yet religious leaders are still called upon to voice their perspective about matters affecting the black community. In the United States for example, when there are riots, when there are racial issues, journalists still tend to consult with religious leaders like Reverend Jackson and Reverend Sharpton. This is definitely problematic as it assumes that times have not changed and that black communities are still homogenous, that we are still all Christian and that everyone still thinks within the biblical framework.

The truth is that our young people have created their own leaders who have strayed far away from the values and teachings of the religious traditions of the black church. Celebrity sport stars, celebrities in the music industry and celebrities of reality shows are now the new leaders. This has resulted from a vacuum of black leadership and even more worrying a vacuum of any cultural concept of community itself. With civil rights leaders aging, with church leaders focused on the business of the church, how can we cultivate moral leadership within our communities?

What has happened traditionally is the church leaders have effectively dominated discussions about the betterment of our community not recognising that there needs to be a broader church of contributors. Understandably, our leaders are steeped in religious thinking but they must allow for common goals to take priority over common faith. If this happens, leadership of the community can be guided by groups of academics, politicians, professionals and popular figures to consider policies and action plans for our community development. Without this commitment to changing our thinking about coming together to elevate ourselves, we will simply continue to protest rather than progress. For the community to move forward, we must allow all voices representing intergenerational, interreligious and interrelated educational backgrounds to make positive contributions to the development of our community. Yes, there will be religious bias, there will be culture clashes but these must be encouraged in an orderly manner for younger people to learn how to reason and think critically rather than simply accept one authority on community matters. Should we form new establishments which are microcosms of community in the same way as the black church has been? Should churches unite to explore ways of cultivating leadership of our community?

Should the black church have a comprehensive examination of the problems it faces in finding forward thinking leaders to reconstruct a form of morality which appeals across generations?

Chapter 36

RELIGIOUS EXTREMES

Peace. Pilgrimage. Fasting. Prayers. Charity. Purification. Animal sacrifice. Contentment. Honesty. Holistic. Individualism. Conflict. Freedom.

In Western culture, there seems to be a clear misunderstanding of Islamic faith and its role and contribution to the world. Not only does it shape the lives and identity of its people, but importantly, Islam is shown to be much more than the practice of a ritualistic religion: it is a religion that promotes a complete way of life which incorporates religion into every aspect of its spiritual, academic, cultural and day to day life experiences. Rather than focus almost exclusively on various restrictions Islam imposes such as the prohibition of pork and alcohol, Western thinkers overlook how the Islamic faith prescribes ways to have a peaceful and happy life. What is enlightening about this way of life, is a completely different premise for logic which shapes different beliefs, values and a contrasting moral system. Because Islam is the extreme opposite way of life to that of the western cultural thinker, that becomes the heart of the problem posed. Islam shows that faith cannot be divorced from culture, upbringing and identity whereas the West preaches the extreme opposite. Crucially, Islam emphasises the philosophy of peace within the self and socialises its followers into an identity of peaceful living; it offers a logical explanation for everything that is prescribed for peaceful living within the religion. By contrast, Science, worshipped in the West, emphasises the religion of conflict of the platonic self, of society and of the world. There needs to be dialogue between followers of both religions to reconcile these extreme differences.

Science and western ideology seem to create a fear of others, an endemic fear of losing material things and of losing life itself. This western cultural indoctrination, rather than promising eternal life has awarded a free life on earth chained to anxiety and spiritual isolation with the ultimate price of eternal fear, euphemistically termed as religious freedom. This fear of a different spiritual essence exists overwhelmingly in the mind of the western cultural thinker and feeds the root cause of the conflict: a clash of ideologies about the nature of the self, society and the world. Essentially, this spiritual deficit can only be reconciled with the true acknowledgement of the nature of the self. The Western cultural thinker must try to find the peace that Islam offers, from another source; they must go beyond their collective pride, beyond the illusion of their religious progress and beyond the institutionalised ethic of the Christ ethic. What will be discovered is the simply stubborn truth that there is no other source of peace.

Should the Western cultural thinker apply some of the prohibitions of Islam to avoid some of the health and moral problems related to alcohol use and overeating? Can the requirement for women to dress modestly help to prevent some of the ills in modern western societies? Should the West include a complete set of beliefs with some form of spirituality at the core? Should the west adopt the charitable Islamic expectation that all savings should be taxed each year to ensure the fair redistribution of wealth? How can the West really address its extreme moral and spiritual bankruptcy?

Black perspective /

In the African diaspora, famous converts to the Nation of Islam include Mohamed Ali, Malcolm X and Minister Farrakhan, who have showed how adopting an Islamic way of life can shape families and allow members to find an inner peace. The real problem for us is that many of our people within the diaspora perceive Islam as the Western cultural thinker does: in race-related terms when Islamic faith specifically states that it is a universal religion not confined to any ethnic group or nationality. The western media maligns Islam in the very same way that it presents misinformation about our people and when our minds are free, we should be able to see Islam with different eyes. What many of us do not realise is the fact that Islam has practical solutions for the problems of the world as it achieves results both at the individual and collective levels. Yes, small percentages of Muslims do not conform but collectively, form the best model of community in the world. As many Muslims insist `don't judge a car by its driver'. If you want to judge how good is the latest model of the "Mercedes" car and a young driver takes to the wheel and crashes it, you do not criticise the car, the blame is with the driver. To analyse how good a car is, a person should not look at the driver but see the ability and features of the car. Everyone should judge Islam by its best follower – Prophet Muhammed (pbuh).

If we study the religious demographics of our motherland, almost fifty percent of the African continent are followers of the Islamic faith with almost forty percent being Christian. Islam has been a central force in the creation of the plethora of African Kingdoms (from Ethiopia, to Islamic Spain, to the largest African empire of Songhai), and has been part of Africa since its emergence. Sculpted by African and Arab agents, Islam is one of the fastest growing religions among

Africans and the largest religion in Africa— accounting for 1/4 of the world's Muslim population of 1.5 billion. Islam and Africa are also the most misunderstood, under-represented, and misrepresented as many fail to observe how different the influence of Islam has been compared to what was imposed for different reasons on our motherland. However, let us not forget that Islam is not indigenous to Africa as it was spread initially by traders and Arab travellers that is why many of us in the African Diaspora tend to see an Arabized Islam or the Hindu influenced Indo-Pakistani kind of Islam rather what Islam is intended to be. The questions them become: should we seek to understand Islam as a cultural and historical site on progressive understanding of its community of people? Should we extrapolate what seems to empower Muslims everywhere with a strong sense of identity, faith and belief? Should we analyse the faith which shows a dynamic, hospital and holistic culture and understand its contribution to African civilisations? Should we extrapolate principles from Islam to build moral values and cohesion for our community? Should we think critically about our multi-faith ancestry with the view of understanding history and progressing for the future?

Chapter 37

RELIGION AS INSURANCE

Life in heaven. Life after death. Life before death.

For the western cultural thinker, the infrastructure of the capitalist system is applied in every institution and in every area of life and the insurance role of religion is no exception. Within this context, it is its strength as well as its weakness: failure to insist on religion for the self, the society and the world has undermined the strength of religion to empower on all levels in western society. Everyone knows that religion or spirituality is great for emotional well-being and inner strength to cope with the life stressors that are on the rise in Western societies as economic hardships increase. Religion insures higher degree of life satisfaction and insures against psychological difficulties caused by unemployment and family breakdown. Crucially, it is perceived by the west as death insurance as all major religions emphasise an afterlife. What the western cultural thinker fails to realise is that for religious people they interpret this life as spiritual beings on a human journey and not as merely a human experience.

Some may argue that the social, political and economic implications of this kind of thinking has paid dividends for the west and helped to maintain control over the lower classes of society. Getting the poor to concentrate on the afterlife and forget about the reality of society in the present, served its purpose throughout history. However, the problem is that ignorance of the motives of religious leaders in selling religion as an insurance policy is no longer a strength in modern society and this policy has created problems for both the self, society and the political establishment. Focusing exclusively on preparing the self for the afterlife implies neglecting the present physical life. No focus on care for the body but exclusive focus on life after death. Consequently, when religious groups congregate there is a sense of contentment with life so much so that religious institutions do not actively focus on creating jobs to occupy themselves on earth. Instead, the focus is on replenishing the earth with more and more people for the workforce.

Here lies another paradox for the insurance policy holders and those who are not. The emphasis by those who institutionalise Christianity in the west is that that there is a better place, a paradise for enjoyment in the afterlife and this life on earth is just like a transitional journey or experience. Can Christians continue to sell the insurance policy by encouraging the endurance of pain and suffering here on this earth with the insurance policy delivering higher levels of contentment, satisfaction and peace of mind? Should the western cultural thinker produce a different insurance policy? Should the western cultural thinker find a completely different way to insure against extreme conditions? With huge rises in unemployment everywhere, should there be a rise in initiatives geared towards increasing ever-falling attendance to churches? Should the West refrain from using religion as propaganda and place emphasis on the meaning offered to its followers? Should the insurance role of religion be reinvigorated, redesigned and renewed?

Black cultural perspective

For us, religion is not an institution, rhetoric ethic or propaganda but rather a spiritual experience that gives significance to our lives. However, what this has insured, rather inadvertently, is that our people have not focused enough on how to have a successful life before death. Yes, the Lord says that we must prosper as our soul prospers. Yes, the church has made our people happier, more forgiving, more personable and more virtuous. Yes, we can never devalue Christianity's contribution not only to our community but to the world. After all, it was the black church that contributed to the whole civil rights movement with its deeply felt moral message; it has even provided strong moral values and principles for political parties both right and left and in between on the political spectrum. However, we cannot deny that if we are preoccupied with the afterlife, then the current life is no longer a priority for us. Consciously and unconsciously, we feel that we can accept the suffering, accept the poverty, accept the hardships in this life because it will be worth it all when we get to Heaven.

This is an essential part of this death insurance policy that our people must be aware of. It seems like we are simply living and waiting to die or as the older people say 'waiting for the Lord to take me home' so that we can claim the death insurance of the afterlife. For those who do not believe, the reward of life after death is regarded as the unique selling point for the death insurance brokers. Our people are thus given an incentive to prioritise life after death rather than focus on life before death. More formally, only our spiritual-emotional needs are being catered for within this policy and that is why many argue that religion has not helped our people, collectively to progress.

If we look at this issue in its social and historical context, we will remember that Christianity was spread by missionaries and used in the colonization of Africa and most notably in the conversion of the slaves. The insurance brokers did indeed use Christianity to occupy the minds of many so that they could have access to the wealthy resources of the continent. As taught in the African diaspora: as we bowed to pray, they took the gold away.

In recent times, many Christians or churchgoers have lost that complete trust in God to solve our problems; they have lost faith in the faith but would not openly describe themselves as agnostic or atheist. Losing faith means losing belief, losing confidence, losing trust in God. This trust is cultivated over time as God proves himself faithful on different occasions. In our daily lives the truth of the faith and the perceived reality – our daily experiences no longer correlate. Put more formally, when we follow our perceptions of what is true rather than our belief in what is true, the struggle is a loss of faith. The apostle Paul admonished Christians to: "Walk by faith and not by sight" 2 Corinthians 5:7 but this is becoming more and more problematic as there is a loss of both faith and sight.

Chapter 38

SPIRITUAL HIGHS

Weddings - Funerals – Prayers - Dreams –Inspirational sermons – Parenthood- ceremonial dancing - intellectual moments – Music – drug-taking

For the Western cultural thinker, who have no spiritual background as culture dictates the suppression of the human spirit, starting a spiritual journey is important as well as necessary. Purposeful meditation or finding spiritual highs tend to be sought and associated with the physical effects of common drugs – alcohol, legal and illegal drugs and merriment through music and revelry. The western cultural thinker wants to engage in an experience that allows them to let the mind go of everyday issues but fail to admit that this involves a direct appeal to the greater powers of the world to come forth and connect for a greater purpose. Spacing oneself out for a while does not really address the spiritual emptiness but rather just takes one temporarily away from the spiritual vacuum that needs to be filled. Spiritual smoking is often cited as a way to clear the mind but that is just a kind of food for the brain as it generates more alpha waves while the individual is high. Connecting body and spirit with a substance in the system creates a false essence of a spiritual high as it implies that the drug has to guide the body and mind to the spiritual experience rather than the other way around as emphasised by monotheistic religions.

The problem for the western cultural thinker is that spiritual highs connect the individual to nature or rather one ends up on a harmonious level with nature itself. This leads into deeply ontological arguments about the nature of the self; whether the human being is more than the five senses, the mind and intellect. If the western cultural thinker does not acknowledge the spiritual self then there can be no full understanding or real connection to the spiritual realm and searching for spiritually high moments would just be futile. The journey to find spirituality would be one that is lost in high state experiences that are meaningless without an awareness of these being intrinsically sacred. To fully develop the paths, the western cultural thinker must learn to embrace the intricacies of the experience without resistance to the destination: interconnectedness with other spirits. The ego will have to be sacrificed as all spirituality involves to some degree, service to others. What will be discovered is the more intense the spiritual high, the more manifest the existence of God becomes. In other words, spiritual knowledge slowly replaces the spiritual ignorance of our true state of existence.

The questions for the western cultural thinker then become: how can spiritual highs be divorced from the spiritual world? How can the five senses, mind and soul connect with a spiritual realm if the object is non-existent? Why are scientists encouraging legal highs on one hand and denying the existence of a spiritual world on the other hand? How can the western cultural thinker find peace within the self without a connection to the spiritual essence of the self?

If spiritual highs are experienced at weddings, funerals and parental birth – is this not evidence of a humans being quintessentially spiritual beings?

Black cultural perspective

Black churches are often identified as those that apply `black cultural' practices to the delivery and order of the service. More emotional singing and dancing which gives church service a more festive feel to it. There is more emotional energy in the delivery of sermons, more emotional energy in the singing of songs, more emotional expressive dancing and more emotional spiritual connection – a frenzy when being `in the spirit' and `talking in tongues'. This emotional investment, this spiritual high presents concerns regarding the engagement of the brain at the same time. If psychologists are correct in their assertion about the relationship between thought and emotions then, we need to redress that balance so that equal energy is spent on both emotional satisfaction and intellectual stimulation.

In Caribbean islands, the emotional energy of the music is almost parallel to that of the Carnival revellers in its intensity, its entertainment value and its rhythms. Choruses are repeated endlessly and more intensely, church members dance vigorously and the music is played loud enough to reach the heavens. One calypsonian referred to this display of spiritual elation as `Sunday J'ouvert' when evangelical churches enjoy the spirit and rhythms of the church music. While this emotional aspect of religious life can be described as the connection to our African past, critics argue that it compromises religion's integrity as the purpose of religion has never been to provide spiritual pleasure for worshippers but rather for worshippers to give pleasure to the Spiritual One. Pure Christianity and pure Islam would undoubtedly stress some form of religious orthodoxy but black churches have traditionally combined different beliefs and syncretised their faiths. The historical underpinnings of this practice must be visited here.

The spiritual highs in black churches cannot be divorced from slave emotionalism, our ancestral rituals and our prolonged psychological suffering. The prolonged song services with endless repetition of choruses, the lengthy devotional prayers and the sermons with or without substance. Such inspiration speakers are never lacking in emotional appeal, physical energy or exhorting eloquence ensuring that the worship sessions are the triumph of style over substance. Critics amongst us may argue that such spiritually high sessions accentuate rather than alleviate the problems of our people. They insist that such worship sessions still reflect the pain and anguish of the daily lives of its members but admit that many enjoy the performance poetry, the vivid imagery and dramatic effects that typify Shakespearian drama. What many fail to realize is the truth about this deep dramatic irony and how it foreshadows what audiences who are well read have already discovered. Those who can fully understand what is being said will say 'Amen'.

Rastafarians have been saying 'Amen' the loudest but rather than address the core of the problem have insisted on a different spiritual high altogether. In fairness, their spiritual high helps to cope with the pain and anguish of life in an entirely different way but like the church highs, there is a failure to acknowledge that we have to return to face the reality of what is causing the problems in the first place. Rejecting Babylon without offering a feasible and comprehensive alternative pathway is not helping us cope with the reality of our human journey. What is worthy of merit is their emphasis on the relationship between culture and religion.

The Black church has highlighted the link between the distinctive African traditional elements embedded in our religious practices and in our music and way of life. We all know that our cultural and religious music is distinct from traditional European sounds and the cultural transfers regarding religion are evident in this context. The problem here is how to we address the pain, suffering and anguish that lead our people to search for spiritual highs in the wrong places? How do we progress from the prayer 'Lord, have mercy'? How do we develop spiritual guidance without the perception being a spiritual high? Should we seek a different source for spiritual highs? Should syncretism, the combining of different (often contradictory) beliefs be incorporated into our thinking of a way forward? Is it a quintessential part of our true African identity to adopt the philosophy of syncretism with indigenous beliefs to construct our personal identity? Is Kwesi Yankah right in insisting that many African peoples today have a 'mixed' religious heritage to try to reconcile traditional religions with Abrahamic faiths?

Chapter 39

OTHER RELIGIOUS IDENTITIES

The image of Science, like Christ, seeks to mirror a model of moral perfection and western cultural thinkers try to form themselves in this image in order to progress and advance. For followers of Science, logic is the way, the truth and the light and no one can come to know the truth except through rationality. What they fail to emphasise is the fact that the light of scientific reason is unable to pierce the force and function of metaphysical darkness.

Science is sacralised as a ritual, a cultural system of beliefs and world view that is given reverence and worshipped by the Western cultural thinker, who seems to be heading single file down the wrong path, chanting his own lies, damn lies and statistics. Scientific leaders insist that this path is the only path to absolute truth about their world and praise their little ones who study the STEM subjects for their dedication to the faith. Parents, totally unaware of the cultural indoctrination, religiously offer up their sons and daughters as sacrificial lambs. They then go off to the spiritual wasteland to slaughter house after slaughter house not knowing their ultimate fate - the destruction of their metaphysical, ontological beings.

Science spiritualises academic power for its followers and commands them to have knowledge for everything. Thou shalt know the truth and the truth shalt set you free but their leaders deceive them into thinking that freedom is free. Orwell reminds them that it is not. Worshippers pray daily to their gods to relieve them of their anxiety but the gods cannot gain control over what controls them. They make different chemical weapons, poison and tablets for their followers to consume; play games with drones and bombs in their attempt to play God. Everyone is seeking fulfilment in Madonna's world not realising that their gods cannot materialise a spiritual concept. It is evident that they have reduced spirit to matter and the ability to manipulate it and; their heaven promises an abstract and oppressive future. Only cyclic (not linear) time will tell.

How does the West rid itself of a religion that is clearly destroying the self, destroying communities and destroying the world? How can science refrain from making meaning mere visible manifestations with virtues being reduced to mere objects for verification? Should the West promote different religious options for society rather than insist on cultural indoctrination? Is the process of osmosis between Science and the more powerful religions causing problems in the hearts and minds of western cultural thinkers? Should scientists invent a science of integration? Should science try to empower its followers with a plan B system to cope with the spiritual essence within? As all other religions insist on gathering together for a collective communal purpose, should Science begin by organising such sessions for communities? Should scientists refocus on the organic interrelationship between the mind, soul/spirit and body in an attempt to understand the workings of the soul?

Rather than create emotional confusion, should scientists research the possibility of creating a rationally ordered universe for everything and everyone? Can scientists invent a science of integration, a science of morality or a science of happiness? Has the monster created by the West pressed the self-destruct button or rather how can Frankenstein Science be saved from itself?

Black cultural perspective

There have been two powerful religious organisations that have been led by black leaders in the African diaspora: the Rastafari belief system and the Nation of Islam. Some may argue that Rastafarianism is the only religious movement that can be viewed as authentically black or Afrocentric in its origins. Some may disagree. What is certain is the fact that it was developed in Jamaica by Marcus Garvey and popularised by Bob Marley, who emphasised the freedom of the mind from mental slavery. What rastafari must be given credit for is their rejection of the quintessential values of capitalist culture – greed, deception and conceit which they branded as Babylonian ideas. Instead, they advocated a way of life that focused on resistance to oppression, simplicity as opposed to materialism and naturalness as opposed to the use of chemicals. Shunning the power structure of Europe which enslaved blacks both mentally and physically, they insisted that the building blocks of the structure must be rejected if black people are to rise. Similarly, the message of Kenyan academic, Ngugi wa Thiong'o insists on decolonisation of the mind and many echo this view.

Another central concept in rastafari belief system, is the spiritual use of cannabis which relaxes the mind and provides a spiritual high. However, one of the problems this has posed, in recent years, is that the spiritual use of cannabis has not been divorced from the criminal use of the substance in our communities. Study the statistics for our black community and it would show a strong positive correlation between criminal activity and those criminals being tested to be under influence of the substance. This is what advocates of the religion need to address comprehensively because many of its young followers are misusing the key tenet of their religion. However, with no formal, organised leadership of the Rastafari movement, revising these values and beliefs would be problematic. What is also problematic is the treatment of Ethiopian Emperor Haile Selassie I as the divine Messiah, romanticizing Africa or rather Zion as heaven on earth and the belief in physical and spiritual immortality, referred to as "everliving". The belief in `I and I' inadvertently, and inadvertently must be stressed here, implies looking after oneself rather than others. This may contribute to elements of individualism, selfishness and disunity that plague our societies.

Just as the Black Church extrapolated from established Christianity, the Nation of Islam (NOI) did likewise from the Islamic faith. The Nation of Islam (NOI) is an Islamic religious movement aimed at improving the spiritual, mental, social and economic condition of African Americans and of all humanity. Its perception as a black supremacist group, its perception as anti-semitic and its perception as a segregationist organisation tend to overshadow its commitment to promoting dignity, providing social and educational programs and transforming black men. Great efforts have also been made to be a stabilising influence in the black community.

Louis Farrakhan has led the Nation of Islam that combined elements of Islam with Black Nationalism since 1978 and is known for fighting all forms of oppression. He has faced fierce criticism because the Nation of Islam does not adhere to the core tenets of Islamic theology but rather is a religion exclusively for black people descended from slaves proper Islam is a universal religion open to people of every race. As the Qu'ran makes clear – "And mankind is naught but a single nation – Qu'ran 2:213

Attempts to find a religion of our own proves to be problematic as shown in the shortcomings of the movements above but how do we progress from here? Should Rastafarianism followers upgrade and document the beliefs by which they live? Should we extrapolate the notion of rejecting extreme materialism and greed as stressed in Babylon? Should we adopt some of the values expressed by the Nation of Islam – particularly those which promote dignity, discipline and the transformation of our men? Should we use the notion of Zion to encourage our people in the African Diaspora to visit the homeland at least once before we die? Should we seek a collective identity that imposes the African integration of self: the human spirit or soul, the mind and natural body working holistically as one? Do we need to redress the balance by reducing the spiritual high elements in our cultural practices and instead by increasing the imposition of the collective decolonised mind? Do we need to reclaim our African spiritual ancestry without romanticising the Past?

Chapter 40

ABSENCE OF FAITH

Atheism – Agnosticism – Scepticism –Secularism – Humanism -Freethought – Enlightenment – atheist existentialism – Non-believers

Atheism seems to be growing in diversity in gender, race and class

Is atheism on the rise because many people don't really want to talk about racism, sexism, homophobia and other bigotries or wrongs.

Pseudoscience like homeopathy

Anyone who declares themselves a nonbeliever does so because of a compelling need to talk about reality. The desire to discard what we perceive as falsehoods and speak honestly about the realities of our lives

Dismiss social justice issues as 'mission drift'-

They have pushed a door open and that represents an opportunity but the real task is to step through that door with some positive proposal of what life after religion has to look like.

I cannot divorce my critical thinking from my blackness, from my femaleness, from my position as a mother.

The practical consequence of this atheism was that there are no a priori rules or absolute values that can be invoked to govern human conduct and that humans are condemned to invent these for themselves, making man absolutely responsible for everything he does. – Jean Sartre

Forthright and articulated things we had kept locked away or simply hadn't found the words for.

Sart

The older dictionaries defined atheism as a belief that there is no God but modern upgraded meanings state that atheism is not a disbelief in gods or a denial of gods; it is a lack of belief in gods or the existence of deities.

Arguments – lack of empirical evidence – rejection of concepts that cannot be falsified -

The problem of evil

Inconsistency in revelations

Humanity as the absolute form of ethics and values and permits individuals to resolve moral problems without resorting to God. Marx and Freud used this argument to convey messages of liberation, full development and unfettered happiness. Denying the existence of a god leads to moral relativism leaving one with no moral or ethical foundation or renders life meaningless and miserable

Feminism and Frankenstein share more than the initial letter

R

They see creationism as propoganda

What we refuse to acknowledge but what we cannot deny is the fact that the Christian religion was manipulated to ensure our mental slavery. We feel guilty just to allow the thought to enter our minds, we feel like God is going to judge us for allowing the cultivation of these thoughts but don't be afraid to reason here. You are not being disrespectful, sinful or irreverent for critically assessing the tenets of the falsification of the faith. Do not be paranoid! Do not be afraid to explore the connections between slavery of the mind and the use of religion in the process. Allow your thoughts to develop. Reason. Examine. Analyse.

Let's favor freedom over faith for a few minutes. Focus on these five features of slavery: blind obedience, dependent thinking, forced labour, total dependence on one's master and systematic/acceptance of oppression. Now answer these five questions in your own mind: Was the Christian religion employed to insist on obedience to accepted words of wisdom outlined in sacred books? Was religion used to teach us what to think rather than how to think? Was religion focused on getting its followers to complete evangelical/missionary/ worship work whether they wanted to or not? Was religion used to state implicitly and explicitly that one could depend on a superior being to take care of everything so we do not have to? Was religion used to state that we are unequal to our superior master and that we had to suffer as part of your experience of life?

One more mental activity. Draw a Venn diagram in your mind: have one circle for religion and the other for slavery. Place the following words appropriately in the Venn diagram: indoctrination, brainwashing, money-making, manipulation, coercion, superiority, inferiority, righteousness, evil, freewill, bondage. How many words did you place in the overlapping sect in the middle? Case closed. To state that there was no comprehensive effort made to emphasize the connection between religion and mental slavery is a rather peculiar species of irrationality.

The legacy of slavery and the legacy of religion cannot be divorced. Slavery promoted subjugation, racism, inequality, dependency, inferiority and critical unconsciousness. It also manipulated our perception of ourselves, our homeland and each other.

It made us dependent on one way of doing things, one way of seeing things, one way of believing things to be. Slavery, then, indoctrinated an entire generation and continues to do so. Can you see the connection between slavery and religion?

Religion prevents us from freeing our minds. It expects us to `do as we are told' without question because that is what is written. Let us not forget what is written in Ephesians 6 verse 5: slaves be obedient to your masters'. It cultivates a sense of acceptance, lack of initiative, it stifles our imagination etc.evation

f half of the focus, money, time and effort put into faith was redirected and concentrated on real world problems we would have a much better society to raise our children in.

Recent events surrounding the Occupy protest camp in the City of London, and its impact on the life of St Paul's Cathedral, have led to many sharp questions about the Church of England's view of capitalism and about how Christian ethics engages with economic issues.

To ask whether the church is for or against capitalism is to pose the question too starkly - there are many capitalisms and a number of ways to analyse it theologically. We offer here some preliminary thoughts to guide ethical and theological reflection and suggest a number of books which can help in taking the question forward.

A NEW paper published by Theos, a London-based religious think-tank, will raise hackles on the right and left alike, if only because of its title: "Just Money: How Catholic Social Teaching can Redeem Capitalism". Advocates of capitalism will certainly retort that the system has no need of redemption. The core meaning of the word redemption is something like "to secure the freedom, or the very existence, of someone or something at a price...." And as a supremely efficient instrument for resource allocation and price discovery, so the argument would go, capitalism should have no need of any external agency to purchase its right to exist. It just needs to be allowed to do its job. At the other extreme, critics on the left will retort that capitalism is so wicked that it cannot be redeemed by anything, least of all the doctrines of Catholicism.

Yet the paper by Clifford Longley is well worth reading, if only because it presents in readable language ideas which normally lie buried deep inside closely argued papal encyclicals and other cerebral writings. Mr Longley explains some of the key concepts in an elaborate body of thought which began to emerge in 1891 with a document called Rerum Novarum which accepted with qualifications the ideas of a free market in capital and labour. They include not just "solidarity"—the idea that all members of society must look out for one another's welfare—but "subsidiarity" or the widely devolved distribution of power. Catholic Social Teaching (CST) seeks to chart a middle way between unrestrained capitalism and dirigiste socialism by stressing the vital role of civil society: all the institutions, from the family to voluntary associations and churches, that stand between the individual and the state.

Mr Longley also stresses the need to cultivate virtues such as trustworthy behaviour and dismisses the idea, which was fashionable a decade ago, that the market has its own mechanisms for driving out untrustworthy behaviour. He recalls the Catholic teaching that accepts the idea of private property ownership, but with the qualification that the proprietor must be a good and socially responsible steward.

The fault that the Church finds with the capitalist system is the fact that each and every human being living on the planet does not have access to a minimum of material goods. So they are not allowed to have a decent life and even in the most advanced countries there are thousands of people who do not eat their fill. It is the principle of the destination of human goods that is not fulfilled: there is plenty of production, it is the distribution that is defective.

And in the present system the instrument that makes possible the distribution of goods and services, the symbol that allows people to get products, is money. It is therefore the money system, the financial system that is at fault in capitalism.

Pope Pius XI wrote in *Quadragesimo Anno* in 1931:

> Money should be a servant, but the bankers in appropriating the control over its creation, have made it an instrument of domination. Since people cannot live without money, everyone: this includes governments, corporations and individuals; must

submit to the conditions imposed upon them by the
bankers to obtain money. Money means having the
right to live in today's society. This establishes a real
dictatorship over economic life and so the bankers
have become the masters of our lives. Pope Pius XI
was quite right when he said in *Quadragesimo Anno*
(n. 106):

Even if Marxism has collapsed, this does not mean the triumph of
capitalism. Even after the fall of Communism there are still millions
of poor people and situations of injustice in the world:

"The Marxist solution has failed, but the realities of marginalization
and exploitation remain in the world, especially the Third World, as
does the reality of human alienation, especially in the more advanced
countries. Against these phenomena the Church strongly raises her
voice. Vast multitudes are still living in conditions of great material
and moral poverty. The collapse of the Communist system in so many
countries certainly removes an obstacle to facing these problems in
an appropriate and realistic way, but it is not enough to bring about
their solution. Indeed, there is a risk that a radical capitalistic ideology
could spread which refuses even to consider these problems, in the
a priori belief that any attempt to solve them is doomed to failure
and which blindly entrusts their solution to the free development of
market forces."(*Centesimus Annus,* 42.) 3

Chapter 41

FOOD CONSUMPTION AND OVERCONSUMPTION

Processed food. Chemical additives. Artificial sweeteners. Artificial colourings. Preservatives. Butylated hydroxytoluene (BHT). Butylated hydroxyanisole (BHA). Sulfites. Pesticides. Hydrogenated fats. Organic foods. Alcohol. Wine. Spirits. Beer. Beverages. Fizzy drinks. Red meat. Sugar. Salt. Carbohydrates. Starch.

Food and drink consumption has a great impact on the state of the body as it creates dryness and moisture. Hot (heat-creating) foods produce heat in the body and cold foods have the opposite effect. Striking a balance between the two is the ultimate challenge as the temperament of the individual ought to be considered along with what is appropriate for their age, the season and the climate. The big problem of food consumption in the West is that globalization caused the demand for food to outweigh its natural supply and consequently, food production had to increase to meet the huge demand. Traditional food methods of production had to be replaced with modern methods of food processing as the demand for profits from the food trade increased. Western cultural food production and consumption is now the new slave trade, masterminded for money rather than for human health, human rights and human dignity. Food choice freedom is slavery but this is not the only Orwellian truth at play here as ignorance is strength for this slave trade to continue to be totally unaware of its far reaching effects.

Many people are unaware of the many additives included in processed foods. Many people are unaware of the effects on the functioning of the body's system. Many people are unaware of how it develops various skin, psycho-behavioral and pulmonary problems. Western cultural consumers are ignorant of the current research into additives in processed food, damage to genetic components and cancer. Google for evidence of this. Google for the links to asthma, hypersensitivity, ADHD and skin conditions. Google for evidence of the ways in which chemical additives can contribute to poor health. Slavery and sugar have a very interesting historical connection and its relationship continues with sweeteners like aspartame replacing the natural sweetness of sugarcane. Many people enjoy this new sweetener without focusing on the controversial aspects associated with its use. Google its link to the toxic compound methanol. Google the number of processed products that contain the sweetener in question. Google individual consumption of aspartame and its potential risks to health.

Colorism has always been controversial in every aspect of global culture and food is no exception. Colored foods attract. Colored foods cause consumers to react. Colored foods cause some children to hyper-react. Google for further details of the many artificial colorings, the additives that are linked to attention-deficit-hyperactivity disorder and those linked to various skin conditions. It is true that western cultural thinkers have always consumed the idea of preservatives so its use and concerns for its use in the production of processed foods will be no surprise. As within the culture, common preservatives are controversial and come with a warning from scientists about damages to cells and potential risks to asthma sufferers and the like. Google for further details. In addition to preservatives comes the associated danger of chemical pesticides and fertilizers that pose additional health risks. Google the effects of organophosphates, organochlorines, thiocarbamates. and organoarsenic compounds. Google the effects of neurotoxins on the brain. Google the effects of hydrogenated fats on the functioning of the body.

Consumption of certain types of food like pork has fat building material because pork has very little muscle building material and contains excess of fat which when deposited in the vessels can cause complications to the proper functioning of the bodily system and to obesity. Obesity is of epidemic proportions in America, Europe and other parts of the globalised world. More weight gain means more health risks with doctors shouting `lose the weight or die'. Doctors, nurses, health workers have been working arduously to develop long term solutions for issues of obesity with an increased number of leaflets, websites, health advisers but still the obesity crisis spirals out of control. Part of the problem is the culture of consumerism. There is the restaurant industry, the fast food franchises, dining in, dining out, Bake off, Come dine with me and all of the above scream at consumers the one western message `you are free to eat as much as you like whenever you like and with whomever you like'. All consumers are advised to do is - just eat.

Eating out has become a mark of success, a luxury of the upwardly mobile and a lifestyle of the privileged so much so that cooking and eating at home almost feels ancient. Western thinkers have even made this cultural practice affordable to the masses with McDonalds, KFC and Burger King providing popular options. However, what restaurant consumerism has created is a series of interrelated health and societal problems which are shouldered by medical doctors, junior doctors and spin doctors. The truth is that popular menu meals contain more saturated fat and more calories than home cooked meals. The truth is that there are risk factors and related health problems from the practice of continually eating out. The truth is that the choice to eat in or out needs to be managed and controlled by individuals being the CEOs of their own health and food consumption.

Education is a great way to start taking control but the western cultural thinker knows that eating out is a welcome way to socialise and have fun with friends and family selecting types of restaurants and deciding on delicious dishes. The problem of this practice slowly but surely becomes one of overindulgence and increased risk of poor health. Everything in moderation is the sermon on the mount but no one seems to be listening and more worryingly no one seems to care. Those who try to spread the word tend to order whole-wheat bread for sandwiches, start with a packed salad of vegetables and choose fruit for dessert. Many avoid the option to eat as much as you like and are reminded that the purpose of eating is not to clean the plate.

The problems of the eating culture are self-explanatory and must be addressed at the very core. How can society eat less while socializing? How can food be made tastier and healthier? How can people gain control of their own food consumption without changing this popular lifestyle? Can society change its attitude to food without changing the system that creates it? Should there be a greater education about processed food? Rather than seeing organic foods as luxury items, should consumers be more informed about the broad issues concerning organic foods? Crucially, how does the western cultural thinker address the immorality endemic within the capitalist production of food and how can the health issues be addressed without compromising the economic issues?

Black cultural perspective

Steeped in cultural roots, food, love and language are universal in their importance to our happiness, health and wellbeing. It is well known that food serves more than one purpose in our culture and traditionally, we have always had a personal and social connection with soul food. To refuse food from friends and family is almost disrespectful and one cannot imagine going to a funeral and afterwards not having fried chicken, rice and peas, macaroni cheese and fried plantain. This is a very culturally sensitive issue as for years and years being `big' has been accepted as a virtually family heritage with our grandparents referring to their grandchildren as `fat and nice' and `they have a healthy appetite' and admonishing us to let the children eat until their `belly full' as eating on such family occasions is culturally appropriate and indeed culturally specific. Affectionately described as soul food, we all love the jerk chicken, the curried goat, the cook-up, the fried dumplings, the roti, the souse. The devilishly delicious taste of these dishes is delightful to the soul but destructive to our bodies. Sadly, the foods that make us feel alive are affecting our minds, our souls and our bodies. Put simply, our food is killing us slowly. The obesity crisis in Black America, the Caribbean and other parts of the African Diaspora is of epidemic proportions and we are dying under the weight of it.

Addressing the issue of healthy eating must begin with looking at the ingredients and preparation of our traditional food more closely as many of our dishes are cooked and seasoned with pork products and our fried dishes are steeped in too much sugar, too much salt and too much oil. Regular consumption of these ingredients without significant exercise or activity to work the calories off often contributes to disproportionately high occurrences of obesity, hypertension, cardiac/circulatory problems and/or diabetes. Yes, eating our cultural food, it is argued, helps us to cope with the stress of our lives; many of us simply comfort cook and comfort consume. The eating of cultural dishes almost has a spiritual element that takes us away from this world to a delicious high but the truth remains that we all have to come back to earth and face the consequences of our overconsumption.

To begin to address this huge problem, we may need to enlist the philosophy of our rastafari brothers and sisters who advocate that we make a conscious decision to avoid chemicals and make eating natural food a way of life. This philosophy will undoubtedly promote good health and a more disciplined way of life which of course demands discipline to follow a specific diet that avoids foods with chemical additives. Instead, foods that are organically farmed or low in chemical elements should be the foods we embrace. However, as we all know, the problems with food in our culture have greater complexities which are linked to the larger legacy. If we trace its historical underpinnings, we will discover the undisputed, undiluted and uncomfortable truth that soul food is slave food. Slaves were fed as cheaply as possible with the discarded and leftover portions of foods from the plantation owners. As a consequence, all the traditional dishes for our people within the African diaspora had to be made from discarded cuts of meat such as pigs' feet, pigs' tail, oxtail, tripe and other such portions while slave owners got the meatiest cuts of ham, roasts, etc. Slaves had to strive to survive and creatively thought of ways to make tasty dishes from what was thrown at them by their masters or from house slaves. However, we cannot hold on to the legacy of the ingredients given and how they had to be prepared with lard, molasses, pigs' feet, pigs' tails, sugarcane, salted meat and oil. Preparation and the diets of slaves were steeped in fat and starch and thirst was filled by consuming sugar cane juice.

Yes, we were resilient over the years in surviving on this kind of food but is it time to lose the legacy of slave food? Yes, it is true that after slavery, many of us, being poor, could afford only off-cuts of meat, along with offal. Our men turned to farming, hunting and fishing to provide fresh vegetables, fish and wild game and our people had to make do with the food choices available to work with. It is also true that soul food style of cooking originated during American and Caribbean slavery and now nearly every black community has cultural cuisine referred to as soul food.

First Lady Michelle Obama told the NAACP to move past the slavery narrative and focus on the threat of obesity that is harming minority children. But can slavery really be divorced from obesity? We are over a century past slavery but slavery is not past us. It is not a matter of holding on to the past but rather the past is holding on to us through our eating habits, our customs and traditions that are anchored in the practices of slavery. Fast food or more precisely junk food is the modern slave food thrown to our black communities and sadly our children simply salivate for it like Pavlov's dogs. We have been conditioned to consume fast food because it is cheap and cheerful and we have been totally incapable of seeing it for what it has become: one of the biggest killers of our people. Fast food seduces our children, turns them into food junkies before the age of ten and causes them to develop into delinquents. They have no energy or inclination to exercise, no motivation to learn and no mental strength to resist the temptation to eat junk food. Have we forgotten the lessons of the past or has history taught us nothing? Let's remind ourselves of how we have been used to maximise profit. Let's not forget how wealth was accumulated on the sweat of our forefathers. Let's just remember that we have always been the objects of capitalism – wealth was built off our backs and now wealth is built off the bellies of blacks.

The legacy of fast food is rooted in the legacy of slavery in every way. Bad food was fed to the slaves just to keep them alive rather than build brain power. It was important that the mind of the slaves did not function so that they could simply react or obey their masters without having the mental energy to question what they were being told to do. Essentially, the minds of the slaves were deliberately undernourished, underfed and underdeveloped through destructive diets. Food thrown at the slaves included discarded parts of the pig, foods high in cholesterol, sugar and salt. Fast forward decades later and the fast food masters are at it again, throwing the same kinds of food drenched in oil, loaded with sugar and tasteless without additions of salt to the survivors of slavery. We have become addicted to salt, sugar and oil as those who are hooked on cannabis, heroin and other substances but we seem totally unaware of the parallel. Both are killing the community!

Fast forward to the present and obesity is shown to be one of the lingering effects of slavery as we simply eat the same foods as the slaves, in the same large portions as the slaves and in the same frequency as the slaves. We have to let go of this link to the past. Slavery was made legal to service capitalism and made illegal when services were no longer needed. When slavery was no longer profitable, laws were passed for its abolition and compensation was made to the slave owners. That same compensation has been invested and reinvested to make more and more profit. Fast food franchises can be seen as one of the ways to continue throwing bad food to the masses. We have to refrain from entering the 'eat as much as you like' food chains and those that offer supersize meals and we have to listen to our rastafari brothers and sisters on how to eat, if nothing else. Eating huge meals and then insisting on a diet coke is not going to help nor is waiting for lunch specials. We must not be slaves to meal deals or to the delusion that fast food is cheaper than healthy options. Children must be taught that an apple is not the forbidden fruit but that fast food is the beguiling serpent.

Moving past the slave narrative is easier to do in theory than in practice as we are not holding on to the past but rather the past is holding on to us. It is like a huge anchor that prevents us from being eagles soaring to majestic heights with our children by our side. Obesity is pressing us down, weighing down our wings and preventing us from flying. We must find the strength of will and discipline to lose the weight before it kills us individually, collectively and spiritually. We must lose this legacy. The question still lingers here, why are we still cooking with large proportions of these ingredients? Even though soul food has gone upscale, doesn't it still hold on to many of the traditions that can be traced back to the legacy of slavery? How do we progress from this detrimental legacy of slave food? Should we adopt a radical approach to changing our cultural and traditional lifestyles in order to change our eating habits? Should we have cookery classes to make soul food healthier?

Should we encourage our cooks to serve smaller portions or use less fat, salt and sugar even though it takes away some of the taste and authenticity of the dish? Should we use shock tactics in the way that advertisers do for smoking – 'Soul food is Slave food' or ' Soul food kills' or 'Soul food may be good for the soul but bad for the body'? How do we address the problem of food and its consumption within our culture? Should we battle the bulge by building brain power to resist the urge to eat unhealthy foods? Should we educate people to opt for the healthier choice rather than the cheaper choice? Should we encourage more weight management programmes? Should we have family fitness support clubs so that all members of the family are supporting each other to change lifestyles together? Should we have a comprehensive, holistic educational program to promote healthy living for the whole being- mind, body and spirit? How can we make the link between nutrition and academic performance more salient? How can we create a program which provides a fast food detox therapy offering alternatives to fast food? Should we teach courses to develop the mental fortitude needed to resist fast food? Should we start boycotts of fast food chains in black communities?

Chapter 42

MENTAL HEALTH

Stress. Depression. Inner conflict. Unforgiveness. Rumination.
Guilt. Fear. Worry. Unfairness. Inequality. Relationship breakdown.
Bereavement. Harassment. Debt problems. Anxiety. Self Harm.
Attention deficit disorder. Sleep paralysis – sleep deprivation – sleep
apnoea – sleepwalking – sleep talking – nightmares – excessive
sleepiness – narcolepsy – cataplexy –insomnia – Dementia-
Depression-Alzheimer's - Post -Traumatic Stress. Schizophrenia.
Suicide

Happiness or utopian bliss can only be achieved, according to
positive psychology, with a healthy mind, healthy body and healthy
soul (spirit). This holistic approach to maintaining mental health
can be contrasted to mental ill health which refers to an impaired
functioning of the mind or its inability to cope with life's stressors
leading to a change in thinking, a change in mood or ultimately
a change in behaviour that may lead to diagnosable disorders.
Leading psychologists, philosophers and other academics insist on
the importance of understanding how to achieve peace of mind. Early
childhood experiences are crucial in developing healthy young minds
that need to be nourished from the cradle to the grave. Religious and
community leaders also insist on early socialisation as psychological,
emotional and spiritual well-being must be nurtured in boys and
girls as mental health affects gender in different measures. Google
for official figures on these differences for validity; there is also a

need to google the different kinds of mental illnesses and how they affect different ages, different genders and different races. It may also be interesting to google results across class stratifications and across cultures.

Preventing mental illness was embedded in the western cultural formula for happiness: achieve success in all areas of your life and that would lead to psychological well-being. Be happy with your family life, your work life and your social life and you will enjoy your life on earth. Herein lies the problem for the western cultural thinker: mental health or rather happiness cannot be achieved with this ` one size fits all' formula which has been recommended for the three core systems – the individual, the community and the world. Applying this capitalist ideology or this capitalist formulation for success cannot guarantee peace of mind and more importantly it cannot provide equal access for everyone. In today's society, the problem is compounded because this system can no longer provide the perceived route to happiness for the global majority. For many the burden of life's anguish, pain and disappointment of being denied equal opportunity for success has become a burden of mental ill health that is costing the western world billions to treat. Even more worrying is the fact that this has caused a shock not only to the familial system, not only to the societal system not only to the global system but crucially a shock to the central nervous system itself: individuals can no longer cope with the inner conflict created by a system that perpetuates it.

Many people have trouble sleeping or difficulty falling asleep and experts insist that such sleep disorders are signs as well as symptoms of medical and psychiatric disorders. Google for studies done on insomnia and functional impairment while awake and google for the research done on primary and secondary insomnia. Google for facts and figures on the effects of sleeping pills causing dependency and substance abuse. Study the differences between medical, psychiatric and environmental causes of sleep disorders and restlessness. Google what psychologists, psychiatrists and psychotherapists all claim to be the causes of sleeplessness whether it be evidence of what lies repressed in the unconscious mind, the pain or traumatic experiences of childhood or unexplained emotion that may be carried in the DNA: all professionals will point to some form of turbulence in the mind.

Other thinkers argue that voices within the head are voices of conscience that force the western cultural thinker to search within their restricted space for peace of mind. In novels, in films and in plays, narratives are presented about disturbances of mind without knowing that peace can only come from a place that offers peace or is defined as peace. Shakespeare's Macbeth is undoubtedly a classic portrayal of inner conflict: in this play sleep symbolises innocence, purity and peace of mind. When Macbeth murders King Duncan, he thinks he hears a voice say 'Macbeth does murder sleep' and indeed Macbeth's inability to sleep after his regicide will always be a painful reminder of the huge price one has to pay to achieve power. Later on in the play Lady Macbeth begins to sleepwalk and Macbeth is haunted by ghosts, witches and nightmarish episodes as his deeds damaged his mental health and left him paralysed by fear and hallucinations. Of all of Shakespeare's plays, this one has countless references to sleep: as a balm of hurt minds, as a nourisher and as the death of each day's life. The play still reminds the world that terrible dreams will haunt those who play most foully for success, whether it be success of women whose partners resemble their fathers as they sleep, success of friends who deny that they dream not of their deeds or success of those who regard the sleeping and the dead but as pictures. Like Macbeth, many people in power will suffer from guilt, fear and the curse of sleeplessness.

Mental health or rather psychological well-being is as unique to each individual as the finger print. Even when faced with similar problems, different people react in different ways. The key questions to be posed must begin with - do western cultural thinkers need a fundamental change of ideology to address the core of the problem of mental illness? Is it true that only a moral transformation of society can help to eradicate mental illness? Does the West need to redefine, re-examine and re-evaluate happiness/ success so that everyone can realistically achieve it? Can individuals really find their personal route to happiness without the guidance of a moral authority or an institution committed to moral integrity however morality is defined? With the established institutions that provided stability for our mental health on decline, how can the West restore faith in the Faith, faith in the family and faith in community? With anxiety on the rise to almost epidemic proportions, how can society be changed to eradicate it? With Psychologists and Psychiatrists prescribing drugs without fully understanding individual differences and attitudes to life experiences, how can practitioners help our mental health rather than hinder it?

Black Cultural Perspective

The problem of mental health and the black community is a complex one mainly because it is painful to talk about the root of the problem for many living in Africa and the Diaspora: slavery and colonialization. Feelings of shame, feelings of anger and feelings of painful unease are evoked only to be cloaked in different defensive mechanisms and behaviours. The hidden truth about mental illness is as concealed as the hidden truth about our past history and about slavery's impact. What is also shrouded in secrecy is the correlation between clinical depression and race. Think about it. Collectively, we face the most difficult situations of all people but yet some of us find ways to cope under tremendous pressure; we are reluctant to seek professional help, take the drugs prescribed and confide in other friends and family members about such issues. If other people were in our oppressed position, they will all be on suicide watch but our people have enormous mental strength, psychological power and physical capacity to cope with oppressive forces coming from all directions yet still we rise as Maya Angelou affirms. However, for those who have not learnt how to harness this power, tend to experience negative mental outcomes, increased anxiety and sometimes psychiatric problems. What must be explored and thoroughly researched is the impact of oppression and exploitation on mental health. Frantz Fanon undoubtedly was the first black intellectual to explore this issue and now our modern day sister warrior has expanded on his ideas.

Joy DeGruy has examined this issue after twelve years of quantitative and qualitative research which she compiled in her brilliant book Post Traumatic Slave Syndrome. She insists that centuries of slavery followed by systemic and structural racism and oppression and unwarranted mass incarceration have resulted in multigenerational maladaptive behaviours which originated as survival strategies. The syndrome continues because children whose parents suffer from PTSS are often indoctrinated into the same behaviours, long after the behaviours have lost their contextual effectiveness. DeGruy states that PTSS is not a disorder that can simply be treated and remedied clinically but rather also requires profound social change in individuals, as well as in institutions that continue to reify inequality and injustice toward the descendants of enslaved Africans. Anger is good for our mental health if channelled appropriately. However, if anger is internalised and forced deep into the unconscious and contaminated by unresolved pain, suffering and anguish it becomes a mental problem. Our daily anger at the current systems of oppression in every institution, in every aspect of society coupled with our personal pain of not being able to change it, causes day to day transmissions of unexplained behaviour towards our family, friends and acquaintances. How do we begin to heal our minds, heal our broken community and heal our world? Do we work on a comprehensive educational system to teach our children how to have healthy minds, bodies and souls? Do we campaign for a change in politics that leads to the moral transformation of society? Do we work with other like-minded groups to effect the changes necessary for a new world order? Do we teach children mental health resilience techniques through social and emotional education initiatives? How can we free our minds to think differently about our past and its impact on our present and our future?

Chapter 43

ALCOHOL

Cirrhosis of Liver - Cancer of the liver (Hepatoma) - Cancer of Oesophagus. Cancer of the head and neck - Cancer of the Bowel – Oesophagitis - Gastritis Pancreatitis – Hepatitis – Cardiomyopathy – Hypertension – Coronary Atherosclerosis – Angina- Heart attacks – Strokes–Apoplexy–Peripheral neuropathy–cortical atrophy-cerebellar atrophy – Wernicke – beriberi- pellagra – Myxodema – hyperthyroidism – macrocytic anaemia- Jaundice

Alcohol seems to be the mother of all diseases and the love of western cultural life with young people waiting patiently for their eighteenth birthday for their rite of passage. This important ritual marks a milestone for young people to officially become social drinkers, then binge drinkers and ultimately alcoholics. Intoxication then leads to all sorts of social problems that are gender related, domestically related and health related. The huge burden on the NHS of this freedom for all has been articulated eloquently by junior doctors whose message to the government is that this weekend freedom can no longer be free. Freedom has to be replaced by responsibility or more appropriately by prohibition. Alcohol costs countless lives and causes terrible misery to millions of families but yet young people are encouraged to consume more and more of it. The doctors need not remind us of the detrimental effects of consumption and overconsumption of this poison to the system; alcohol is toxic and every drop of poison is doing just that to the body.

Consuming alcohol inhibits the inhibitory centre in the brain which serves to prevent a person from doing things that are considered wrong. That is why people found to be indulging in behaviour that is completely uncharacteristic of them: using abusive language, poor communication, general misbehaviour show that they have lost complete control of their minds. This behaviour becomes more concerning if you google the cases of adultery, rape, incest and AIDS found more among alcoholics. If you also google the number of crimes committed when the offender is in a state of intoxication, you will see the real extent of this problem. If you also google the number of cases of offenders later regretting their acts, you will find that the guilt of both the perpetrator and the victim are irreparably and irreversibly damaged.

The diseases associated with alcoholism need some mention here as these are the most scientific reasons for the prohibition of consumption of this poison. The maximum number of deaths in the world related to any one particular cause is undoubtedly due to the consumption of alcohol. Serious complications, different types of cancers, liver problems, amnesia, endocrine disorders and all kinds of deficiencies have all been associated with alcohol. The question is not why is this poison still legal but rather why are our politicians more concerned about making money than securing our national health? Is the solution to the problem treating alcoholism as a disease rather than an illness or banning the substance altogether? Is the solution to continue to sell the poison in bottles, advertise the poison in the media and license more outlets to circulate it? How can the government prevent violent deaths, lessen its destruction of the family and reduce crime whilst producing revenue for the government? How can the West find the courage to tell the truth, the whole truth and nothing but the truth about alcohol and its effects?

Glynis Glasgow-Kelly

Black cultural perspective

Many black people in Africa and the Diaspora grew up with the belief that alcohol was sinful. The Bible clearly prohibits the consumption of alcohol in Proverbs Chapter 20 and Verse 1: Wine is a mocker, strong drink is raging; and whosoever is deceived thereby is not wise. The bible further states in Ephesians Chapter 5 Verse 18: And be not drunk with wine. However, with a whole generation being tempted by the secularism of the West, how do we reach a generation of young people who do not even know that the bible still exists. The prohibition of alcohol is clearly forbidden in Islam as it is seen as the scourge of human society costing countless human lives, and causing terrible misery to millions throughout the world. Followers of the Islamic faith insist that alcohol is the root cause of many problems facing society with soaring crime rates and increased instances of mental illness to prove the destructive power of alcohol. It was reported by Anas (may Allah be pleased with him), that Prophet Muhammad (pbuh) said, "God's curse falls on ten groups of people who deal with alcohol. The one who distils it, the one for whom it has been distilled, the one who drinks it, the one who transports it, the one to whom it has been brought, the one who serves it, the one who sells it, the one who utilises money from it, the one who buys it and the one who buys it for someone else". Put simply, alcohol is prohibited by all major religions.

The problem is that many of our people are no longer religious and simply consume western practices and rites of passage. Young and older black professionals are now social drinkers, binge drinkers and alcoholics; they no longer believe that alcohol is Satan's handiwork. However, they must all be aware of the fact that the resistance to disease and the immunological defence system are compromised by alcohol intake. Chest infections are also notorious in alcoholics: pneumonia, lung abcess, emphysema and pulmonary tuberculosis are all common in alcoholics. Google the ill effects of alcohol consumption on women who are more vulnerable to alcohol-related cirrhosis than men. Google the severe detrimental effect on the foetus during pregnancy that alcohol has. Google the skin diseases related to alcohol indulgence and google eczema, Alopecia, nail dystrophy, paronychia (infection around the nails) angular stomatitis (inflammation of the angle of the mouth) as common diseases among alcoholics.

Simply consuming western practices and rituals is not the way forward for our community. We must find a way to tackle the issues that are driving us to drink. Should we educate our young people more about the dangers associated with the alcoholism, like the spread of STDs like AIDS? Should we have a moral transformation of our community? Should we merge all interest groups to form an umbrella organisation to address the problems that are leading many of our young people to drink instead of think? Should we promote prohibition as stringently as Islam? Should we incorporate recommendations within a comprehensive rites of passage education system that encourages everyone to eat and drink for the healthy upkeep of the body?

Chapter 44

HEART DISEASE AND DIET

Coronary heart disease – Diabetes - Heart attack - Hypertension/ High blood pressure - Angina – Arrhythmias – Heart failure.

Heart disease is one the leading causes of death worldwide. Prevention of disease and illness is better than any cure but knowledge of the causes of diseases must precede both prevention and cure. We all know that the communication system within the body is the blood and the blood's job is to carry oxygen and nutrients around the body for its proper functioning. Blood takes food to the vital organs – the brain, the heart and the lungs and if the system fails to work properly, the result is illness, disease or death. Too much sugar (glucose) in the blood is described as diabetes. Type 1 diabetes results from a bodily malfunction that arises from failure to produce the hormone insulin and type 2 diabetes results from either the body doesn't make enough insulin or it cannot use the insulin properly. Medical experts insist that people with diabetes often suffer from feelings of fatigue, tend to lose weight, are often thirsty, need to urinate more often at nights, have problems with vision, have itchiness around their private parts or get thrush often and discover that wounds and cuts heal slowly.

The heart and brain both need oxygen from the blood to function properly and to keep the main organ or the heart healthy, one has to do three things: control blood sugar levels, keep blood cholesterol levels low and control blood pressure; these are necessary to protect arteries and prevent clogging up with fatty material. If blockage happens to the heart, it causes a heart attack and if the brain is clogged, one will have a stroke or a brain attack. The problem for the western cultural thinker is that there is not enough focus on preventing these major diseases as the culture insists on promoting profits over people. The most profitable foods in western culture are the ones that damage the system the most. The consumption of pork for example causes several diseases. Did you know that a person can have various helminthes like roundworm, pinworm and hookworm and one of the most dangerous is Taenia Solium, which is in lay man's terminology called tapeworm; this harbours in the intestine and is very long. Its ova (eggs) enter the blood stream and can reach almost all the organs of the body. Did you know that if it enters the brain it can cause memory loss and if it enters the heart it can cause heart attack, if it enters the eye it can cause blindness, if it enters the liver it can cause liver damage. It can damage almost all the organs of the body. A common misconception about pork is that if it is cooked well, these ova die. Google the studies which show that the ova present in pork do not die under normal cooking temperature. Another point about pork is that it has fat building material and contains excess fat which when deposited in the blood vessels can cause hypertension and heart attack.

How can the West prevent such blood related diseases without cutting the profits from the foods which cause the diseases? How can the western cultural thinker detoxify the cultural practices that lead to ill health? How can the West move away from the value system of money over morality or profits before people? How can the west think of another way of making money other than capitalising on ignorance of the foods they love to consume?

Glynis Glasgow-Kelly

Black cultural perspective

Hypertension or High blood pressure. Diabetes 2. Sickle Cell.

The heart pumps blood around our bodies and how hard the blood is being pushed through the arteries is referred to as blood pressure. High blood pressure or hypertension is when the pressure on the walls of the arteries is higher than it should be. Having high blood pressure also means that one is more likely to have a heart attack or stroke. We know that we are more likely to get high blood pressure if we are overweight, have too much salt in our diet, fail to do enough physical activity, drink too much alcohol or a family member has high blood pressure. Our problems with these blood diseases are directly related to the lingering effects of slavery on our thinking, our eating and our lifestyle. We are well aware that the traditionally prepared foods contain far too much starch, too much fat, too much salt, cholesterol and calories and fast food favourites are appealing in the same way. The legacy of slavery lingers on here and studies abound in this area.

Google for studies which show a consistently higher prevalence of hypertension in blacks than any other racial group. Google reasons why there is a higher prevalence of hypertension in blacks living in the United States instead of Africa. Google why researchers insist that environmental and behavioral characteristics are the more likely reasons for the higher prevalence in blacks living in the United States. Google the "slavery hypertension hypothesis" which states that the higher prevalence of hypertension among blacks could have resulted from an enhanced ability to conserve salt by slaves, protecting them from fatal salt-depletive diseases during the stormy Atlantic passage, such as diarrhea and vomiting. Google why researchers think that this condition would induce hypertension when they and their descendants consumed the much higher sodium content in American compared with African foods.

In the Caribbean (former European colonies), Diabetes two is still affecting over 90 percent of our brothers and sisters there. This has been blamed on the long lasting legacy of slavery and it is very difficult to airbrush this fact. Google what the Caribbean Health Research Council has found about this health problem. In addition, google the Pan American Health Organisation studies into the number of people in the Caribbean plagued by this type of diabetes. Yes, it has been over 180 years since the abolition of slavery but if we are still chained to the eating habits of the slaves and still shackled by the colonist conditioning about gratification, then we cannot address these challenges until we free our minds. If we do not treat this as a public health crisis and tackle it in the education system, then the problem will worsen rather than improve. It is well known that environmental facts and genetics must contribute to its occurrence. After so many years of pioneering research into coronary heart disease, how do we use this knowledge to improve our cultural attitudes? How do we fight this huge battle for our heart? Do we begin with a battle for the brain and educate our people to think differently? How do we take control of our collective culture life in the present so that the next generation can look forward to a healthy life in the future?

Chapter 45

EXERCISE

Exercise for health. Exercise for heart. Exercise for headache. Exercise for fitness. Exercise for stress relief. Exercise for mood change. Exercise for reduced risk of diseases.

Everyone is encouraged to live a healthy life by engaging in regular exercise. It is a prescription for good physical, mental and spiritual strength, depression, stress and classed as the most underutilised antidepressant. The benefits of an active life are stressed especially at the start of a new year when we make our annual resolutions. In good faith, everyone resolves to make even basic exercise a priority on the long journey to physical fitness. Some sign up for weightwatchers, others begin or renew gym membership while others commit to simply walking in the park. The benefits of physical activity or bodily movement is good for the body as it causes warmth to the body by increasing the rate of respiration and helps us to burn off those unwanted calories, control the weight, reduce risks of cardiovascular disease, type 2 diabetes and metabolic syndrome, reduce the risk of some cancers, strengthen the bones and muscles and improve mental health and mood.

Separating the problem of lack of exercise from the cause of the problem is virtually impossible. Everyone knows that exercise is great not only for the body but also for the mind but everyone also knows that you need to have time, motivation and commitment to engaging in physical activity. If the day is packed with home chores then work tasks then home chores after work, then there is literally no time to exercise and this lack of time to exercise has detrimental effects on all levels. With increased workload comes increased stress coupled with less time and less ability to prioritise exercise. The relentless pace of life these days compounds the problem of not having time to exercise and many are left to wrongly eat more and more unhealthy food to numb the pain of life stressors. The problem of lack of exercise and lack of time and therefore ability to participate in such activity cannot be divorced.

Other dimensions of the problem include failure to see the correlation between good exercise and mood boosting as many fail to see the need to exercise socially and prioritise it in the same way that they prioritise eating out. It is well known that exercise does give a better emotional lift than food as all experts claim that physical activity stimulates various brain chemicals that leaves one feeling happier and more relaxed. Everyone knows that exercise boosts energy, boosts muscle strength and endurance and boosts the cardiovascular system. Everyone knows that exercise provides the feel good factor. However, no one seems to know how to address the issue of dedicating and prioritising time to such physical activity. The issue here for the western cultural thinker to address is how can exercise ever be prioritised over professional priorities? How can people be given enough time to live a healthy life when they are expected to work longer for less money? How can commonly held attitudes to perceived mood boosting activity like eating be changed to allow exercise boosting activities to replace them? How can people convince their friends to go for a swim or to the gym instead of dining out at a restaurant? How can young people be fully educated to learn how to make exercise a daily priority rather than a daily chore?

Black cultural perspective

As a collective, our community has an issue with weight gain and this cannot be separated from the issue of lack of exercise. We all know that exercise can prevent excess weight gain and maintain weight loss; we all know that burning calories depends on the intensity of the workout as the more calories that we burn the more weight we lose. It is not news to us that exercise combats health conditions and diseases and being active boosts high –density loporotein (HDL) or good cholesterol. We do not need reminding that exercise helps to decrease the risk of cardiovascular diseases and helps us to prevent or manage a range of diseases or illnesses. We know that exercise and physical activity deliver oxygen and nutrients to our tissues. We also know that it boosts mood which leads to improvement in sexual activity.

The problem of lack of exercise cannot be seen in isolation as for us it is multidimensional. For us, exercise must begin with freeing our minds or changing the way we think and this will enable us to eat properly, to prioritise our health and to commit to sustaining the long walk to freedom. Seasoned gym veterans amongst us will insist that developing your strength involves discipline and you must be prepared not to surrender. They will insist that we push harder and harder to achieve the desired effects. Our gym trainers will tell us that we must feel the ache in our legs and listen to the voice in our head that urges us to keep going and never give up. They will encourage us to go through the hardships and the moments when we sometimes feel defeated but encourage us to be determined to achieve our goal. Exercise involves big challenges that demand inner strength to develop through the struggles and still be determined to win the prize which is undoubtedly seeing the beauty and strength that our black bodies are capable of in all its ancestral glory.

We struggle with exercise because of our mental slavery which affects our attitude to eating and subsequently our attitude to exercising. If we are not prepared to stop eating unhealthy food, then there is no point exercising because that would be counter- productive. As ladies, if we are worried about our hair styles rather than the benefits of the workout, then our thinking needs to change prior to changing our lifestyle. Healthy eating and exercising are brought together in love by a healthy mind with arranges the marriage. If the couple is not prepared to understand the terms under which they are brought together then it becomes a marriage of convenience rather than a marriage arranged through love. Together eating and exercise will be fruitful and everyone would admire the fruits of the labour. This labour must not be confused with the labour that our people endure from the dawn till setting sun because that labour prevents us from prioritising and preserving our people's pride. That labour is designed to undermine our spiritual, psychological and physical power and we must resist the temptation to eat too much of that forbidden fruit.

That labour is designed politically to prevent us from finding time to empower ourselves in this way and we must see exercise as a prescription for mental, spiritual and physical freedom. Lately, our people seem to be working more and earning less, slaving on modern day plantations and left with little time to spend with family, friends and ourselves. If we can trace the origins of this back to the legacy, we will see that this practice has always been the intention and we must find ways to workout rather than be victims of other people's workouts. The thinking that we can still be working out all day and not reaping the right rewards is testament to the fact that the owners of these gyms are taking most of the benefits while we gain hardly anything to show for our six and sometimes seven day workouts. What little benefits we are given has to be given back to the government whose workouts are to balance their success on our backs.

How do we make resolutions to collectively commit to our long walk to freedom? How do we boost each other's energy and stamina for this huge undertaking? How do we build spiritual, mental and physical strength to combat depression, stress and all of life's struggles? How do we eat less and exercise more? How do we learn to work out our minds in the same way that gym advocates work out their bodies? As a collective, how do we build a gym workout business that develops and stimulates our children's mind, soul and body from the womb to the tomb? How do we ensure that we have the physical and mental fortitude to endure the pain and struggles but yet sustain our collective strength?

Chapter 46

POLLUTION OF THE AIR/TOXIC AIR

Particulates. Sulfur dioxide – Nitrogen dioxide – Ozone - Rubbish–Car pollution. Industrial pollution. Smoke pollution. Gas pollution. Human pollution. Pet pollution. Germs. Waste. Carbon dioxide –emissions- global warming

Air, as long as it remains pure, is the human lifeline and a great protection for the body but in the world's modern cities, air pollution is rising at an alarming rate, wreaking havoc on human health. Oxygen within the air is used by the body to transform other nutrition into useful energy and depending on the temperature and moistness of the air can have different effects. Change in air quality can often be the cause of disease but attention must also be paid to the quality of one's own breathing as headaches, tiredness and irritability can often be a result of insufficient oxygen. Not only that but the air that one breathes out removes waste products such as carbon dioxide, a gas that is essential to plants. Seasonal changes can also have an adverse effect on the body. Exposure to extreme conditions can be severely dangerous and so special care should be taken that an optimum body temperature is maintained.

Emissions of greenhouse gases contribute to climate change and ozone depleting substances cause damage to the ozone layer. This type of pollution also increases the acidity of the rain which causes damage to buildings, land, fresh water and sea water, wildlife and plants. Not only that but there are many associated risks to human health from air pollution – those who are exposed to poor air quality can face an increased risk of developing or exacerbating a range of illnesses including lung and breathing problems, skin conditions, cancer and organ damage. Google the number of early deaths related to air pollution or rather Chronic Lower Respiratory Disease (CLRD). Google the effect of tobacco, chemical fumes and other emissions on or health.

Businesses are also at risk of creating air pollution at the workplace, genetic factors and respiratory infections also play a role. Google the list of contributors: manufacturers, farmers, construction, building and demolition trades, vehicle repairers, welders, mines and quarries, printers, haulers and other transport businesses, waste management businesses, dry cleaners, laboratories. You may also wish to google the additional pollution from business premises such as emissions from burning fuels in furnaces and boilers, burning material in the open, dust and fumes from poor waste storage and ventilation systems, ozone (an air pollutant which can be harmful to human health) from office equipment such as copiers and laser printers – exhaust fumes and dust from distribution and delivery vehicles.

How can the West improve air quality without reducing the quantity of finance for each heir? Should the Western cultural thinker consider giving up tobacco since it is the main pollutant? Should the Western cultural thinker consider sanctions on the highest global polluters? Should such countries, businesses and individuals be forced to pay a green tax or rather a green charge? How can the West reduce exposure to air pollutants in the home, in the workplace and in the world?

Black Perspective

Africa and the Caribbean islands are known for fresh air and unspoilt natural environmental beauty. We can enjoy drinking coconut water under the trees and living the simple life but now, thanks to slavery, colonisation and social media, we are staring enviously at the Western world and want what they have. Sadly, we are now enjoying what we wished for as the price for living in these countries is increasing at the same rate as global warming. In fact, our people are experiencing the sociological equivalent of global warming itself and the long term effects are going to be astronomical. With our people living in poor housing conditions, with our people living in the polluted areas of the cities in the African diaspora and with our people having access to poor health education our problems will increase before the opposite occurs. We are victims of all sorts of Chronic Lower Respiratory Disease (CLRD) which is a collection of lung diseases that cause airflow blockage and breathing-related issues, including primarily chronic obstructive pulmonary disease (COPD) but also bronchitis, emphysema and asthma. Tobacco still poses the biggest threat in the development and progression of COPD, although indoor air pollutants like wood-burning stoves, cleaning products and fresheners can contribute. Google for further evidence here.

Home-produced toxic air contain tiny particles that we take into our bodies causes immediate problems for some individuals such as those with asthma and contribute to longer-term problems for most of us in the form of heart disease and stroke. Signs and symptoms of COPD may include difficulty breathing (breathlessness) especially when active – a persistent cough with phlegm – frequent chest infections but the causes also include genetic factors and respiratory infections. Doctors insist on using preventative methods like quitting smoking, avoiding second hand smoke, avoiding air pollution, avoiding chemical fumes and of course, avoiding dust. This advice is easy to give but hard for us to prevent considering our daily access to air pollution. We are being killed slowly and we must find a way to provide a healthier environment for our children. Keeping children indoors can offer some protection against outdoor air pollution but it can also expose us to other air pollution sources. Google for further information on this and also google how to make homes more energy efficient.

Pollution is a global killer and countries in the developing world are not an exception. Developing countries will suffer the most from the weather-related disasters and increased water stress caused by global warming and we have to be prepared for the consequences when this happens. Garbage pollution in many parts of the world is also increasing as a factor or real concern so too is the gradually increasing manufacturing industry in these parts. What we must realise is the fact that pollution is not only a major factor in disease but women and children are especially at risk. Our children are more vulnerable and more susceptible to pollution as a high percent of the global disease falls on them. Google for statistics from the world health organisation and others on the estimated figures for global pollution. Google some of the possible ways we can all work to reduce pollution. Google the facts about how pollution is caused by other means in the Caribbean and other less industrialised countries in the diaspora.

How do we begin to address this plethora of problems created in the areas in which we live? Does the solution involve an intellectual revolution and an alternative route to economic prosperity? How can we preserve resources and limit carbon emissions without a technological revolution? Should we pray for God to save the planet or is this the sign of his second coming? How can the world survive with a carbon capacity that simply cannot allow us to continue on this path?

Chapter 47

DRUG USE AND ABUSE

Heroine – Cannabis-Marijuana – Hashish-Opium- Cocaine-Amphetamine-Methamphetamine-Methylenedioxymethamphetamine- ketamine illegal drugs – Club drugs – Prescribed drugs –Dissociative drugs – ketamine hallucinogens – LSD - Other Compounds - anabolic steroids

There is a burden of drug problems and a vast range of challenges associated with the abuse of substances and these affect different demographics in Western societies in different ways. At the heart of the problem is the need or the perception of the need to find another reality, another mood or rather another spirituality because life is a complex web of psychological, emotional, spiritual and physical interactions. Many use mood-altering drugs, hallucinatory drugs, prescribed drugs and spiritual drugs like cannabis to experience a different reality. Examining the problem of abusing these substances cannot be seen in isolation of the causes and challenges that users face psychologically, emotionally, physically or spiritually. It is well known that mental health problems all stem from some kind of inner conflict, negative feelings or unhappiness; emotional problems all stem from conflict within being triggered by stimulus outside the self; physical problems relating to gender, ethnicity and age and spiritual problems related to belief or lack of belief. Diversity and drug use is also another issue worth exploring so you may google for facts and figures to confirm whether or not the overall drug use is lower among minority ethnic groups than among the White population. Google for evidence to support or refute the claim that drug use prevalence is highest among those from mixed ethnic background. Google to see if the lowest overall levels of drug use are reported by people from Asian backgrounds (Indian, Pakistani or Bangladeshi).

Another part of the problem for the Western cultural thinker is that substance abuse must be described as a progressive disease rather than a habit marked by a state of powerlessness and the inability to manage one's life. Dependence on mind-altering drugs to cope with life's problems is not only addictive, but destructive to the body and mind. Encouraging young people to subscribe to this way of thinking that traps them into this downward spiral of self-destruction is deleterious to their mental and physical wellbeing. Peer pressure and western rites of passage pressure to experiment with these substances both affect the fundamental freedom of young people to choose a different path entirely. Think about it. If another path is presented instead of drug treatment and prevention programmes, then our young people can see that life can be enjoyed without addiction. The West has lost many young celebrity icons to this habit and there needs to be a different way to peace and enjoyment of this life. Failure to provide an alternative to mood altering, the western cultural thinker has to resort to potentially lethal dosages of drugs. How can frustration, boredom and anxiety be prevented? How can people be encouraged to face unemployment, isolation and social exclusion without resorting to drug taking? What alternatives to drugs can the Western cultural thinker resort to? How can preventative measures help the police and criminal justice system reduce drug related crimes? What if drugs were socially stigmatised as self-harming? What if explicit information about drugs was made available in schools and social gatherings?

Black Perspective

Drug taking in our community comes from personal philosophy about culture and belief. Those who believe that we have no culture and therefore we have to simply consume all aspects of western culture without filtering it first, would simply have the same attitude to drugs and its use. Those who believe otherwise, in some form of spiritual essence informing our existence would only use prescribed drugs for specific reasons. Rastafarians prescribe drugs for spiritual use not for abuse and those who believe in a specific religion would work on prevention of problems rather than cures. The problem for black people living in Africa and the Diaspora is that if we do not teach our children a culture distinct from the western paradigm, they will have no other path to choose except the one offered by the dominant culture of the West. The prevalence of excessive drug use in our community is a part of the paradox of living in a western society. If we look at the huge number of variables related to socio-cultural factors in drug use and abuse, then you will see a clearer picture created by gender, age, income/wealth, geographic locations and cultural patterns. If we google the number of black youth arrested for drug crimes at a rate ten times higher than any other race, you can begin to see the socio-cultural vacuum that exists for our young people. Google the contexts of drug use and abuse in our community and you will find that study after study identifies poverty, illiteracy, limited job opportunities, poor education, high availability of drugs, and stresses of the urban lifestyle as key factors.

Many of our young men have turned to cannabis use hiding behind the spiritual use of cannabis which is one of the key tenets of the Rastafarian movement. Many of our young men who do not subscribe to the teachings use and abuse cannabis to give them a high to commit all sorts of crime. Others hide behind the perception that it is safe and less harmful than other drugs and feel they could abuse its use on that basis. Many others in our community have a history of marijuana use within families and just do it as mindlessly as smokers do in the West. This consumption without filtration always links us back to the legacy of just doing things without questioning why things are done and for whose benefit. We have to find ways to move beyond the slave mentality and question everything that we do and everything that is dangled in front of our eyes to do. We must question everything and think of ways to move forward rather than holding on to customs and norms.

Poverty and its related socioeconomic determinants definitely have an impact on the use of drugs in our communities. How can we save our children from this decent into drug use? What if we explore some other form of spirituality for our children to experience, one which is culturally specific? How can think of a way of living that negates the hardships of young people and old? How can we treat our collective cultural pain without resorting to substances that are doing more harm than good? How can we design educational programs with coping strategies to prevent the need to take drugs in the first place? How can we alert our community to the burden of drug taking and how can we change perceptions towards drug use and abuse? How can we use mass media to spread preventative messages to our young people?

Chapter 48

HOUSING AS A PUBLIC HEALTH ISSUE

Housing. Hygiene. Squalor. Overcrowding. Homelessness. Inequality. Loneliness. Shelter. Safety. Security. Settlement. Warmth.

Physically, the western world has not been known for possession of natural or spiritual resources so rationality dictates that home or property ownership be one of the main aspirations of the western cultural thinker. Property is the main indicator of class, status and happiness so whether the properties are glass houses, mansions or filing cabinets of human lives, an Englishman's house would always be his castle. Lately, it seems that most houses are being built on the sand and that is causing huge problems for the social, spiritual and natural environment. The central role of the home has always been to provide shelter, warmth, love and security to all those who inhabit it; the cornerstone on which families build a quality psychological, spiritual and physical life. Sadly, the home is developing into a place of painful alienation, chronic loneliness and devoid of human interaction. Properties are now isolated in every way like vast wastelands, barren of the human spirit. The only spirits which reside in these estates are those of fear, phantoms of capitalism that haunt those bastards in their mansions and those of Havisham hate for the beloved sweetheart ones. Security is summoned to throw stones at those foreign spirits who attempt to shatter the glass, not to cause harm but to simply save the residents from themselves.

The huge impact of housing on people's mental, physical and spiritual health is often understated. Many are encouraged to make a twenty five year financial commitment to this endeavor which imprisons their freedom to finance anything else. The Western cultural thinking that one possesses the house when it cannot really be owned until you are free from the shackles of the mortgage, validates the Orwellian view that freedom is slavery. This twenty five year commitment to freedom tortures many minds and forces them to slave in work places from the dawn to setting sun. Physically, many have to rise in the dawn, and kneel and blow, some have to wait until the fire will glow, while others scrub and bake and sweep, till the stars begin to blink and peep. This song of the old mother must be the only spirituality that keeps hard workers honest as they watch in envy at those who lie long and dream in their bed as their day goes over in idleness.

Living in cities comes at an additional price with less natural space to enjoy clean fresh air and less pollution. These built environments pose additional problems to both mental and physical health in terms of size, conditions, proximity and location. Unhygienic conditions which accommodate rodents, insects and other creepy creatures not to mention the stench of some environments. The state of dilapidation and poor structure are real causes for concern for health visitors everywhere. How can poor housing be prevented from becoming Dickensian slums? How can the housing crisis be solved without restricting the freedom to have as many children as one pleases? How can more houses be built without sacrificing the green belt areas? How can the owners of massive estates be persuaded to share their excesses with others? How can overcrowding and all the ills that come with it, be resolved?

Glynis Glasgow-Kelly

Black cultural perspective

Housing for those of us living in the African diaspora will always be a problem related to issues of location and dislocation. Until collectively we return in spirit, in mind and even in body to our homeland, our motherland, we will never be at peace physically, culturally or socially occupying someone else's territory. Home is where the heart is, home is where you feel wanted and home is where you belong. If we do not feel part of a society, then we can never really call it home. If our children are denied a holistic education, if our young men are denied access to higher education, if we are stopped and searched travelling around a city and discriminated against in the workplace at every level, then this can never be our home. Our place in the western world is almost like District Six: No board says it but we know where we belong and for many of our boys their hands burn for a stone to shiver down the glass.

The issues of poor housing, which multiplies inequalities in areas already segregated by income, are well known: dilapidated housing, asthma triggers, mental health stressors, overcrowding and its plethora of impacts in terms of health, education and family, the threat of crime that keeps many people indoors, obesity and many other problems dealt with separately in this book. Let us not forget the problems of ill-health associated with poor air quality, cold homes and overcrowding. Illnesses that increase the risk of cardiovascular, respiratory and rheumatoid problems as well as ill health related to allergies and asthma. The profound impact of poor housing on our collective community cannot be overlooked nor can it be separated from the ideology that believes that our place on this earth is at the bottom of the social ladder. We have to do our part too by addressing the culturally entrenched view that the earlier we have children, the better it would be for all. This view needs to evolve at once. We need to encourage our children to delay parenthood and work to improve the housing crisis rather than compound the problem by adding to it. It can no longer be appropriate to have as many children as we please especially at a young age, with no job prospect, no housing prospect and no partner prospect. The home needs to play a central part in improving health and reducing inequality rather than add to overcrowding which forces our children to end up on the street.

Poor housing and squalor has historical underpinnings as everything was done on the street during slavery for the inspection of the master. We also had to live in shabby, shanty shelters in squalid conditions and now we have to be careful not to sleepwalk back into those days of severe squalor. Our living environment, no matter how modest, must be kept clean. Let us not forget that during slavery we were devalued, demoralised and dehumanised to the point where we paid no attention to hygiene, health or housing conditions. We were not simply told we were inferior but the whole slave system conditioned us to feel that way. Fast forward to the present day, how do we improve our living conditions to bring up our children to enjoy a better life? How do we improve our thinking about the environment in which we live? How to we teach our children to cherish their area and treat it like home? How do we change our thinking about housing, hygiene and health?

Chapter 49

SEXUAL HEALTH

HIV – Chlamydia – Genital Herpes – Genital warts – Gonorrhoea- Syphilis –

Sex was once sacred, secretive and spiritual but nowadays thanks to the liberation movements, sex has now become an adventure, an experiment or a casual encounter between two strangers on a Saturday night. Modern attitudes to sexual activity are parallel to attitudes to religion, morality and marriage. Abstinence is now a huge dinosaur scoffed at by the young western cultural thinker as modern sexual adventurism empowers with celebrity status. The western woman mocks the best and the worst of her conquests: the peacocks, the dolphins and the performing seals all of whom were great lords of the past adventure. Sexual activity between males and females occurs when both fall under the spell of the delusion of romantic love, sex working or more euphemistically private dancing. The problem with this lifestyle then becomes the problem of the State, the problem of society and of course the problem of the self. With huge financial burdens on the cost of caring for the consequences of sexual freedom, the western cultural thinker is faced with the free choice to burden junior doctors or change this costly lifestyle to one of responsibility.

Tracing the root cause of this problem leads undoubtedly to the decline of Christianity to platonic philosophy and of course to Freudian analysis of personality development. The latter has always involved repression of real feelings and many western cultural thinkers battle this deep conflict with the Oedipus complex, sexual ambivalence and displaced aggression. These culturally unacceptable feelings manifest themselves in sexual activity instead of directing violence against other people and perfect examples can be found in one's observation of priests and to a lesser extent intellectuals, who seem less sexually active and therefore less fertile.

Sexual ill-health cannot be divorced from sexual lifestyle choices and religious leaders would definitely advocate abstinence from extensive activity with numerous partners would be a reasonable path to take. Sexual promiscuity is rampant in society today and many are simply living by their sexual urges rather than having a meaningful relationship. This leads to all sorts of problems for the individual, for the community and for wider society particularly in the area of healthy living. Young people especially fall into all kinds of problems with having sexual activities way too young and forced to pay the price for their sexual pleasures.

The big questions then become: how does society persuade the younger generation to act responsibly when it comes to sexual health? How can the western cultural thinkers reduce the plethora of problems caused by poor sexual lifestyle choices? How should wider society address the issues of poor sexual health that is spiralling out of control?

Black cultural

Having children is an honour of participating symbolically in the primordial act of creation. It is a spiritual necessity, a cultural obligation, since birth represents the continuance of the group and of the self our own immortality. Our ancestors and origins are repeated in sacred symbols through which we unite with them, not compete with them.

Our spirituality is the recognition of spiritual connectedness, beyond lineal, ordinary profane time. This recognition energises our humanity, influences our priorities and prevents the alienation that Europeans experience. The issue of sexual union arises from the need to connect to our deep inner feelings of love and deep connection with another human being.

Sexual union is a spiritual legacy and it involves the deep connection with another human being to produce an offspring. We value the product of the sexual union as we always see children as a blessing or a gift from God just as the sexual union is meant to be a spiritual connection that involves the mind, body and spirit. The interconnectedness of mind, spirit and body is demonstrated in the sexual union as the bond takes them to a spiritual high sexual union is sacred and involves future legacies and the continuation of the species. In our culture it takes a village to bring up a child and that village is the black community.

We need to see children as a blessing and love them not just when times are good but through thick and thin and someone who we love is more than a deep emotion but an inner energy and a lifelong passion. We see dearly a heart felt emotion, a powerful inner feeling of love that causes us to want our legacy to live on forever. If we love ourselves we also love our children and want them to carry on our legacy forever. We love ourselves and want to see our children or offspring happy in the future. Future legacies are what we live for as having children is a lifelong commitment. We want to see them grow up to love and be loved. We want to see them make good lifestyle choices being happy with their sexual partners.

The questions then become: How do we ensure that our young people learn to love the partners with whom they have sexual relations. How do we foster a sense of pride in their ancestry and how do we strengthen ties with partners? How do we get young people to value the sexual union as sacred in a world that often sees sex as casual?

love our ancestors

Chapter 50

CANCER

Bladder cancer – Bone cancer – Gastric cancer -Breast cancer cervical cancer – ovarian cancer – vaginal cancer – vulvar cancer –Uterine cancer –primary peritoneal cancer –pancreatic cancer - Colon/rectum cancer –lung cancer – anal cancer – appendix cancer -skin cancer – kidney cancer -prostate cancer

Cancer is the leading cause of death worldwide and the second leading cause of death in the United States with lung cancer being the most common cause of cancer deaths in both male and females with breast cancer becoming more prevalent among women. It is not just a problem, it is not just an epidemic but it is also a huge international burden as cancer affects people of all genders, ages, races and ethnicities. Particular cancers are related to infectious agents such as human papillomavirus (HPV), Hepatitis B virus (HBV), Hepatitis C virus (HCV), human immunodeficiency virus (HIV) and Helicobacter pylori (H. pylori) –these changes may be prevented through behavioural changes and use of protective vaccinations and antibiotic treatments. Skin cancer cases that are diagnosed annually could be prevented by protecting skin from excessive sun exposure and avoiding indoor tanning. Screening offers the ability for secondary prevention by detecting cancer early, before symptoms appear. Early detection usually results in better outcomes and a decreased need for extensive and invasive treatment. Screening for cervical cancers can prevent cancer by allowing for detection and removal of pre-cancerous lesions. To improve early detection of potential tumors, people are encouraged to regularly carry out personal examinations of their breasts skin and testicles

As cancer affects people of all genders, ages, races and ethnicities, there needs to be a comprehensive examination of the causes of this terrible disease. Investing millions into curing the disease has not been successful so far but investing in preventative measures may have a better outcome. There is a lot to research here about many aspects of the disease and its continued proliferation around the world. Google for facts and figures for more about the collection of different and distinctive diseases all related to cancer. Google the billions and billions for direct medical costs and google for indirect mortality costs. Google for the numerous agencies committed to research in this area. Google what all the experts insist should be done to prevent it.

Leaders worldwide need to be more honest about the causes and work more strategically on preventing cancer than researching for the cure. As many western cultural thinkers are aware preventing cancer especially those caused by cigarette smoking and heavy use of alcohol is achievable if extensive investment is made into its causes but that would involve prevention of another kind of cancer, the one for which the Western cultural world does not really seek a cure. If Western cultural thinkers are serious about curing that cancer then one must address the causes and the effects of capitalising on a lack of knowledge about the cancer which causes all of the other types. How can cancer be prevented without preventing a pothole in the economy? How can the western cultural thinker free his/her mind from the slavery of freedom in lifestyle choices? With the cancer landscape shifting, should the roadmap for change involve a key which highlights the source of the problem endemic within the system itself?

Black cultural perspective

The cancer that all statistics state is most prevalent in our cultural group is prostate cancer. The figures are high. The figures are alarming. The figures are a real cause for concern. Did you know that we have the highest death rate and shortest survival of any racial group for most cancers? Did you know that very few studies, relative to the huge numbers afflicted by prostate cancer have been carried out to find out why prostate cancer is so widespread in our community? Cancers can involve any tissue of the body and may have different forms in each body area as most cancers are named for the type of cell or organ in which they start. By definition cancer refers to any one of a large number of diseases characterised by the development of abnormal cells that divide uncontrollably and have the ability to infiltrate and destroy normal body tissue and spread throughout the body. Google for evidence of studies done in this area of research. Google the many theories that exist about the cause of it. Google the controversial studies that link its cause to slavery and genetics. Google black men's attitudes to testing and treatment. Google how lung cancer affects our community too even though we do not smoke as much tobacco as other groups. Google the links to diet and lifestyle. Google for forecast of increase in cancer cases by the next two decades. Google those types of cancer that affect by gender, race and age.

Avoiding cancer is paramount and all medical experts yell at everyone to eat and exercise and avoid tobacco and alcohol. What seems to be avoided is that what is hugely toxic for our bodies is hugely beneficial to capitalism. Capitalism and cancer have more than the initial letters in common here. Cancer arises from one single cell just as capitalism arises in one single human's socialisation. Wherever capitalism is introduced the cells of the community automatically result in uncontrollable division. The transformation from a normal cell into a tumour cell is a multistage process and these changes are an interaction between a person's genetic factors and three categories of external agents – physical, chemical and biological carcio-nogens. There seems to be a striking resemblance between capitalism and cancer and its destruction on the individual, the collective and global body of humans everywhere. If we look at the behavioural and dietary risks often cited for cancer: high body mass index, low fruit and vegetable intake, lack of physical activity, tobacco use and alcohol use we will see the deeply disturbing connection between the two diseases. How do we rise above the flames of these two fires which are both consuming our people and the world?

Do we return to the Rastafari tenet that we eat all naturally grown foods or do we just resign ourselves to our fate? Do we listen to reason about healthy living and prioritise it – if not for ourselves but for our children? Do we find another way to survive other than be victims of a capitalist system that is inadvertently and intrinsically a cause of the problem? How do we prevent the spread of these cancers in our communities and around the world?

Chapter 51

BEAUTY

Aesthetics – Plato – Kant – Philosophy – Religion – Good – Universality
Conception of beauty –positive emotional responses –self-image- self-
concept– Kantian philosophy- Standards – Class- Status- Success-

Beauty is in the mind of the beholder and the mind of the western
cultural thinker has been ideologically obsessed with Platonic notions
of absolute beauty, rationality and religious validity. In the twenty
first century, such standards of beauty are still being blared from
front covers of magazines, fashion catwalks and other media. This
beauty brainwash continues to permeate western cultural thinking
ever since Plato originally associated the concept of beauty with
perfection and universal truth. By doing so, he imposed a standard of
beauty that western cultural thinkers are conditioned to embrace but
many realise that setting such standards of beauty has now become
problematic on many different levels and has caused a plethora of
gender-based, societal based and spiritually based problems for the
girls living in Madonna's world.

Young people are fatally attracted to the beautiful image of a partner;
others are desperately seeking someone's possessions while others
are sleeping beautifully for financial success. Celebrities role model
this concept of beauty which has become as cosmetic as the system
that promotes or rather applauds its achievements. The red carpet is
laid for all to admire the universal standard of beauty with young
girls, young women and even men all at home in the knowledge that

they would never be allowed to go to the ball. This Cinderella turned Barbie Doll concept of life in the booming beauty business creates a false consciousness that fails to acknowledge the fact that a universal standard of taste or beauty can never be achieved. Feelings about beauty vary by gender, by religion and by culture; they can never be really dictated by the powers of objectification.

Black Beauty Defining Black Beauty

Living in the materialistic world that the West has created, conditions many of us to see ourselves through whitewashed lenses rather than through the lenses of our African heritage. Our ancestors have defined all people as kings and queens in our own right; as equal in dignity rather than the intrinsically negative concept of black beauty propagated by western cultural thinkers. Until we decolonise our minds, we will never celebrate the essence of black beauty that must be defined within our own racial and cultural frameworks. Western notions of blackness automatically devalue, demoralise and destroy our perception of ourselves because their positive self-image is dependent on the negation of our true cultural image. This false dichotomy serves to permanently destroy the self-esteem of our people as we are conditioned to see ourselves as having the wrong colour, the wrong shape and the wrong personality. Our journey to redefining our beauty must happen on the same journey of collective cultural identity. This journey is a long walk to free our minds but we must begin with an acknowledgement and recognition of the beauty of our physical differences: we are curvier than women of other races, we have fuller lips, we have distinctive noses, our natural hair is unique and our dark skin is more resistant to wrinkles. Within our cultural and biological frameworks, we must seek to construct an identity that our men and women can realistically embrace rather than try to adopt western standards of beauty which we can never, ever, ever tailor to our cultural needs.

How do we empower our women to define our own beauty without having feelings of body comparison? How do we insist on the black body being kept in shape with its beautiful ancestral curves but losing the excess weight that spoils its appeal? How do we be healthy and happy rather than too big but beautiful? How do we learn to resist the temptation to eat knowing that it leads to obesity? How do we empower black women to accept our classy curves and detox our minds from the western beauty brain wash? How do we repossess our rightful titles of black kings and beauty queens? How do we build on Michelle Obama's legacy of brains, beauty and body image? How do we encourage our men to keep fit and fabulous? How do men and women both maintain a healthy body, a healthy mind and a healthy soul in the face of the avalanche of adversity?

Chapter 52

HAIR

Blonde – Brunette – Brown – Bronze -Red- Flaxen- Grey – Frizzy-curly- straight- long-short-Hair-beauty- Tones- Highlights- Depth-International Colour code ICC

The global hair care market is vast and worth billions and billions as it values ideals of beauty, ideals of nourishment of hair and ideals of prevention of hair damage that men and women buy because they are worth it. With an ever increasing array of products that are nice and easy to use, the hair business promises future growth and development. Because the market has divisions of products, applications and geographical locations, its structure can be researched and analysed in detail making it an industry that provides equal access to all whose hair can access to the spectrum on the international colour chart. This global numbering system was designed to create a more precise definition of hair colour and uses numbers that convey what the depth of the colour is, and what tones (if any) are in the colour. On the scale of 1 to 10 (with 10 being blonde), men and women everywhere can purchase colouring products according to their place on the spectrum and manufacturers can use their own in-house system. Depth or level and tones are carefully numbered so that every product is carefully and precisely categorised with double tone meaning a greater intensity and vibrancy of that particular tone. This whole system of standardising creates problems for the western cultural consumer whose natural hair identity denies them access to the range of colouring products.

If the western cultural thinker researches natural hair colour diversity that has been prevalent in Europe only then she may find a spectrum of possible causes from natural selection to intermixture or inter-genetic factors. The cause for naturally different hair colours is not the problem because everyone ends up with shades of grey. However, the effects of the obsession with designs within the system to promote hierarchy over taxonomy must be addressed. The fact that a select few have different coloured hair does not or rather should not justify the ideology of imposition or rather standardising ideals. The thinking that blondes have more fun is rooted in the ideological obsession with perceived perfection and thus exists as a fabulous footnote to Plato. For the western cultural thinker to convince the global majority to believe in an ideal of hair colour that denies access to this notion of ideal beauty reflects the degree of mind programming in operation from the cradle to the grave. Being brought up to perceive perfection in this way, has led to further dimensions of this problem relating to self-esteem, bullying and mental health issues across genders and across cultures. Yet, the western cultural thinker fails to address the problems at source.

How can western cultural thinkers begin to see the beautiful hair without negotiating ideals? How can perceptions of hair colour and class be divorced from the ideology which sustains the obsession with it? How can western cultural thinkers be persuaded to tone down standardization of outer beauty ideals in order to give legitimacy to inner beauty ideals? How can ideals of hair beauty be presented as a western value rather than as a dominant, global standard that denies access for many?

Black hair perspective

Attitudes to hair and beauty are rooted and grounded in our view of our culture, our history and our heritage. These are also linked to important issues of self- esteem which cannot be divorced from the politics of race. Rastafarians have always insisted that wearing the hair in its natural form without the addition of any chemicals makes a political, cultural and religious stance. Now, political hair leaders have started all sorts of movements notably the Natural hair movement to echo this left-wing sentiment by encouraging our women and men to shift affiliations but it seems like the majority, particularly the younger women are moving towards the right rather than occupying the centre ground. There are those who wear their natural hair but straighten it with a comb to make it more manageable; there are those on the complete opposite end of the spectrum who have embraced weaves, wigs and western straight hairstyles and to some extent the ideology of assimilation/integration. In hair politics terms, we have the far left, the centre ground and the far right.

Over the years, the ideology of racial identity has not been challenged in this context but continues to be associated with hair and beauty. Without careful examination and acceptance of our differences, we cannot address the other people's hair and that is why we have found ways to manage it; everyone knows that our hair is also more vulnerable to damage from chemicals but yet we relax the hair for beauty reasons without investigating the beauty standards that dictate this behaviour. For women of mixed heritage, their texture varies from fine to medium to coarse and different haircare treatment reflects the variety of hair types for women who are described on the colourism spectrum. Colourism and cultural perceptions of beauty cannot be separated in this context nor can the underlying plethora of problems of identity associated with it. Colourism is not just a matter of colour but a matter of facial features, facial shape and hair. Hair then poses problems of good hair v bad hair – long hair v short hair, curly hair v kinky hair. The problem is then compounded by issues of ideal beauty. Feel free to challenge on this one, but some hair styles and hair colours do not suit certain shades of black. Picture a bright red or blonde wig on the heads of sisters along the colour spectrum. Do you see what I see?

Similarly, some braided styles do not really suit certain head shapes. We cannot simply wear our hair without thinking of suitability. Some colours match other colours better and we should aim to coordinate the hair colours accordingly. The same principle applies for men too but the brothers seem to know what styles suit their facial features more so than our sisters. Some older brothers wear the bald head quite well, some wear the square; younger brothers wear the Mohican and fancy tops quite well and our rastafari brothers look gorgeous with their locks. Like the men our women should wear hair styles to match their head shape and complexion; women should apply the same thinking behind choice of hair colours. Negotiating hair ideals should always be a matter of suitability and personally perceived standards which should be culturally rooted or should it? Let us look at our hair and care in its social, cultural and historical context here.

Some people argue that we have embraced the hairstyles and standards of beauty of our oppressors; others see it as the use of our unique creativity and African braiding roots that produce the styles to form an artistic new standard of beauty. As black women, we have different hair care and beauty issues from fragility that can result in breakage and hair loss, medically termed alopecia to the complex issue of vanity. Some of us love to braid our hair but when it is done too tightly, it can lead to breakage, hair loss or both. Feel free to google about the occurrence of hair loss on the front temples and on the back of the scalp. You may also wish to study the effects of the long term use of chemical hair treatments and straighteners. We may all be rushing to the natural hair movement quite soon and with good reason. Or we may simply convince ourselves that time has moved on with more important issues to address; it is not what is on the head that matters but more what is inside it. As president Mugabe joked `it is hard to bewitch African girls these days; each time you take a piece from her hair to a witch doctor, either a Brazilian innocent woman gets mad or a factory in China catches fire'. Our hair business is no laughing matter anymore as Chris Roc has pointed out: it has now become a booming business worldwide.

From no major treatment for the dryness of our hair in the fields during slavery to using Vaseline or coconut oil during the period of colonisation. Older sisters have come a long way and would remember enduring the heat of the hot comb, then sleeping with rollers to perfect the curls. Who can forget the battle with the edges, the battle washing the hair and battle to keep the comb from breaking in the end. We smile at the memory of the burn of the perm which we have swapped for the burn of the bum sitting hours in the salon. Another generation may relate to avoiding workouts because of the expensive hair style or daring not to go straight to sleep without wrapping the hair. Our partners know that we often avoid after-hour aerobics because of the effects on the hair. For those who dared to go natural, we had to avoid those sisters thinking out loud `there goes a broke bitch'. Thank God for the emergence of the natural hair movement. Other sisters who head wrap their hair to be African queens get falsely accused of `having a bad hair day' rather than receiving applause. We cannot forget the other ladies who love touching our hair but we just glare which says do not even go there. Seriously sisters, our hair business is big; it is such a shame that we don't own it.

Should we have movements for each kind of hair care with tips to boost healthy hair and issues of identity? Should we pressure black music artists and other media to promote positive images of black hair and beauty? Should this issue be addressed only if sisters prioritise hair care and maintenance over family care and child sustenance? Should we take the problem seriously when sisters invest hours in the salon and invest minutes on their child's cultural education? Should we prioritise tackling this problem when we consider the cultural effects this styling industry is having? Should we tackle this problem when sisters prefer to miss exercise workouts because they do not want the hairstyle to blow out? Should we stress what is in the head rather than what is on it and depoliticise the whole issue of hair altogether?

Chapter 53

SKIN ISSUES

Moles - sun damage-rashes-dry skin- lumps and bumps-irregular pigmentation-Acne-Rosacea, Shingles-eczema- dermatitis-

The maxim that beauty is only skin deep only holds grains of truth in this context as skincare is big business for the western cultural thinker. It is no surprise that countless cosmetics, countless creams and countless celebrity faces dominate advertising of skincare products that target mainly women who perceive beauty standards of skin tone, skin type and skin health. Ideal beauty skincare assumes healthy eating, healthy environment and healthy understanding of the root causes of skin problems which vary across gender, class and cultures. The skin of the human body responds to its physical environment of air, water, earth or whatever occupies the inner or outer space around it. Hence what goes in the body can also affect the skin as much as environmental pollution. The latter is particularly high in western countries where contact with other people in the hustle and bustle of crowded cities is inevitable; this leads to a spectrum of problems from mild to those of high magnitude. Such problems persist from initial contact in public spaces to problems in unhealthy homes, ignorance of the pollution of products like harsh soaps, itchy clothing or errors in understanding of the skin problems which results in misuse of moisturisers, misuse of hot showers and baths and of course misdiagnosis and misuse of medication. The huge problem with skin conditions has negative impact related to self- esteem, self-worth and self-confidence of young and older western cultural thinkers. Breakouts, spots, acne and various skin disorders lead to different degrees of depression and a spectrum of lifestyle habits including eating out, smoking and guzzling gallons of alcohol. The curious paradox that the most valued lifestyle choices destroys the most valued material possession, the physical body, is definitely one to ponder.

The thinking that the skin must be perceived as beautiful has roots in the ideological obsession with beauty standards and the pursuit of perfection. Judging and living on physical appearance whilst ignoring the poisonous substances both inside and outside the body systematically deviates from any form of logic. The relentless drive to treat effects of skin conditions without acknowledging the rooted causes seem to reflect the lack of logical validity in western cultural constructs. Maintaining good skin care is diet environmental and lifestyle factors including home environment and clothing which implies that if preventative measures are applied then good skin care can be maintained and developed naturally.

The questions then become: How can body image, beauty standards and perceptions consider skin care from within the self? How preventative measures for skin care problems become the priority over treating the effects? How can beauty identity be redefined to include inner beauty? How can the western cultural thinker address environmental issues that cause a plethora of skin problems without undermining the financial gains that come with polluting the atmosphere in the first place? How can the western cultural thinker change the ideology of the maxim that beauty is only skin deep to one that insists that beauty within is deeper than skin?

Black cultural Perspective

Forget shades of grey, what arouses controversy in our community is shades of black: jet black, chocolate, deep coffee, beige, toffee, high yellow and the list goes on and on based on the principle that those with lighter, fairer skin are treated with a higher regard than those with darker skin, referred to as colourism, happens both between racial communities and within them. The light-skinned, dark-skinned skin tone spectrum poses a combination of problems for the black community: prejudice, discrimination and complexes. However, colourism tends to mask the emphasis that should be placed on addressing the issues associated with skin care and skin health problems which prevail in our community. It is a fact that our different experiences of prejudice in the African diaspora can be traced to our different skin tones, reactions and attitudes to each other within the community but skin conditions affect us all in different ways. Dry skin has always been one of our main skin deep concerns and we have tried everything from Vaseline to cocoa butter to natural oils to harsh soaps and moisturisers but still dry skin persists. A number of us are totally unaware that medical conditions like diabetes can cause dry skin, that there are medical recommendations on how to treat dry skin and dietary ways to prevent the skin from becoming excessively dry. Skin dryness may also be due to something in the environment or something leaving the skin unprotected and the cause may be internal from genetic predisposition. Feel free to google for evidence here.

Other skin conditions that overwhelmingly affect our men are mostly experienced when shaving to prevent the development of ingrown hairs or getting razor bumps. As hairs curl back into the skin, they can cause irritation and inflammation, which is made much worse by continuing to shave after razor bumps have developed. The body responds by producing collagen to repair the damaged skin. This can sometimes lead to keloid scarring, where the collagen spreads into healthy tissue to leave a noticeable scar. Darker skin types are more prone to keloid scarring than lighter ones, which means that black men are not only more likely to suffer from razor bumps, but they are also more likely to develop scarring as a result. We are bound by the shared ancestral pains of slavery, separated kin, sexual assault by enslavers, and the pervasive impact of an unfair capitalist system that was designed to intoxicate our minds. Skin care products to lighten darker-skinned folks in order to make them more appealing to the masses cannot be viewed as a tree without these deep historical roots. Lighter-skinned black people have been given opportunities to work in the house, while darker-skinned people have often been sent out to work in the field. This parallels what happens in the workplace, in the home and in the human body and has caused problems in our community that are akin to brain and skin cancer. These cancers need a political cure, an ideological solution and a historical healing that offers us some kind of view to a bridge. Sadly, it is a bridge that President Obama, our biggest case in modern history, stands powerless to provide. How do we begin a new narrative on issues of skin tone, skin colour and skin conditions? How do our men and women begin to heal when the issues are more than skin deep? How can we learn effective techniques that treat Keloid scars that can be very noticeable on black skin, and can be a real blow to the confidence of black men? How can we work together to address the internal and external problems that are affecting our skin health?

Chapter 54

SIZE ISSUES

Fashion models- Hollywood, Sport, - police- politicians-taller women-privileged property – size of credentials – size

The world of fashion thrives on promoting images of beauty as taller and slimmer on the beauty spectrum and this mirrors the western cultural thinking that the taller the better. Size has been used to dominate the arts, media, academia, religion and fashion by selling the notion that quantity means quality. However, this has served to deny people access to aspire to the value of certain occupations especially those within the beauty industry like modelling, media and acting. Fashionable women's clothing ranges in size from zero to thirty two with size zero being the one often promoted with the most high profile prestige in the dream world, the underworld and the material world. From posh to classy lines, the world of fashion thrives on line to promote certain lifestyles, certain ideologies and certain ways of thinking about the materialistic world. The ideology that it is all about exclusivity of material wealth, of outer beauty and of outer appearance seems to drive the western cultural thinker. In what seems to be a relentless pursuit of perfection, the beauty brokers try to encourage more styles, more clothing and more products. The consumerist way of thinking continues to affect attitudes to normalised standards of beauty and this has an impact on everyone across the spectrum of society from childhood to babyhood, from sisterhood to brotherhood, from motherhood to fatherhood.

Without accumulating inner beauty, without belief in other fashionable ways of viewing the world, the western cultural thinker focuses on exclusive styles and promotions of a value system that has lost its value. Imposing this western standard of beauty through size standards, has served to deny access to different people that many young women may have aspired to be part of in the world of art, the world of religion and the world of fashion. Many young women have been denied access to power because of this hashtag of Size matters. The patriarchal power brokers have enjoyed these images of taller means better whilst admiring those who do not conform. Size then adds to status to secure power rather than really empower those who seek it. The size of this game mirrors the size of the model and many often dream of the leggy ones in Mercedes rather than those who look like scavengers in a truck.

The big questions then become: how can the western cultural thinker negotiate beauty ideals without concealing the size of the matter that needs be concealed? How can this size myth that has served to perpetuate patriarchal power be used to share power with those who seek it? How can this size myth be dismantled without diminishing the dignity of those who have created it? How can this size myth that has been used to preoccupy the minds of those without a model size change to accommodate those who do? How can this size myth that has been used to build the consumerist value system of the western cultural thinker now serve to help those who do not have the model size of thinking?

Black cultural perspective

Our ladies are larger than ladies of other races and this has far reaching implications for health, fashion, relationships and other aspects of everyday life. We have accepted our body shape with our beautiful curves but the size of our bodies has a natural capacity or framework for being big. Our people and writers use all kinds of descriptions: black women are big-boned, thick, larger than life, large and in charge, slimly challenged. Put formally, they mean the same thing: our bodies are bigger than the bodies of other people. This does not mean that we are better or worse than anyone else but rather that we are different just as there are different parts of the human body. Our bodies show that we can be curvy and large but breathtakingly beautiful. We can be small and seemingly unattractive but what matters is the size of the inward beauty that we possess not the size of the imposed beauty value of the societies in which we live.

The reasons why our women are larger are well known: diet, genes, childbearing, lack of exercise, stress, discrimination, socioeconomic status and environment. We all know that our diet needs to change and we all know that we need to eat healthy foods in order to cultivate healthy minds. We know that we have to work out before and after childbirth rather than let ourselves go. The stress of life can be minimised if we make different life choices but some of our people do not have a choice and therefore are left with a huge bill of stress which accumulates and accumulates. Socioeconomic status and environment can only be changed with a collective and holistic government led approach to education for elevation to bring out the best in everyone.

Our men are also large physical specimens but the size is often only highlighted for mythical reasons but size matters for our black men do not begin and end there as our men are naturally bigger which presents difficulty with fashion that has not traditionally been designed with them in mind. Thankfully, some retailers have been considering the larger man on all fronts and fashion is making some changes for the greater good. In terms of the mythical issue, we will have to quote Chinese research here. According to freelance writer, model and sex educator Glamazon Tyomi, there are ways to tell genital size without seeing the genitals. Let us read directly what Taoist matchmakers have said:

Taoist matchmakers in China have had an understanding for centuries that great relationships are rooted in a great sex life, so when pairing couples together, they made it a necessity to pair men and women together according to their genital sizes. The Chinese understood that genitals that fit together perfectly would produce great sexual experiences, and so they developed a system to determine the size of genitals by using facial features and hands. (And believe me, this system is spot on.)

> Believe it or not, a man's thumb is a direct mirror of the shape and size of his penis. The length of a man's penis is twice the length of his thumb; the shape and width of the base of the thumb is the shape of the shaft of the penis; and the tip of the thumb correlates to the shape of the penile head. When it comes to women, a small mouth and short fingers correlates to a small, short vagina. A woman with big, thick lips is said to have a wide, thick vagina. There are a number of features that reveal genital size, and you can read more about them on her website (see below).

So the answer to the age-old question of "does size matter?" is yes, it does! Size matters, but not in the way of being large and in charge. Size matters in the aspect of being able to fit perfectly with your partner to perform in an experience you will never forget. Be confident in what you have, because someone, somewhere out there was created to fit with you exactly as you are.

If the mythical narrative is viewed from a historical perspective and in its entirety one may understand why slaves were fed with foods to ensure that they became as large physically as ever under the mantra of carrying out slave labour. If one examines why male slaves had to toil in the fields, working in back breaking jobs to ensure a reward of something to eat or a special reward by a female slave owner. If one looks carefully at the size of the problem with size on the plantations and beyond then one would see how those in the house and those in the field survived. Female slaves had to bare children, drag them up to be slaves again; there was no time to look pretty, braid hair at will or do anything that would boost self-esteem. Slave men and women had to toil in the field rather than sit pretty in the house with all the privilege of gazing at slaves working in the field. Back to the present and the gazing has developed into a huge art and the eye is now making a fool of the other senses.

The key questions here then become: How can we negotiate on this huge issue of size when the size of the problem is the problem itself? How can we promote size positively without overemphasising, overinvesting or overusing rhetoric? How do we find the language to express the real hurt caused by the original sins of the past? Should we embrace the curves and fight against obesity? Should we deny or officially confirm that black men are mythical? How can this issue ever be resolved?

Chapter 55

FASHION AND COLOUR

Fiery Red - Imperial blue- pearly white- ebony- hot pink-buttercup yellow-jade green- blueprint-bright colours- dull colours-autumn line- winter wear-spring wear-summer wear-high fashion-classics-

Colour and fashion have always had an interesting relationship and one could argue that one cannot exist without the other. Colour wheels enhance the relationship and colour clashes on the catwalk simply. It is a fact that colour enhances or ruins the beauty of an outfit and convey a certain sense of style. The colours designers choose make or break the fashion line and that is why designers take care in their colour combinations. However, colours have certain cultural connotations of which designers are very aware. They are aware of the seasonal colours and the bright colours associated with summer and the dull colours associated with the winter line. They are aware of the colour combinations that match and those that do not.

Fashion has had a long, complicated yet stable relationship with its consumers over the years but now this relationship is suffering from the strain of the limelight and social media. The market for making consumers look more and more beautiful is bursting at the seams and designers from all houses know that keeping the truth behind closed doors is of utmost importance. Like consumerism, fashion's fortress is faced with forces of gluttony that threaten to destroy the empire itself as more and more design houses are being erected everywhere. Designers are trying to make their houses standout by dressing celebrities, dressing certain classes and dressing real women. However, the problem of what constitutes being high fashion still remains carefully coded.

Colour coordination is weaved into the tapestry of designing and lines of clothing can be destroyed when colours, prints or patterns clash. In clothing and the fashion world of colour is compared and contrasted to create that sense of what one perceives to be style. Houses of design are built on this foundation of perception and association of class and beauty with the cloth and pattern prints from which the style permeates. Grand designs imply imposed perceptions from which the blueprint for style, beauty and glamour emerges for the red carpet. Showcasing different colours is tantamount to the design of the line that relies on the glitz and glamour of the clothing. Ladies in red always reminds one of certain dances and conjure a certain class and radiance for the western cultural thinker.

Colours have positive and negative attributes and people integrate colour into careers and daily lives. Not only that but we wear colours consciously and when the right colours are worn the effect is harmony. The problems for the western cultural thinker are how do fashion designers deal with culturally sensitive colours in fashion and models? How can the connotations of colours be divorced from the fashion industry? How can the psychological effects of colour and fashion be used for positive effects?

Colour is the first thing noticed

Colour can express an emotion

Colour can convey a brand or an image

Colour has cultural connotations

Ladies in red are good for dancing

Colours have psychological and physiological effects- colour therapy
Men and women are attracted to certain colours

Western cultural thinkers wear white for weddings as it symbolises
peace and purity

Colour affects mood – mood affects choice

A glow – radiance

Colours are meant to complement and enhance

Colour consultants use the seasons

Colours have a calming effect

Colours have different tones

When we are wearing the right colours the effect is harmony

Choose consciously the colours

Each colour has positive and negative attributes

Integrating colour into our careers and daily lives

Fashion's relationship with black consumers continues to be
complicated. It's the dream of every fashion designer to be carried in
mainstream department stores and dress celebrities, yet Tracy Reese
is really the only black designer who's currently living this dream. I

love wearing Reese's clothes; her modern approach to dressing real women has made her a standout in the fashion community and not just as a black designer. That said, Reese isn't the only black designer working. There's also Kevan Hall, b michael, Byron Lars, Patrick Robinson and, the baby of the bunch, LaQuan Smith, just to name a few. All of them make beautiful clothes, but unfortunately they aren't always easy to find. Design houses clamor to showcase Michelle Obama's powerful arms in their clothes, yet African-Americans are still not reflected in advertising, on the runway or even behind the scenes. The kumbaya moment hasn't happened yet. But as a brown girl from Harlem who has sat front row at fashion shows in Paris,

Black cultural perspective

Do you have that little black dress for special occasions? I bet you do. Black represents authority and power - According to Fashion selection, black, as a colour, makes us all look slim. Think about it. The western world of fashion has great difficulty accepting black models as a rule but of course there are exceptions: Iman, Naomi Campbell, Tyra Banks, Joan Smalls, Jourdan Dunn who are successful in supermodel world but known more for their status as black models than supermodels in their own right. Would you like to challenge this statement? Before you do, answer this question honestly - how many more black models can you name? We will be waiting for a while. Sisters, let us face it, modelling was not designed with us in mind. Our natural curves do not belong in those dresses worn by the supermodels, and we can even say that to Kim K and Queen B who can both afford to have dresses designed exclusively.

`It is all about money' the fashion industry would insist. The fact of the matter is that featuring black models on the front covers of major fashion magazines will reduce the sales. Featuring too many black models will lower the perception of class attached to the House of Fashion. Striding down the catwalk is not for black cats: for some, it is a runway and for us it is a runaway so put your trainers on. Seriously, the fat cat designers of all houses know that this is the truth that meows and roars simultaneously. Please refrain from the temptation to shoot the writing cat. We have designed the billionaire dresses by spending billions on urban, hip-hop and street wear forgetting we created the street style in the first place. We are fashion cats forgetting that black cats are not welcome on the runway. Hip hop cats are writing odes, building fashion houses and wearing designers yet none of the cats are building houses for those who toil out in the field. Field cats are left in boyhoods, motherhoods and babyhoods designed for fabulous neighbourhoods. This has designed trendy and lucrative problems that have to be addressed before we can no longer fit into the fashions.

Fashion, throughout history, has created a unique identity within black culture and the church has always been a significant driver for style and fashion. From the hats to the pretty dresses, we have always oozed style in our daily lives of service and socialising; church has always been a place for information dissemination and mobilization. Fashion is a statement and speaks volumes with little to no words. Within the black community, everything from cloth to churches to the forming of political movements (The Black Panther Party) and hair has elements of style. Today, the significance of "hashtag politics" and the viral capability for an image to instantly reach millions as well as the social impact of political pieces like the "I Can't Breathe" t-shirts create a whole new dynamic in the social and fashion space.

Let us face it our black designers are only known for who wears their designs rather than for the designs themselves. Ask the designer of Michelle Obama's pink dress as instant fame followed because the first lady looked so radiant in that dress. Yes, we love the fashion industry but the fashion industry does not love us. We are a viable market with huge purchasing power yet there are major issues with not being able to access virtually every market. There have been many attempts to stop and search for fashions in the major Houses but we only end up being stopped and searched instead. To stand out in the crowd is essentially our relationship with fashion as black consumers so to build a new relationship will prove difficult because beauty is in the eye of the beholder.

Ever wondered why there is not a line of clothing for us as black booty queens? Let me be more formal, with so many curvaceous figures, why has there not been a line of clothing modelled by curvy models for curvy women? What about the size issue, why is it virtually impossible to see models for those under a certain size? Why is it that we are made to feel that our beautiful bodies are exclusively invaluable while others are made to feel that their bodies are ideally valuable?

During times of slavery and especially post-slavery, black women looked forward to dressing up for church on Sunday. Monday through Saturday they were restricted to their work uniforms; Sunday was the opportunity to step out in style. Professor Josef Sorett, an academic of religion and African-American studies at Columbia University, explained,

"Sunday was the morning where the slave or the sharecropper was transformed into a saint. They went from being a servant to a deacon.

By naming each other as brother and sister, and by putting on their finest attire, black folks both affirmed their own humanity, and imparted respect to one another. They did all of this, with style."

Church style is now embedded in Southern culture and one can see its influence of wide brim hats and ornate details permeating throughout the fashion industry. Living in Harlem, every Sunday becomes a classy, colorful fashion show. I see older women dressing with a style and flair that is created through pride and dignity. The oversized church hats with delicious details of bows, ribbon, and wide brims; the colorful church suits accented with brooches and hand-sewn details. It is truly a site to see as I sit with my coffee on a Lenox Ave. stoop and watch a Harlem Fashion Show.

Fashion within the African-American community permeates from the cloth and pattern design. Kente cloth began to garner the attention of African-Americans in 1958. Ghana's first president, President Kwame Nkrumah, visited Washington D.C. wearing Kente, fueling inspiration for African-American people. According to *Stitched With History: African Textile and Fashion*, photos of President Nkrumah adorned newspapers and magazines, helping to establish the African cloth as a symbol of African heritage and pride.

IAnd they have become Internet-age fashion polymaths: stylists and models, but also writers, preservationists, photographers and editors — and soon, designers and retailers.

Already they have wide reach: Street Etiquette receives 20,000 page views a day. The two men are the most prominent public faces of a new burst of black dandyism taking root in small retail outlets, niche fashion lines and thoughtful style blogs.

"There's more than one cool now for black people," Mr. Gumbs said on a recent Tuesday at the Bergen Street studio, wearing a slight wisp of a goatee and dark glasses that sharpened his round face. "When we were growing up, it was just one kind of cool."

That was hip-hop, with its hegemonic style. But the men of Street Etiquette and their peers practice a deliberate elision of hip-hop style (except in the site's early days, when the two were still shaking free of their Air Jordans). They even eschew the prim eccentricity of an Andre 3000, or the cosmopolitan flamboyance of Kanye West.

Instead, this generation emphasizes the basics: great fabrics, aggressive tailoring, thoughtful accessorizing. It's a return to style as a source of dignity, a theme that has run through generations of black American style, from Reconstruction to the Harlem Renaissance to the civil rights era to the mixed messages of the hip-hop era.

"I used to wear size 42 jeans," Mr. Kissi said. "Coming from that to a tie and shirt, people perceive you in a whole different way."

When Michelle Obama stepped onto the stage at the Democratic National Convention in 2012 to talk about her husband and the coming election, the Internet went into an effective group swoon. Words like "spotlight stealing" and "dazzling" were used with abandon. Not about the first lady's speech, but about her dress: a shimmering pink and silver sleeveless number by the designer Tracy Reese.

> Though Mrs. Obama had worn Tracy Reese before, she had never worn the brand in such a high-profile forum, to such universal acclaim. Consensus was, another career had been made — just as Jason Wu shot to prominence after he created Mrs. Obama's first inaugural ball dress — and a role model born: Ms. Reese is African-American, and her newfound fame would, the chatter went, have repercussions when it came to diversity in the fashion world far beyond the evening.

Continue reading the main story

RELATED COVERAGE

> Fast- forward two years, however, and the schedule for New York Fashion Week, which begins on Thursday, tells a different story. Of the 260 shows on the men's and women's wear schedule, only three with any global reach are by African-American designers: Tracy Reese, Public School and Hood

Chapter 56

HOLLYWOOD ISSUES

Hollywood is the entertainment capital of the world and the heaven of the materialistic world which has a pleasant seat in the land of dreams. Setting universal standards in style, fashion and beauty, Hollywood can be described as the bastion of western cultural glitz and glamour. The Platonic view of Beauty reigns supreme in Hollywood with lavish lifestyles of the rich and famous condoned, condemned or commended. Marriages are more money mergers and power partnerships than those made in heaven with focus more on weddings of style more than stability. Hollywood gossip is more about the beauty of the bodies than the compatibility of the couples and the fact that most marriages are shortlived proves the point. Hollywood wives do everything to conform to the Platonic standards of beauty from plastic surgery to endless hours in the gym while men muscle their way into masculinity. It is all about the reality of appearance for success with a relentless pursuit of the pleasure principle and more of everything; satisfaction is never guaranteed. For the younger generation they learn the values of life in this glorified glitzy and glamorous world that has created a negative impact on those who can never ever go to this ball.

Hollywood values have created a negative impact on society culturally, morally and politically especially through the movie industry which has worked wonders in wooing audiences with films that promote action, violence and sex. Many blame the industry at least in part for the proliferation of acts of violence in society such as shootings and killings as the adage states that violence breeds violence. The movie capital of the world influences to a large extent what happens in wider society in terms of trends and other norms and has the strongest impact on the younger generation. James Bond films make violence seem cool and science fiction films often equate acts of violence with intellectual prowess. Even the latest games and gadgets promote violence as almost normal which is disturbing in the current climate. Sex is almost synonymous with the film industry and according to the western cultural thinker that is what sells. In an industry where money matters more than morality on every level where do the younger generation go for moral guidance?

The problems then become if movies reflect the latest scientific ideas, should science fiction explore a future without violence or the science of a utopian world? Should Hollywood address the violence in films by showing less violence? With younger men everywhere seeking new ideologies should Hollywood explore a new ideology outside capitalism? Should the Oscars also provide a political platform for those committed to improving society? Should the younger generation be influenced by official Hollywood role models- those with moral values?

Black cultural thinker

Hollywood is the entertainment capital of the world which sets imposed standards of style and acting performance. The academy has always been made up of a certain class, a certain sex and a certain age of thinkers and their minds have been programmed to see talent that conforms to the established order of things. It is just a fact that the established order of Hollywood has traditionally not included us. Over the years times have changed from the single black actor in films to films with an all black cast but the core problems still remain that the standards were not made with us in mind.

The universal beauty ideals of Hollywood often simply cause our women to look at ourselves through a different lens instead of through the lens of our African heritage. We are bigger and curvier than other women so let's face it no matter how much plastic surgery our women have we will never look like the standards specified by Hollywood. We have to be proud dignified and accepting of our selves as African queens and do not feel like we have to conform to standards that just do not suit us.

We have to acknowledge the fact that our young men especially have lifelong dreams to have a career in the entertainment business but this dream is often unrealised. Our men are left chasing unreachable dreams as they meet setback after setback from the lack of acknowledgement from the academy. Failure to have a dream in the land of dreams cause people to perish and our men are left living from day to day without hope for the future. In addition, the lack of dreams, hopelessness and exclusion can be blamed at least in part for the amount of gang violence in the wider community. If the system excludes our young men in principle those who cannot cope with it would lead to mental health problems and depression as from day to day they wake up having no hope for the future. It could also lead to violent crime especially in inner city areas when many feel like they have no choice but to hustle and resort to crime.

The problem remains how can we make it in the entertainment business that is so difficult to infiltrate? Should the few actors and supporting actors who receive nominations use the platform to inspire young black actors by describing their journeys? Should we try to secure a whole new academy dedicated to address the needs of our people; a Mollywood like Bollywood to appreciate our African talent? How do we work with the western cultural thinkers to reduce the black on black violence in inner cities? Should we promote the young men who are actively promoting positivity in black communities everywhere and help them to mentor those without dreams?

Everything is about outer appearance and Hollywood women strive for outer beauty by any means possible. Plastic surgery is on the increase as there is a relentless pursuit of perfection or to achieve the ideal look in Hollywood standards. Violence has barged its way through society with become the norm and this is reflected in the events in wider society: school shootings, domestic violence and drive by shootings. They do not In Hollywood there is the relentless pursuit of materialism as opposed to inner beauty glamorised the belief that money matters most in this material world. Everything is about the glitz and glamorous lifestyle that been hailed as the bastion of the capitalist system with style, fashion, secularism and the ultimate materialistic world.

Hollywood pay gap gender inequality – even in a world where the capitalist thinkers are pursuing large sums of money and trying to achieve equality in an unfair system it cannot work

Glorifies gun violence

Marriages do not last freedom to those in the system of capitalism. Slaves to the freedom of Capitalist society has been hailed as the everything from the capitalist heaven for those who have belief in the material world. The Hollywood is the

James Bond poses with a gun – Fifty cent does likewise and it causes outrage. army gangsters – those in banks who use pens rather than pistols to inflict personal - injuries of the mental kind - hurt on families and communities / journalists – armed with technology and the tools of false representation – their jobs are to the white collar criminals - use scaremongering and scare tactics as curtains behind which they conceal themselves– knives from the draw board versus than keys on the key board – War lords are in solitary confinement in secure prisons while the real war lords are seated in the House so aptly named.

Chapter 57

BODY IMAGE ISSUES

Body image is very important to men but is especially true of women everywhere who want to appear attractive for themselves, for other women and for the opposite sex. For the western cultural thinker, body image is mostly what matters over everything and universal standards are used to assess one's assessment of that body image. When one's body does not conform or fit the image that society dictates all kinds of emotions set in. How one views him or herself always depends on the societal standards or images that are laid outlined by the culture. These standards can be traced back to the thinking that there is universality and absolute truth in standards of how the human body should appear. The ideal that the taller the person the better the body excludes rather than embraces the majority of western cultural thinkers as many are not living up to those standards of beauty any more. If originate in the Platonic notions of universal standards

How one sees himself has always been an issue for the western cultural thinker and has caused a lot of interrelated problems for the thinkers in Madonna's world. The world is consumed by the belief that outer beauty is everything and there is a standard of beauty that everyone should try to aspire to. If one's natural body does not come close to the ideal standard then issues of negative body image leads to low self esteem and stress especially for the minds of the younger generation who have been preoccupied with the outer beauty rather than looking at inner beauty. Distorted body image or negative self image has led to a series of problems facing mainly women. If all the attention is paid to the outer body image, what about the feelings that are within. One may argue that it is all about striking a balance between the inner beauty and the outer beauty or it depends on the way one sees herself. If one is reliant on societal standards for the way bodies should be viewed then there is a permanent pressure to conform to standards that are often unreachable. If many do not believe in themselves and if many do not conform to universal standards then they will feel frustrated and resort to doing things out of sheer negativity over their situation.

Being dissatisfied with oneself can lead to a plethora of problems associated with severe body hatred which include eating disorders, self esteem issues and depression. This is especially true for the younger generation who to a large extent depend on their body image for self worth and validation. Without a positive image of themselves they descend rapidly into depressed states and for some it can lead to mental disorders. The feelings associated with this negative state can lead to other major disorders and these can often have detrimental effects on the psyche. The thinking that body image equates to self esteem has negatively impacted many in this appearance driven world. The focus on appearance in magazines and the wider media driven world has not helped or rather has compounded the problem of low self esteem. With images blaring from billboards many with body image issues are left to sink further and further into depression.

The problem for western cultural thinkers remain how can wider society cultivate the view that body image is a matter of mind over matter? How can young men and women appreciate their bodies in the image in which they were created? How can the western cultural thinker avoid pressurising people into thinking that outer appearance is all that matters? How can body image issues ever be resolved without looking at the underlying issues endemic within society itself?

Black cultural perspective

Our bodies are bigger in size than other races and often our women especially struggle with body image issues. Many women dread going shopping for fashions as often the dresses are not designed to enhance the body shapes of our sisters. Often our sisters are left feeling depressed and devalued by the constant bombardment of images of slim models in magazines and on television. Some insist that we should just accept our body image the way we were made and do not feel frustrated or depressed when we are larger than other women. Others insist that we should work out in the gym and change our diet in order to lose the excess fat while there are those who say that life is too short and we should just be fat and happy. Whatever the viewpoint we have to face the reality of life in the western world and the pressure placed on us to focus on physical appearance.

Many black celebrities try to set good examples of ideal body image for us to aspire to by being role models but often their message falls on deaf ears. Some give their personal stories of their journeys from negative body image to accepting themselves for who they are. Others tell their stories of their battles with the bulge and how they won in the end. Talk shows abound on the subject of positive body image but some of us are not listening or rather we just maybe do not care. We abuse our bodies by eating and drinking in excess and it has taken its toll on our minds and our souls.

In fairness many of our sisters comfort eat to deal with the stresses and low self esteem issues rather than go to see someone about it

How do we cultivate positive thinking about our bodies? Should we stop avoiding our bodies and start focusing on improving it? Should we stop comparing ourselves to others and accept ourselves the way we are? Should we stop criticising our bodies and learn to love the body we are in? Should we recognise the influence of the media and question the messages conveyed? Should women join together to gain confidence in our body images?

Chapter 58

MEDIA ISSUES

The Internet-Social Media-journalism-facebook-youtube-fake news-twitter-snapchat-whatsapp-instagram- messenger

The Internet-Social Media-journalism-facebook-youtube-fake news-twitter

Some may argue that the internet is one of the great inventions of modern times and one of the achievements of the West. The western cultural thinker has been able to connect with the world in a way that has been unprecedented in recent times. The pace of change is accelerating and the world is now a smaller place with everyone being able to make use of the modern world of technology. Businesses boom thanks to the advertising on websites and multimedia outlets. Young people are hooked on social media websites and the world has become totally reliant on modern technology. It has become a world of making everything public from mundane daily routines to quintessentially private affairs of the home and the bedroom. With Donald Trump again complaining that social media companies are silencing millions of people, what can be said of a world of freedoms being threatened. Modern technology has revolutionised social life, work life and family life and the world is now in a place that some may say is beyond redemption.

One of the biggest problems affects the family as a unit. Families are no longer conversing as before as young people are sitting for hours on social media in their bedrooms and some are becoming addicted to the internet. With psychologists calling on parents to monitor screen time and parents looking to experts for guidance while children complaining that they have no other form of enjoyment, the western cultural thinker has a long way to go to monitor the situation. Gone are the days of family games and conversation around the dinner table as the phone is almost as important as the forks and knives. Gone are the days of meeting friends to play games as gadgets have taken the place of direct social interaction. The internet is vast in its appeal and has won the hearts and minds of young people everywhere. Many are likely to even change their minds on issues because of social media. With this huge cultural shift how c an the western cultural thinker reverse the current trend of social media? How are young people going to get practical skills on how to be parents when both parents are busy on the phone? How are the younger generation going to be creative again and think of things to do rather than be totally reliant on social media?

The advantages of modern media are vast from being baby sitters to gathering ideas for business and the like. However one has to look at the problems caused by recording everything and leaving privacy as an ancient treasure. With everything and anything available on the internet how can the western cultural thinker slow down the rampant surge in nothing private. The pace of change is accelerating and the future is set to be even more frightening. How can the world slow down or is there any slowing down to the rampant social media charge? How can young people find love in relationships at home rather than over the internet? How can the world slow down the pace of the social media charge? Should there be more open forums where young people can share their frustrations with other young people or should there be more places where how to love when social media fails? Do we need a moral transformation of society?

Some may argue that the internet is one of the great inventions of modern times and one of the achievements of the West. The western cultural thinker has been able to connect with the world in a way that has been unprecedented in recent times. The pace of change is accelerating and the world is now a smaller place with everyone being able to make use of the modern world of technology. Businesses boom thanks to the advertising on websites and multimedia outlets. Young people are hooked on social media websites and the world has become totally reliant on modern technology. It has become a world of making everything public from mundane daily routines to quintessentially private affairs of the home and the bedroom.

With Donald Trump again complaining that social media companies are silencing millions of people, what can be said of a world of freedoms being threatened.

Modern technology has revolutionised social life, work life and family life and the world is now in a place. One of the biggest problems affects the family as a unit. Families are no longer conversing as before as young people are sitting for hours on social media and some are becoming addicted to the internet. Gone are the days of family games and conversation around the dinner table as the phone is almost as important as the forks and knives. Gone are the days of playing outdoor games as gadgets have taken the place of direct social interaction. The internet is vast in its appeal and has won the hearts and minds of young people everywhere. Many are likely to even change their minds on issues because of social media. With this huge g

The advantages of modern media are vast from...... to ...... However one has to look at the problems caused by recording everything and leaving privacy as an ancient treasure. With everything and anything available on the internet how can the western cultural thinker slow down the rampant surge in nothing private. The pace of change is accelerating and the

How can the world slow down or is there any slowing down to the rampant social media charge? How can young people find love in relationships at home rather than over the internet? How can the world slow down the pace of the social media charge? Should there be more open forums where young people can share their frustrations with other young people or should there be more places where how to love when social media fails? Do we need a moral transformation of society that takes young people back to traditional standards of morality?

Chapter 59

ETHICAL ISSUES

The ethical issues which affect the western cultural thinker are huge with large sections of society believing that ethics and morality belong in the religious department rather than in the mainstream. With society in a dystopian state at present how can ethics be established when all morals have broken down. There is the issue of whether the government should be taking the moral high ground and insisting that teachers do the parenting role by teaching sexual education and other personal social and spiritual issues. However, one may argue if parents are not in a position to do the deed who is going to do it. Many teachers protest about having to do the parental role but the government finds ways of implementing change after change. The changes are evident in every segment of society and one area worth discussing in a bit more depth is the field of fashion.

Fashion

In the context of fashion there are issues caused by exclusivity and inequality which are endemic in a capitalist society. Only some people can afford to buy certain fashions so they are exclusive as only a select few can afford to buy the particular lines. Glamour and a degree of status is added to those who can.

To secure this exclusivity many fashion houses have to manufacture these goods in developing countries where young children are often exploited in child labour . This practice known as sweat shop labour helps to highlight the problem of living in an unfair world where the world is operating with an unfair system.

The fashion industry also raises issues of standards of beauty and whether or not it is ethical to have thin models when that is not the norm for most women. Most women do not meet the standards of beauty laid out by the fashion industry and holding up a standard for the select few at the top is grossly unfair on women . This causes additional problems of body image issues notably eating disorders as women are trying to look as thin as the models in the fashion industry. Women where many women are faced with low self esteem and has led to many eating disorders. The question of ethics is truly pertinent here.

Another related field of fashion and ethics has to be problems with the fur trade where real animal fur is used within the industry and many complain about the unfair treatment of animals. The fur trade like many other trades are based on exploitation of some sort either on the part of the developing countries or the developed countries. Then there is the issue of the rights of animals where activists have long fought against the use of fur in the industry.

Advertising also persuades people to buy things that are not necessities and the issue of ethics comes to play here with respect to fashion as people are encouraged to consume as much as possible. The new line of clothing is always preferable to the previous one and one is forever searching for the latest fashion. The latter is almost always advertised as more desirable than the previous fashion line. The connection between advertising and ethics of the fashion industry cannot be divorced.

301

The questions then become how does the western cultural thinker address the unethical behaviours connected to the fashion industry? How can ethical issues be considered without looking at moral ethics? How can the fashion industry right the wrongs of an intrinsically unfair system that operates it? Should the industry have its own regulators or should there be an independent body to hold it accountable for unethical practice ?

Black cultural perspective

The issue of ethics and culture stems from the fact that we are living in an unfair system with people at the top of the fashion world imposing various standards on the e rest of the population. When only a few thin models exist and that select group usually being western thinkers there needs to be a rethink on issues of fairness and equality for our women. Let's face it most of our women are not tall and getting into the supermodel world is an uphill struggle. Being of the elite few of models it is hard to see how this could have been allowed to affect so many young women who are excluded from this elite group of supermodels. The question as to whether it is ethical to virtually discriminate on the basis of size is part of the system that exists within society. The system favours the select few over the majority, the system pays the select few in stead of the majority. In the world of fashion ethical issues like these exists and one has to be ready to accept the consequences of capitalist society that breeds inequality and unfairness.

If models and consumers are being treated unfairly then fashion executives have an ethical responsibility to change the situation. Unfair treatment or exploitation cannot be allowed to foster poor standards of ethics in the industry. In terms of cultural exploitation by those who purposely exclude the majority in the fashion world by having clothing that is exclusive for the select minority. These exclusive goods are expensive and price out the majority of our consumers who simply cannot afford to be part of the group at the top.

Body image issues are also causing poor self esteem for many who try to become as thin as some of the models on the runway. The extreme thinness of many models can be blamed for many eating disorders and poor body image. If being thin is condoned by the fashion industry then there are issues as to whether other young girls are being influenced negatively by the media images of models. If the fashion industry is there to set a standard of modelling beauty then there needs to be responsible standards that are set for the majority to follow. The problem here is the same as the problem with the infrastructure of capitalism that the elite few set standards for the majority and the majority are trying to emulate the elite.

Eating disorders have plagued the industry and many insist that the industry cannot be saved from itself. For the black cultural thinker eating disorders of this kind are not really widespread because our women tend to be slimly challenged and not afraid to eat so eating disorders of this kind do not really affect our women on a large scale.

Other issues with the fashion industry and ethics include the inclusion of women of colour on the catwalks. It was once said that the fashion world was not made with us in mind model clothes do not usually cater for the black woman's body but there has been much talk about the industry doing lines of clothing for the larger woman. The issues then become how can the fashion industry address the questions that linger in the mind about the influence of eating disorders on communities and individuals? How can the industry right the wrongs of women having negative body images issues? How can the industry have faith in itself to right the wrongs of the past?

Chapter 60

BRAND NEW ETHICAL ISSUES MILLIGRAM AND OBEDIENCE

The question of milligram and ethics is one of obedience to authority figures where there are many people in society who are doing what they are told rather than what they really want to do. In many western societies people don't have the resources to resist authority because they simply have to submit to the authority figure rather than do what they really want to do. The curious paradox that people are born free yet everywhere there has to be a submission to authority rings true here as there are authority figures in government, in churches, in police, in schools, in forces in the media and in other places of authority rings true as people have no choice but to submit to figures of authority in every arena. There needs to be a real change of attitude to authority by both the figures of authority and those in submission. The submission to authority must be in accordance with certain laws and principles of society otherwise there will be no order in society as a whole.

Obedience in the home is one of the main areas of the home where the bedrock of society is formed. Children are encouraged to obey their parents and accept what they are told to do. Many young people protest and feel that they have their own mind and that they have their choice and direction in life so that they can choose their own path. Others say that sometimes parents encourage children to do the wrong things and obedience to parents should not be absolute.

Parents insist that if there is no discipline then children have no upbringing and no guidance. If parents are not strict or insistent with their children then there will definitely be anarchy.

Obedience to authority also extends to education and school where many young people are being excluded from school and sent to special units. What tends to happen after exclusion is that boys especially resort to crime and other activities as they have no hope or purpose in life. Many resort to gangs and other things out of boredom and a sense of worthlessness. Obedience to police when being arrested is problematic as there is consistently no respect for authority.

The questions then become how can capitalist society get children to obey their parents when there is simply a breakdown in obedience on a massive scale. What can the western cultural thinker do when all morality has broken down? Should there be a moral transformation of society where there is a focus on values that teach young people how to obey authority figures.

Black cultural perspective

The question of obedience to authority is one which dates back to the history of slavery and colonisation where our ancestors had to be obedient to their masters and where there was a culture of domination. Fast forward to the present and there is still a clear distrust of authority especially amongst our young brothers who feel that they are victimised by the system. This dates back to the whole history of the capitalist society in which we live where those at the top dominate those at the bottom where there is a clear divide between the powerful and the powerless. The rich and the poor have a special relationship of dominated and dominant, where those at the bottom have to be obedient to those at the top. The thinking that all are equal but some are more equal than others rings true here, Being obedient to our former masters is problematic for many of the oppressed people but we must fight on and seek justice for all. The issue of being obedient to authority will always be problematic for us because of our position in society and capitalist thinking insists that some must be in submission to others while others insist that there should be a rejection of the whole system that perpetuates the obedience to authority.

The obedience to authority is one of the issues in the novel Of Mice and Men written by John Steinbeck. Candy and Crooks had to obey the authority of the boss and so too did George and Lennie. Obedience to authority is something that has happened throughout the history of mankind and continues to happen today. The rules and laws have been made to ensure that society conforms and anyone who steps out of line with authority will receive their due punishment. If we trace obedience to the legacy of slavery and colonisation we will find that our people tried to reject the authority of the masters and met with force of the oppressors. Those who tried to resist must have been beaten to a pulp or killed but they still fought hard to resist all forms of oppression. If we fast forward to the present many still distrust the authority figures and only obey just to survive in modern society. Capitalist society still operates on the same principles of the past and there needs to be a concerted effort to change our thinking about obedience of this kind. If there are no rules and laws in society there will be anarchy and the world will be characterised by chaos.

The questions then become: How can we survive in today's society without some form of conformity to authority? How can we forgive the origins of the laws which led to obedience to authority? How can we lose the legacy of the past without considering the present and the future? Do we forgive the past and have strength for the present and the future or do we live in the past and not be prepared to face the future with confidence? Where do we go from here?

Chapter 61

CELEBRITY AS ROLE MODELS

Celebrity culture is more prevalent in today's society than in generations past. Social media has helped to popularise this obsession with those who have the power and the means to influence young minds. Idolising celebrities dates back to the period when most revolutions happened, the good old sixties and from then on modern reality shows and new forms of entertainment heralded the rise of the celebrity culture. America sees the widespread effects of this phenomenal popularity but like other craves, celebrity rises and falls.

Many celebrities from the jungle to the football pitch from the board room to car racing are hailed as heroes but the pressure to live a standard of morality is really high on the list of expectations. Many celebrities are willing to be heroes but the expectation to be moral leaders is sometimes too great. Celebrities are not Christ and should not shoulder the moral responsibility to give guidance to the younger generation yet Western cultural thinkers are virtually worshipping their celebrities as gods. How can the western cultural thinkers realise that celebrities are only different to the majority through their purses?

Should celebrities really be involved in setting example to the rest of the world or should they concentrate on morally leading themselves? Should celebrities get involved in political issues to show the younger generation that it is good to get involved in issues that matter? Should the western cultural thinker concede that all morality comes from dare it be written the original source? How can western society solve the problems of celebrity culture without conceding that one is born free yet every area of life one is chained to the thinking that celebrities are the way, the truth and the life? How are celebrities going to show examples of love to the younger generation when many of them will never ever ever get back together with their partners?

Black cultural perspective

Problems are created within the black community as many of our young people are seeing our celebrities as role models. This new trend of idolising black celebrities can be traced back to a decline in black leadership post Martin Luther King era. Nowadays, because media technology has made celebrity influence a 24/7 reality, our young people are using celebrity entertainers to fill that void. The problem is all black celebrities in sports, music or television are not positive role models nor should they be expected to shoulder that responsibility. Our black entertainers are burdened with the task of morally leading our young people.

It is true that celebrities, by being in the public eye may be motivated and inspired to be good role models even if they are not naturally inclined to be. In fairness, many black celebrities have tried to respond to the pressure to give back to the community in this way. However, they are human beings like all of us and should be allowed to learn from their mistakes.

This 21st century reality is a world we don't want to face but we have to. Our children are being influenced more by facebook, television, you tube and music than by parents. The parental role is slowly being overtaken by the media role and it is therefore important that celebrity role models help in the fight for hearts and minds of young people. Yes, whether we like it or not, celebrities are slowly and inadvertently taking over, leaving the role of parents almost null and void. Competing against such media influences that have grown in strength and appeal is an uphill struggle for parents. The popularity of the media is climbing with effortless ease leaving poor parents battling a fierce and futile fight. Positive role models are scarce. Black parents and the community at large are slowly losing this war but we must fight on.

The question remains should black celebrity figures use their celebrity status to promote positive values and to support black activism? Advocates of this role modelling belief insist that it is all about what celebrities can do while in the spotlight: it is about what they can do professionally for the fight for young minds. However, some argue that this trend to look up to celebrities is counter- productive as young people identify with the celebrity rather than focus on examining the issues that are being promoted. We have to refrain from promoting celebrity over their causes.

Celebrities might not be able to champion the cause for which we fight in terms of articulation but they can use their status to help support those who wish to voice concerns for the good of our people. However, one should encourage caution because celebrities are celebrities because of mainstream support and therefore need to tread very carefully when the ground on which they tread is the colour of snow. The questions still persist concerning whether or not celebrities are in a position to set good examples for the younger generation. Do celebrities need to concentrate on giving donations to causes rather than championing the causes themselves? Should celebrities leave the moral guidance to the traditional bodies rather than act as role models? Should celebrities simply support causes rather than get involved in activism? Should celebrities encourage fans to get active in movements to which they subscribe?

Chapter 62

MUSIC AND SEXUALISATION

Music is known as instrumental sounds combined in such a way as to produce beauty of form is characteristic of every single culture; it may be classical, country, pop, rock, urban and love. Many look back on the era of the 60s while others hail the 80s as the decade of the best love songs but the younger generation will have much to say about that with their modern day singers blast out in many tunes. It may be argued that music transcends culture and as Shakespeare writes it is the food of love with different tastes reflected by age, sex and class; this food feeds millions around the world. Like many other cravings, the younger generation salivate for this food the most savouring their favourite tunes loudly and proudly. Nowadays, it is more about the taste rather than how healthy or unhealthy it is. Put less figuratively, it is all about one's personal preferences than about what was conventionally applauded as good music lyrically. Feel free to google the changes that have happened to music over the generations.

Many claim the 60s were the golden age of music, while others hail the 80s as the best period in the history of music, millennials may have a different point of view but all in all music changes from generation to generation but is enjoyed by all. There are boy bands and girls aloud singing to the rhythms of music. DJs are told not to stop the music as young people rock to the beat. Music makes the people come together. Music sooths. Music relaxes the mind. Music is used to put babies to sleep. Music matters to all generations.

There is a huge music industry as a result of popular demand and mega bucks to be made from the music business. The problem with the music industry is that it has been taken over by fat cat music moguls and companies that have rendered the industry corrupt to the core. The values of the industry of money, power and greed are part of the infrastructure of a capitalist society where there is the dog eat dog mentality prevalent in the industry. Money matters more than the artists, more than the art and more than the acts. Sex sells and no matter how degrading the videos are to women, it does not seem to matter. It seems the more vulgar or extreme the outfit or the act the better for the video and the stars are rising to the challenge as music videos are becoming more and more sexual. The lyrics of some of the songs aimed at the younger generation leave much to be desired but DJs are told not to stop the music. Morality does not matter in these music videos as the more sexually explicit and the more raunchy the better nowadays.

Should the western cultural thinker acknowledge the source of the original contributors of music? Should the money that is made from the big corporations be redistributed to the workers or charities? Should music producers consider making videos less sexual? Should music that degrades women be boycotted? Should the western cultural thinker promote music that edifies society rather than focus on music that has no moral content? Should music producers do more to help in political, social and spiritual education of the masses? Should celebrities in the music industry unite to promote the truth about the fusion of music in cultures?

Black cultural perspective

For us we have had a long history of music and culture which dates back to the legacy of slavery where the slaves used to sing spiritual songs to heal the soul and to entertain the slave masters. Music has been used ever since as a political, educational and entertainment platform to showcase the talents of our people and is still an intricate part of our culture in Africa and the diaspora. If we trace the history of music, we will see that our people have made a huge contribution from drum playing to negro spirituals to rhythms and blues, to gospel to calypso, reggae, rap, hip hop and to urban sounds. Music is definitely in our souls.

One of the most popular genres of music is hip hop and this has been an international cultural phenomenon. If we look at the heart of hip hop more than the mainstream portrayal of hip hop we will find that the purpose and function of this art form was to edify, uplift and educate young people and give a voice to the voiceless. It seems like the soul of hip hop has been hijacked by the big music companies and now it has lost its former self.

The present problem with hip hop is its increased sexualisation and the images associated with it. Hip hop has virtually become porn with clothes on. Created in the 1970s to showcase rapping, D Jing, breaking and other elements of the reality of life in the ghetto, it has now turned into a global movement that has lost control of its purpose, its positivity and its phenomenal self. Hip hop is now struggling to showcase the music, the business, the fashion, the style, the morality without negativity attached. It has lost the platform it once provided to black youth without a voice of expression; it has also lost those elements of the black underclass culture that once appealed to the mainstream. In the 70s, it emerged as a cultural force that influenced everything from attitude to style, from fashion to Sports advertising, from church activities to mass media. But now, the portrayal of glamorised ghetto culture, perceived as black culture, has left far reaching effects on our community. It has become porn with clothes on. Hip hop that was once regarded as a capitalist tool has now be come a capitalist weapon that is massively destroying our community.

The hip hop culture has been perceived as a culture that maintains values of street culture, materialism, sexual misbehaviour, brand consciousness, a spirit of rebellion, gun iconography (American) and acceptance of ignorance as a lifestyle. Originally it was a capitalist tool: it sold immorality, it sold reckless promiscuity, it sold degrading stereotypes – it sold misogyny all as creative commodities. Now it has become a weapon destroying marriage, obliterating education and gunning down legality.

Black communities are deeply affected by hip hop as it has led to a number of interrelated problems: drugs, promiscuity, incarceration, sport, hustling and above all language and education. In Nelson George's words, `where young African-Americans step into an arena to verbally, emotionally, physically bash each other for the pleasure of predominantly white spectators worldwide To extend his metaphor, black people step in and out of the arena, proudly parading negative stereotypes, glamorising immorality and showcasing vulgarity under the banners of creativity, originality and cutting edge.

The questions then become how can we reverse the negative stereotypes associated with the image of hip hop? How can we elevate the music without the negativity that is almost an intricate part of it?

Should we insist that artists tone down the way in which dances are portrayed for the younger generation? Should we teach our children that the values of hip hop and the values of the slave masters have a strong negative correlation?

The values of hip hop and the values and motives of the slave masters have a strong negative correlation. The behaviours of slaves and those of their masters cannot be divorced.

Chapter 63

THE POLITICS OF ENTERTAINMENT

Hip-hop culture portrays that money equals power.

Entertainment- singing- dancing-drama-social media- television-soap operas-sport- music- readin g- writing

Everybody needs to be entertained and all the experts and all writers recommend it. All work and no play makes Jack a dull boy. Psychologists like Freud insist that we are here to work and to play and many psychologists study children's play patterns to look at early entertainment and human interaction. There is art therapy that studies children's play and there are also studies of socialisation that examines the ways in which we can enjoy ourselves and relax the brain. Some find relaxation watching television all day others find relaxation reading books and the younger generation find entertainment on social media so much so that the traditional modes of entertainment have lost their ideological core. All forms of entertainment are on television nowadays as whatever one's interest one can just turn to the particular channel to watch whatever they want. The ability to laugh and have fun is a basic human necessity and one must find something or someone to make them laugh. Some people find pleasure in different things like watching themselves on social media and sending images of the self to see how many likes. Others find pleasure simply laughing and talking with friends and family. Others find entertainment in simply reading or writing books. The truth of the matter is that one has to find a love of something or someone to keep them going from day to day. Life's journey would be very dull if there is no kind of enjoyment or something or somebody to love.

The problem with the entertainment industry in the western world is that it is dominated by the ideologies of those in power who try to impose standards of the lives of the rich and famous on the masses so that the masses are forever trying to aspire to be famous aspire to be like someone else and aspire to have more and more money. The more one has the more one desires so there is a relentless pursuit of capital which has led to many diseases such as depression and anxiety. Trying to be like the rich and famous rather than loving the individual self, and loving others can be a very dangerous path. How does the western cultural thinker find their own individual entertainment without thinking about celebrity lifestyles? How can one find a different kind of enjoyment that teaches how to love the individual and the collective? Should one just find peace and contentment in the original source of peace?

Black cultural perspective

As a collective our culture has revolved around finding entertainment in music, and dance storytelling and the like and this can be traced back to the legacy of slavery. Musically, our sounds have evolved from drum rhythms that accompanied African folk songs to gospel, to the blues, urban jazz, soul, disco, street funk, pop, hip hop to urban music. Soul still shines over the expression of black music. We have been singing in church worship, we have been singing to entertain ourselves and others over the years. The angelic voices of Diana Ross, Michael Jackson, Whitney Houston and many others came from the singing in the church choirs but the soul of our culture must be changed from singing to thinking about what we sing. There must be a strategic shift to intellectualise more and use songs as social commentary as many reggae and calypsonians do. We have to explore the art of thinking about the lyrics, the rhyme and the dance - what we sing and what we do when we sing.

Twerking, working up, jamming, gyrating can be done in an artistic way rather than in a vulgar way. Many will admit that some elements of dance hall or shacking out or butterfly are extremely vulgar. Have you ever attended a Caribbean carnival event (Calypso or Queen show) staged in the Caribbean? If you have, you will know that the more vulgar the act, the more audience applause one receives. The jamming in the streets is meant to be a cultural event but those who take it to its vulgar extreme turn it into street synthesis of the sex act. It becomes porn with clothes on!

Chapter 64

CREATIVITY IN ENTERTAINMENT

Entertainment is a form of activity that holds the attention and interest of an audience or gives pleasure and delight. It can be an idea or task but it is more likely to be one of the activities or events that have developed over thousands of years specifically for the purpose of keeping an audience's attention. People are doing all kinds of activities to be entertained and hoping to find peace and happiness in what they do. Some find pleasure in reading, others find pleasure in writing. Some find pleasure in singing and dancing. Some find pleasure in simply watching television or pleasure on the internet. Human beings are forever searching for pleasure and have been searching for pleasure since the beginning of time.

The younger generation are all searching for happiness and each generation seeks enjoyment in different places to the same places that their parents did when they were young. Now with the advent of social media, entertainment has been revolutionised but problems of a different kind persist with the entertainment of social media. Nowadays with entertainment on the go, how can social media be used to teach love and not hatred? How can there be creativity in entertainment that is innovative and inspiring?

In the west, all entertainment is celebrity driven and the western cultural thinker is cultivating a system that only the top percentage of society can realistically achieve. If happiness is found in studying what the celebrities have done or what has been done in the past how can society move forward and study a different form of education and entertainment? Should society study a form of entertainment for elevation, for entrepreneurship and for education?

Entertainment can be in many forms what everyone craves after working hard during the day or at weekends. The ability to unwind after working hard is what everyone tries to do to occupy themselves. Hollywood and the entertainment industry have worked arduously on trying to create pleasure for people in this materialistic world and now the entertainment industry makes billions. Everyone wants to operate on the pleasure principle of living and having fun.

What if the western cultural thinker focuses on entertainment of a different kind that teaches how to love the self, the community and the world? How can the younger generation learn to love when the entertainment industry is no longer to a large extent teaching this core value? Do we need to focus on entertainment of a different kind that uplifts society rather than denigrates it? What if we had entertainment that left the younger generation feeling high on morality or high on love? What if there was a focus on learning to love community and self rather than the focusing exclusively on loving the self? What if we had entertainment that focused on the mind, soul and body?

Black cultural perspective

Entertainment for us as a collective has always been singing and dancing with storytelling. We are known to love enjoyment and pleasure as we keep saying to each other not to worry but be happy. Our songs of redemption and belief have always been in our hearts and souls as first world people. This can be traced back even before the legacy of slavery as we brought our rhythms and drums from our African ancestors. Music was and is definitely in the soul of our people individually, collectively and globally. Our women have beautiful curves for the display of beautiful dance routines and our men know how to enjoy themselves in music and dance. With music also being used as a platform for social commentary, we know how to entertain ourselves well and carnival or street partying is evidence of this.

Social media has also helped to entertain our young people these days but we have to look closely at how our young people are being entertained. Putting everything on social media leaves nothing as private or sacred any more. Our young people need to explore different ways to be creative in the use of social media to promote positive well being in the community and in the wider world. We need to motivate each other about positive entertainment that could challenge our thinking about our past, our present and our future. We need to be creative in what we do to bring out the best in everyone. Our young minds need to be challenged everyday with new ways of thinking and capitalising on their intelligence. What if we have our young people create entrepreneurial ideas for creative new ways of keeping themselves occupied? Instead of regurgitating old ways of entertainment that have been dated, what if our young people be creative in thinking about ideas to improve or change entertainment to make it appeal to other young people? What if we think of ways to make dull topics in education more interesting and appealing to young people? What if we change the way we think about entertainment in our society and the community at large? What if people think of interesting ways to tell our history so that it is entertaining and educational at the same time?

It is long overdue that we regain our cultural resistance, identity, and mediums, in order to serve our struggle for human rights, liberty, and social justice. It is time we gathered all of our "drums" (and voices), to begin the necessary process of mentally liberating as many of our brothers and sisters from the corporate media plantations on which they subsist. Hip Hop is not for oppressors. We should never allow it to be utilized against our own collective interests. However, we cannot free those who are willing to be liberated if we refuse to speak out. We must boycott any music that denigrates people of color, women or supports senseless structural violence. We must be willing to organize and educate as many misguided rappers as we can – converting them into Emcees aptly educated to deliver lyrical daggers at systems of oppression. Hip Hop must be ripped out of the hands of the Ku Klux Klan music groups, and placed back in the hands of the people.

Let the spirit of our ancestors guide us. Forward Ever, Backward Never.

Education essentially enables students to study and plan for their future. It is like an investment of time, of money, of commitment and of hard work which operates on the principle of deferred gratification. Rather than being driven by short term thinking, investors have the discipline of this long term thinking and forward life planning. Hip hop rejects this and instead presents our young people with a short term, quick money YOLO mentality. It teaches our youth to have one plan: get rich quick or die trying. Enjoy today. Forget tomorrow. Have fun.

In order to save our young people and change this mentality, we have to tackle these overt and covert messages conveyed by hip hop.

Anti-intellectualism as a mindset must be changed as it destroys the potential in our boys. Girls too.

Yes, mainstream education excludes us. Yes, you have to alter your identity in order to survive. Yes, it is frustrating. Yes, conformity is met with chants of 'coconut' or 'sell out'. However, black underachievement cannot continue at the rate it is. Getting into the mainstream for blacks is a hard knock life but you have to be tough, be smart and be strong. We cannot blatantly defy the mainstream and then expect the mainstream to embrace us.

Chapter 65

IDEOLOGY AND ENTERTAINMENT

Music and Sport

The ideology of power and control is no where more dominant than in the area of music and entertainment which thrives on the values of the powerful over the powerless. The entertainment industry has thrived on the infrastructure of the capitalist system and the music moguls have taken the driving seat in all aspects of this form of entertainment. Those with power in the industry manoeuvre the masses and those beneath them into buying into certain ideas and thinking about music and entertainment. The idea that sex sells is one of those perpetuated by the industry. Women in the industry are forever trying to conform to a certain image, a certain beauty ideal and a certain way of performing that has almost become the norm in music videos. The raunchier the act the more it seems to sell. The less clothes females are allowed to get away with in these videos the more one seems to applaud the act but that is not the whole story as real life for these music artists seem to imitate the art. The pressure on them to conform to these standards see them resort to all kinds of addictions in their quest to cope with the pressures being placed upon them. Their lives even seem to be more and more unhappy as they try to cope with the more money they accumulate.

The problem is that the younger generation especially are looking up to these celebrities in entertainment and want to emulate what their favourite artist does. With the celebrities feeling the dual pressure of great expectations to be role models and to climb the capitalist ladder to success they are often left struggling with the conflict within the self. The ideology of the entertainment industry rests on the same assumptions as that of the capitalist ideology with everything being about money and power. The thinking that money makes entertainers happy has proven to be fundamentally flawed as many are resorting to all kinds of addictions to numb the pain and prove that they are still searching for something that the entertainment industry cannot provide. What is left is a moral void that needs to be filled and with so many thinkers having nothing to believe in but themselves, society is left with the challenge of finding a different ideology that gives the younger generation a future to believe in.

Should the western cultural thinker devise an ideology that does not pressure its entertainers to be role models? Should entertainers focus on their particular art and keep their private lives private? What if entertainers focused on doing acts that proved love for themselves, the community and the world? Should entertainers refrain from or embrace social activism?

Black cultural perspective

Entertainment on a global scale for the black community has focused almost exclusively on the hip hop phenomenon. Hip hop implicitly states that respect is gained by the accumulation of quick money and the evidence of this must be shown through appearance and possessions. What the brother wears must be designer, big and branded with bling on the finger, on the chest –everywhere. They must also have arm candy who develops a likeness for particular lollipops. Don't forget the arm candy is expected to be a lady in the street, though not necessarily from the street and of course the candy must be too delicious for the brothers who are preoccupied with the candy shaped by the boot while the candy is focused being bought with the loot. Get me? This thinking is the root of many of problems especially when it plants seeds of baby fatherhood and baby motherhood. If the starting point for a relationship is based on the look good feel good factor, we are heading for the cultural disaster factor.

Seriously, there are other negatives associated with only wanting the brothers for what they have and how they look. The pressure on our brothers to live up to this bad boy, bling bling, braddagocio image is causing related problems of drug addiction, hustling, criminality and failure to invest in jobs that require long term commitment. It is also denying the discipline needed to endure in long term relationships. Short term thinking that pressures our brothers to get money quick is a blood disease circulating in the body of problems that plague our community.

Worthiness for sexual unions should not be made on the basis of bling or materialism or for giving of a favour. Cases have been cited where young girls are having sex for a telephone top up. The original sin is definitely the desperate situation that many brothers and sisters find themselves in. Yes, cynics may argue that it happens in other communities through legal marriage where unions are made as a financial merger. To those who argue along these lines, there is long term commitment and upbringing of children involved so such a comparison must not lose sight of that fact.

Our brothers and sisters must rise above the negative image of hip hop and opt for a new way of thinking about our brothers and our culture. We should live for the present as well as the future. We should have long term plans in mind especially when we are thinking about the children. We cannot continue to feed into the stereotypes that have hindered our progress over the years. We must be prepared to fight for our community to get better educated through entertainment rather than let the entertainment have no particular value.

The questions then become how do we have entertainment for elevation of our people? Do we boycott musicians and artists who have misogynous and degrading lyrics? Do we insist on artists cleaning up their acts and appeal to the inner person instead? Do we focus on education, entertainment and entrepreneurship for our community to move forward?

We have to get educated or be prepared to die trying.

Chapter 66

GENDER AND ENTERTAINMENT

Hip hop cannot escape the charge of its sexualisation of our girls, its negative depiction of women and the unhealthy sexual lifestyles it promotes. Black Entertainment television plays 15 hours of music per day, Caribbean stations play calypso and other forms of music virtually 24/7. The constant bombardment of this negative sexual imagery is affecting the functioning of our young black girls. If we endorse a form of entertainment that promotes us as `hoes and bitches', depicts us as sexual objects and exploits us through misogynous lyrics then we are part of the problem.

Our attitudes to brothers with bling must be changed. We cannot let the brothers feel that we can be seduced by such symbols of success. Instead we must favour faithfulness over frolicking, brains over bling and commitment to cultural causes over criminality. We can no longer let our young girls be attracted to the bad boy with bling. We must not ask if boys could pay the bills but rather do you have the skills to help US pay the bills. We must refrain from getting with the brothers for what we can get but rather for stability and security in a relationship. We should learn to love the brothers with or without the material goods.

Sisters must be smart and we must not allow ourselves to be sexual objects. Gone should be the days when we are simply gyrating or synthesising the sex act in cultural events and for the purpose of entertainment. There could be dancing that is not vulgar and tasteless.

We should conduct ourselves like the African queens that we are and do everything in good taste. Gone should be the days of the dancing that was done during slavery for the entertainment of our masters but instead we should opt for dancing that showcases talent rather than dancing that showcases vulgarity. Our entertainment should be going forward rather than backward. How do we right the wrongs of the past? How do we focus on loving ourselves as individuals and as a community? Should we have entertainment that celebrates as well as educates? Should we have brothers respecting the sisters and sisters respecting ourselves? Should we lose the legacy of slavery that is holding us back from going forward?

Chapter 67

MUSIC AND LANGUAGE

Music has always been known for rhythms and beats and the sounds of the drums in certain cultures. It has been known for the musical arrangements but also for the messages, lyrics and words associated with it. With specific reference to hip hop and rap where the message, words and images are all fused together certain images are conjured up in the mind of the listener. Undoubtedly some artists have positive messages in their music while other artists have negative messages in their music. What is interesting to note is that the negative images of the numerous artists appeal to younger generation who are growing up in a world that has lost its moral navigation system and as a result most of them have lost their way. Love songs are no longer what they used to be and many have opted to listen to music that degrades, devalues and denigrates women. Music with positive messages are definitely on the decline.

Many artists argue that they produce what popular culture want to consume and if there is no longer a market for positive music then they have to go with the flow. The flow is dictated by the big music moguls and the artists are simply doing what they are told. Some rap songs use all kinds of metaphors that simply glorify wrongdoing and vulgarity. Words have power and can hurt. Words have strong connotations and the choice of words can cause all kinds of emotional problems. Rapping about drugs, misogyny and violence tend to go with the territory but the question is where do rappers go from here? Do they continue to influence young hearts and minds negatively or should the community insist that they clean up their acts? Should young people be encouraged to boycott the music that is hindering positive attitudes to life and long term commitment where the family is put first? Are young people going to learn morality from these rappers or should they take guidance from the original source of morality?

Chapter 68

CULTURAL ENTERTAINMENT EVENTS

Cultural festivals and vulgarity

<u>Move to hip hop section</u> -Dotun Adebayo (Voice columnist and Black radio talk show host)

Carnival is a festival that takes place in many parts of the world and is viewed as the only emancipation from slavery and this has long been the celebration of our freedom from physical enslavement. This was a cruel, vile and evil act of human history but we survived. Slavery was definitely a crime against humanity. Slavery was a holocaust. Slavery was undeniably an evil act. For generations we have celebrated our physical emancipation from slavery by singing and dancing in the streets but is it time to change the way we celebrate. We are not worrying about life now but just being grateful for our emancipation in the past. We have been freed from physical slavery but fast forward to the present is it time to free our minds of mental slavery? Does carnival make us believe that we should only celebrate what happened in the distant past? Is it time for us to think of a way of improving for the future? Is it time we celebrate heroes of the present in carnival and minimise on the excessive gyrating in the streets? Should we have troupes of modern entrepreneurs or troupes of civil rights activists past and present parading the streets giving messages of hope for our youth? Should carnival lose the skimpy costumes and opt for an array of our cultural traditional dress and have messages for our young people rather than simply singing and dancing? Should there be talks about looking towards the future rather than being stuck in the traditions of the past? Should there be a real education of the positive aspects of our people the mental resilience in the face of all odds? Should carnival be elevated to include educational elements like our true African history? Should we also include black heroes of the struggle against oppression? Or should we have a festival of ideas on how to move our culture forward by engaging our young people especially our young black boys.

According to Dotun Adebayo, columnist from the Voice UK `What good has carnival ever done for us? - We are the `talent' – We are the entertainers, We are the purveyors of the culture – We are the minstrels. Carnival has given us a bad name – we continue to be the happy, clappy, gyrating mass of flesh and sweat in colourful costumes.' Questions the condescending view of black people – we like to party- loudly and to the excess. According to Adebayo, carnival conditions the mind of employers that black people are not serious - If there were rival expressions of black culture and black people it would not be such a big deal. But carnival is the only one that ever makes it into prime time and to be frank it's not a good look.

In order to elevate this form of cultural entertainment we need to focus more on black inspirational achievement – Political troupes, School Troupes, Music troupes, Drama and the Arts, Food troupes, Celebrity Troupes etc. We also need to make celebrations a family event so that the vulgarity that is part and parcel of the carnival should be considerably reduced so that families feel comfortable taking the whole family to the event. Is it time to find an entirely different expression of black culture? Is it time to find ways to celebrate present achievements rather than focus on the emancipation of the past? Should we extrapolate from other cultural festivals and move our celebrations forward? Should we really consider something more educational and entertaining at the same time. Should we consider something that will equip our young people with skills for entrepreneurship?

Chapter 69

ENTERTAINMENT AND CRIMINALITY

Entertainment and crime have always been interesting bedfellows engaged together as partners. They have slept together for generations and seem to have a long term relationship. Put more formally, entertainment has always had negative associations with drugs and alcohol addictions with violence and sexual exploitation. No where has this been shown than in the world of hip hop where the charge is that it makes use of lyrics and images which condone aggressive and lawless behaviour. Connected to this is the fact that some artists have been victims or perpetuators of crime. Case in point the dual deaths of Tupac and Biggie both icons that were victims of violent crime. The hip hop culture spreads the message that money equals power and there is the implicit thinking that one ought to get rich quick or die trying. This thinking is prevalent in the world of entertainment and we ought to try to change this mentality. The problem with rap is not really the music but rather the words and images that are woven into them. In the case of rap and hiphop the words and images conjure images of the glorification of criminal behaviour, promiscuity, drugs and images consisting of the most ugly, most degrading black stereotypes. These stereotypes are part of the problem that our people have to cope with on a daily basis because when acts feed into stereotypes they are strengthened in the minds of many onlookers. In America, the Caribbean and the rest of the African diaspora, entertainment and crime are definitely related. Feel free to google for evidence of the correlation between the two.

Glynis Glasgow-Kelly

Every one could remember the poster of 50cent holding a gun and a baby which caused public outrage and fierce criticism from the Advertising Standards Authority. There has always been a connection between hip hop and crime because of the common denominator of believing that money equals power. Many rappers see their art as the only way of getting out of poverty and criminals resort to lawless behaviour out of desperation to get out of their situation. Some may argue that this is oversimplifying the issue but both share the same DNA.

Glamorizing lawlessness through lyrics which condone rather than condemn the use of drugs, guns and gangster lifestyle needs to be re-examined. Yes, hip hop originally aimed to reflect reality of life in the ghetto but that should not be the same as glamorising it through rhyme and rhetoric of criminal exploits. MCs should aim to avoid criminal records rather than relish their criminal credentials. Our young men are throwing their lives away by committing mindless crimes rather than committing to a college career. This problem can be addressed and needs to be addressed.

The key questions then become: is there any truth to the claim that there seems to be some kind of street credibility award to artists who have committed crimes, served sentences and survived shoot outs? Is there a hip hop led culture of criminal solidarity encouraged through the stigmatization of snitching? Does beef between black artists lay the foundation for violent clashes? .

Do hip hop radio stations fuel feuds over the airwaves to boost ratings? Does the hip hop press condone the culture of criminality?

Chapter 70

DRUGS AND ENTERTAINMENT

Drugs and entertainment have a long and interesting history as artists tend to turn to drugs to take them away from reality or rather to create a temporary reality. This has been a practice ever since music became an important aspect of popular culture. Music genres like hip hop have been tied inextricably to drugs. Cocaine is probably the most discussed drug in rap music, if not marijuana and lyrics in many songs show that the genre almost celebrates all things intoxicating in modern society. This love affair with drugs has resulted in many broken individuals, many broken communities and a broken world.

Many insist that the nature of the entertainment industry causes many to seek escape from the reality of life in the public eye, in the full glare of the media and in the full glare of publicity. The pressure on artists in the field of entertainment has been tremendous and many have insisted that it is very difficult to divorce one from the other.

Some of our men have been seen to smoke all day and not have any interest in entrepreneurship or anything meaningful that could benefit the community. There is no meaningful discourse about what to do to provide for our families and so mothers are left with the responsibility to bring up our young boys who are finding role models from the rappers who themselves need some moral direction. Without a holistic education for reparation our boys will continue on the downward spiral of entertainment for instant gratification and no hope for the future. Instead of being entertained by those who are addicted to drugs should young people think of different ways to entertain themselves? Should we encourage our young people to boycott music that promotes the use of drugs in our community? Should our young people be encouraged to think differently about themselves and their future?

Chapter 71

LACK OF POLITICAL VISION

Democracy. Conservativism. Liberalism. Socialism. Human rights. Communism Austerity. Transparency. Political partisanship. Punch and Judy politics – Grievance mongering – Deficit denial – Poverty denial – Economic deprivation – political wasteland

Democracy is the key political concept which promotes equality and human rights for all western cultural thinkers who genuinely believe that this ideal, this rhetoric, this utopian vision will one day reasonably resemble reality. Young people today, being of the exposure generation continue to campaign for this popular reality show but some clever ones call for changes to the system that will give them a future to believe in, a future of fairness and a future of social change. The problem is that democracy as a political concept has lost its appeal even to its key visionaries and now it merely functions as propaganda, as the only western cultural tool or rather weapon in their fight to maintain a free market. For the vast global majority this American dream of success has become a delusionary nightmare akin to the dystopian world it has now created. The bitter irony is that the Orwellian slogan of 'ignorance is strength' rings true here as many people from around the world are fighting desperately to get into these besieged states while those within fight for fortitude. Google the number of failed democracies around the world. Google the problems experts associate with democracy itself.

Google the recommendations that opponents insist need to ensure a fairer democracy.

Many advocates for a change in the system call for more transparency but confidentiality or secrecy is a necessary capitalist asset without which it simply cannot secure success. Transparency is therefore incompatible with capitalism which thrives on dodgy deals, unfair trade, fiddling of figures and masterful manipulation. Put simply, transparency is counter-productive. Yet, many insist on it as a prerequisite for political procedures without having the vision to produce a different regime with new policies and core procedures that would pave a path to a new vision. There needs to be a better way forward that ensures fairness in economic institutions, fairness in the criminal justice system, fairness in religious exposure, fairness in educational, medical and family institutions and above all fairness for all the people of the world. All that is happening is that politicians are preoccupied professionally protecting the established order, the status quo or the value of democracy.

How can democracy change from idealism to realism? How does the western cultural thinker prevent the perception of democracy as being overstated, overrated and outdated? How can liberalist thinkers progress from the legacy of grievance mongering and narcissistic victimhood? How can conservative and republican thinkers begin to see their traditional politics more objectively? How can labour and democratic parties reform socialist thinking without creating a false essence? How can parties like the Greens gain more support for their different standpoints? How can political leaders everywhere restore faith in politics itself? How can the western cultural thinker create an alternative vision without maintaining society's stratified system and the toxic dependence on the ideology which informs it?

Black cultural perspective

The portrayal of our leaders, like the portrayal of our history has served as propaganda to destroy our collective belief in our African ancestral power to create a vision for ourselves that is different to that of the West. Toussaint L'Ouverture, Fidel Castro and President Mugabe have shown that a decolonisation of the mind, in the words of Ngugi Wa Thiongo must precede any major change in policy among the leaders of our nations. In the African diaspora, particularly in America the civil rights movement paved the way for modern movements to fight for an equal society. Sadly, the old vision of protest politics no longer represents a strategic way forward as its original form and intention have both been hijacked by other movements. In fairness, protest politics has led to a change in laws to allow fighters to challenge unfair systems and structures by the opposing camp. However, our fight against structural oppression needs more that sticks and stones of grievances, victimisation and limited resources. Let's not forget that we are fighting against opponents who have nuclear weapons of capitalism, classicism, conservatism, control, platonic ideology and Christianity. In effect, our protest politicians are effectively asking us to fight without arming the troupes, without training the lieutenants and most importantly, without specifying a commander in chief. As a consequence, the war under this old vision has become nothing more than an exercise in futility with our soldiers being more and more frustrated by an unwinnable war strategy.

Veterans like Sharpton, Jesse Jackson, Louis Farrakhan and others are still fighting but sadly the troupes have lost confidence not only in these fighters but also in the fight itself. We are now facing a future with an army of untrained fighters, ill-equipped to form an effective opposition and the problem is the new generation of fighters have selected their own leaders from the world of sport, music and television. There have no strategic vision. They have no moral compass. They have no guide to provide. New generation fighters fly the banner borrowed from their opponents of 'there is no such thing as community only the individual' and these fighters are determined to survive on their own by whatever means possible.

If we look back to the legacy of slavery, the only successful slave revolution happened in Haiti and many forget the enormous sacrifice, wit and strategic planning that led to its success. Today, what we see now in Haiti, is the by-product of decades of sanctions that serve to remind our world of western power and influence. Fighters like president Mugabe, who defy that enormous power structure have to be prepared to cope with the consequences of their defiance. What we need is a new kind of fight with clear political, cultural and moral vision that can resonate with our race no matter which place they may be. A fight for freedom of mind, a fight for freedom from irrelevance and a fight for freedom from seeing ourselves differently to the way we are portrayed. How can we start this huge new visionary movement? Shall we begin with promoting our true history of our people's enormous strength of intellect, spirit and body? Should we insist on an education that presents us as subjects and not as objects? Should we promote our collective cultural consciousness and human spirituality as the missing piece of the puzzle that has led the wider world into dystopia?

Chapter 72

CLASSICISM

Plato. Power. Privilege. Personality. Progress. Practices. Preference. Policing. Prejudice. Politics. Partisanship. Pandering. Nepotism

Social stratification or the class system structures western cultural democratic societies to cultivate feelings of sophistication, maintain power structures and hinder equality. What western cultural thinkers fail to admit is that perpetuating inequality is a necessity in any democratic or capitalist society. All economic, political and western cultural systems demand that there are powerful and powerless people otherwise such societies would not progress. Progress involves moving from one class to another, from one job to another from one milestone to another. Without the concept of otherness, without the dichotomies created, without the urge to be better than someone else, classicism cannot consistently resonate in society.

Classicism begins in the mind and is the brainchild of the Platonic ideology of control. The relentless determination to control the inner horse, the id or the human spirit is transferred to the need to follow principles associated with restraint control of other people, things and other nations in the pursuit of membership of the ruling class. Class then becomes a state of mind in addition to a state of society and a world order. Classicism also transfers to aesthetics and the use of strict forms in literature, painting, architecture and other arts. In literature, there are the canon writers and those who cultivate the cultural heritage view of English teaching; painting, architecture and other arts all operate on the same principles of rationality, restraint and righteousness. People insist on associating themselves with what they perceive to be the upper or upwardly mobile class, usually of the upper rungs and this practice leads to nepotism.

The 'p' in nepotism can refer to a plethora of practices among privileged people in power to protect property of partners, peers and pals by pressuring police to protect them from progressive protesters. People within the professional power structures of politics, education, medicine, law and intelligence merely function as agents of social control and overwhelmingly favour family members and friends in the workplace. Nepotism then functions, like the class system to structure inequality rather than hinder it; it serves to encourage rather that undermine the notion of superiority. It is a key building block for the infrastructure of the capitalist system which thrives on capitalising on the ignorance of those at the lowest rungs of society. The big questions linger for politicians, educationalists, police, lawyers and doctors: How can the western cultural thinker create a system of classlessness in society? How can the mindset of those whose families and friends have been culturally indoctrinated by the belief and practices of their class ever be free from that way of thinking? How can meritocracy become a reality rather than a delusion? How can the oppressed classes ever fight back against the powerful forces above them? Is the American dream that people can rise from rags to riches by dint of hard work and creativity applicable to the individual rather than a strata of society? Is the American dream functioning as propaganda, like the history to which it is confined? Should the western cultural thinker concede that collectivism of some sort is the only way forward?

Black cultural perspective

The class system is one of the structures within societies that hinders equality or encourages the notion of superiority. Within black culture, there seems to be a complete abandonment of the underclass or the lower working class and the failure of those in the black middle class to help them up the rungs of the ladder. As Cornel West puts it `The present day Black middle class is not simply different than its predecessors -- it is more deficient and, to put it strongly, more decadent." This is because the black middle class seems to be more concerned with their professional and personal achievements than with collective, community achievements. This pursuit of individualism over collectivism has created problems for related issues of solidarity and cultural cohesion. Every other culture has a strong middle class that effectively leads the lower classes. Somehow we have used class in the same way that western society uses it: to underscore inequality and underline deep division. Stronger language may be required here to describe the price paid for the individual successes which devalue our collective minds, our collective hearts and our collective body. We know the price of success but not the value of our lower class connections in paving the way to get us where we are.

For those of us in the African diaspora, we have forgotten that we owe our individual successes to our forefathers of the civil rights movement who fought for justice and lost their lives in the struggle for our equality. We owe our success to the resistance of slaves like Toussaint L'Ouverture who led a well-planned and successful slave revolt in Haiti. We owe our success to modern African heroes like Nelson Mandela, Kwame Nkrumah and President Mugabe who fought for our African heritage to be subjective.

The purchase of middle class status must not be seen a Faustian transaction; we do not have to sell our souls, we do not have to sell our collective consciousness and most of all we must sacrifice the present to secure a future for our children and the next generation. Let us work together to build our collective cultural consciousness. How do we begin to fight against classicism that is so prevalent in Africa and the Diaspora? Should we begin with a systematic change in thinking about the definition of class? Should we embrace our African essence of genuine equality? Should we resist the western value system of inherited status and wealth affording class? Should we think of a collectivist system of ensuring classlessness?]

Chapter 73

ORGANISED CRIME

Corruption – money laundering – administrative corruption –whitewashing - white collar crime -Black Gold – Violent crime – Domestic crime – Crimes against humanity

Money laundering is the generic term used to describe the process by which criminals disguise the original ownership and control of the proceeds of criminal conduct by making such proceeds appear to have derived from a legitimate source. Western politicians are the gate keepers of corruption, scams, dishonest schemes that allow industries to rip off the world while they make laws to manipulate the minds of the masses who have been misled, hoaxed and conned into believing the exact opposite. It is a known fact that such criminal activity involves the use of a wide variety of methods to launder money. These methods fall into two key categories: cash-based money laundering - which can involve the physical movement of currency over national borders, as well as the use of companies with high cash throughput as a cover, with payments being broken down into smaller amounts to avoid detection and high-end money laundering – which is specialist, usually involves transactions of substantial value, and involves the abuse of the financial sector and so-called 'professional enablers'. Speaking more euphemistically, politicians operate within this system to ensure that western economies are the best in the world. The more sophisticated the professional enablers, the more successful the economy so on a global scale all western countries are created corrupt but some are more corrupt than others.

The NCA and partner agencies has a proven track record of tackling cash-based laundering, and a good track record of recovering the assets of organised crime but it is understood that there is a need to target high end money laundering. Without mentioning the Panama papers, major frauds, schemes, scams, tricks, policies or rather crime is often electronic and cash is only used further down the laundering process to disguise audit trails or extract profits. The ability of criminals to launder large sums of money themselves without attracting attention is limited. Therefore, criminals need someone professional, capable and trustworthy to make the necessary arrangements. Friends in high places are often called upon by lobbyists to make laws and pass regulations to enable complex processes of criminal activity. Accomplices guarantee anonymity for the offender and ensure that all tracks are well covered. Partners in these cosy cartels meet up for a drink and buy each other rounds. Other professionals working in the field of theft include lawyers, investment bankers and accountants who wittingly and unwittingly flash the cash from their hoists in big properties and other investments.

Petty criminals from the lower classes simply end up in prison while the white-collared workers gang up in the financial institutions with regulators as scared as prison officers to prevent further occurrence of such crimes. Other crimes against humanity such as war, unfair taxation and poverty are dealt with in other Chapters. The big question for the western cultural thinker is who is going to guard the guards, police the police, sue the lawyers, deselect politicians and free the petty prisoners since all morality has broken down? How can the criminals and their accomplices refrain from wallowing in inherited privilege afforded by these dodgy dealing? How can western society be saved from this self-destructing force of criminality, euphemistically referred to as capitalism?

Black cultural perspective

Whitewashing is a metaphor meaning to gloss over or cover up vices, crimes or scandals or to exonerate by means of perfunctory investigation or through biased presentation of data. It is especially used in the context of corporations, governments or other organizations. Our problem is that our identity has been completely whitewashed by our black leaders who, with very few exceptions, seem to forget that when it comes to playing the game of capitalism we need to tackle the player as well as the ball. Our leaders seem to lack the balls to do what needs to be done; as a result we are simply consuming western corruption wholesale and regurgitating it in our black communities worldwide. Black corruption is not a pretty sight even though the Chinese euphemistically call it black gold and Cameron calls it fantastic. Our leaders tend to forget that western corruption is subtle, covered in euphemisms and verbiage with everyone involved signing agreements to keep the deeds in the closet. Our leaders, on the other hand, present it raw, uncovered as if we are on a nudist beach. Our leaders, in Africa, the Caribbean and the diaspora tend to forget the main rule of the game: Cover up the corruption! Whitewash it! Launder it! Hide it! Instead, our leaders are blatantly naked and this graphic exposure of the deeds, that were intended for the closet, are glorified in full view of the stunned poor, who are left standing with their begging bowls. Seriously, we do not need to see what was done in private to secure and maintain power but we do need to see some traces of moral integrity from our leaders.

Google the most corrupt African and Caribbean countries to prove or disprove this charge. Google what is done to cover up corruption.

Corruption is a billion pound industry in many of our countries, benefitting the political class and their comrades. These leaders suffer from a loss of moral and strategic leadership to build our communities. Instead they are destroying them with the implementation of such corrupt practices on every level. The bitter irony is that most of our countries claim to be religious in the devoted sense of the word and refuse to follow the main teachings of 'love thy neighbour as thyself' and 'the love of money is the root of all evil'. The fact is that Caribbean islands, African nations and to some degree black church leadership all operate on the following principles: failure to listen to reason, failure to follow the rules of the game, failure to lip seal the deal on concessions made behind closed doors.

Money matters are on the political table while security knocks on the door to allow nepotism and cronyism to stroll in hand in hand. This palm-greasing love affair from oil revenues ensures that their happy marriage built on selfishness, greed and corruption lasts forever. Honestly, there needs to be strong transparent unity of political purpose that will lead to a divorce or the outlaw of these kinds of marriage. Google the most corrupt African and Caribbean countries and find evidence of these popular marriages.

How do we end such widespread corruption? Do we address the cause of the corruption and try to solve the problem at source? Do we change the whole ideology that informs this corruption? What if black nations tried a different system as Castro did? What if we forwarded a strategic vision to end corruption? Is political corruption really the cancer of capitalism for which there is no cure?

Chapter 74

TAXATION

Principles of tax confidentiality – Tax loopholes – tax treaties – corporation tax – bedroom tax – road tax - sugar tax – tampon tax – Sin tax – poll tax- tariff- toll- charge – arbitrary burden on the poor

The tax system, made in the interests of a self-serving elite, operates on the same principles of the class system: tax exemption for the rich and arbitrary burden on the poor who are exploited by the upper classes as beasts of this burden. Everyone knows that tax oppression is inflicted by the unequal structure of society which allows generations of domination and elitism to further embed inequality. Everyone knows that politicians work to protect the established order of society to balance the books on the backs of the poor whilst allowing sweetheart deals for the corporate class. Everyone talks, writes and comments on the sense of injustice the tax system allows yet the western cultural thinker seems unwilling or rather incapable of providing a fairer way forward. There needs to be a system that allows a level playing field that demands dignity, self- worth and identity for those who contribute to the creation of wealth but do not reap the rewards.

With aging demographics, housing crises and diminished job opportunities, the western cultural thinker is faced with a huge dilemma of fair distribution of wealth. Socialist thinkers offer alternatives and so too are communists but these calls are falling on deaf ears. However, society cannot continue with less than ten percent of a population living virtually tax free to send their money overseas for future investment. The problem for the government is how to strategize for the poor while having to panda to wealthy campaign contributors who would withdraw their support if taxed highly. Instead, western politicians tax the minds of their script writers to produce more rhetoric that does not correspond to the reality. The language, though politically correct is superficial and far too transparent so everyone sees the gimmick, the scamming and the deceitfulness. Instead of the political posturing, politicians should aim to think outside the box and get to the details of what needs to be done consistently to improve access to genuine change. Access ought to include genuine fairness and equality of opportunity to build aspirations and heal the physical and emotional wounds of the Orwellian postulate that freedom is slavery. If many people are living under Dickensian conditions, then progress has only been made for the elite and society must find the courage to campaign for a change in the ideology that has led to this income disparity.

How can the western cultural thinker alleviate the burden of the poor? How can future generations be challenged to think differently? How can the political class have the courage and selflessness to work across parties to address the taxation unfairness? How can the tax system work with the aging demographics and social changes that affect its stability and sustainability? What if the western cultural thinker thought of an entirely different system of taxation? What if taxes were restricted to payment by the rich to adopt a Robin Hood policy of taxation? What if the poor were to be given tax breaks for a year to alleviate hardship? What if politicians decide to think of a different strategic vision that does not involve austerity?

Black cultural perspective

Unequal taxation is embedded in an unequal world that is enshrined in hierarchies; western capitalist societies are structured to exploit those of us at the bottom of society. Those who work for minimum wages, those who work for the government agencies and those who work for themselves all experience unfair taxation because of the structure of the system: it was designed to manipulate, exploit and oppress us. As a people, we have always been hardworking and that is why the government continues to make us work like slaves and then take all our money in taxes. What we should aim to do as a people is refuse to be continually regarded as beasts of burden and find a way to demand some degree of dignity in the workplace. We must refuse to be spoken to like Crooks in Steinbeck's `Of Mice and Men' and refuse to do jobs that the system has designed with us in mind. We are not beasts of burden. We must not let the powers that be balance the books on our backs. The abomination of slavery must remain in the past; we must not let it be reincarnated in the modern day workplace. As a people, we must create jobs not just for ourselves but for the collective so that taxation is not unevenly distributed.

The big problem is that we cannot ignore the wider context; the unequal structure of society with those at the top wallowing in their inherited privilege of paying less taxes and laundering wealth abroad. Never forget that the present context is not unambiguous; everything can be traced to the legacy of slavery when slave owners were compensated for loss of property. Think about it. Without that compensation to the thousands of British slave owners, life for the upper and middle classes would not have been so grand for them. Without that initial investment, without that family investment, without that freedom to dominate us economically, the world would have been a very different place. Like the banks, those who were compensated are simply living off the interest whilst insisting that the money was achieved through hard work. It is like living off the benefits of the Hatton Garden heist whilst insisting that it was earned through dedicated hard work, clever skill and sheer genius.

We all feel the deep sense of injustice and we have been fighting for reparations ever since but a reparation of the system must precede financial reparations otherwise such payments would simply be counter-productive. Essentially, we must be determined to address the root cause of the problem: the ideology which informs the capitalist system of unfairness. If we do not address the issue at source, then future generations will be consistently fighting for their share of reparations. Rather than insist on financial compensation, what if all that energy was reinvested into thinking of ways to ensure fair distribution of wealth? What if in the meantime, we insist on pressuring our politicians to ban tax and asset collectors who simply act as money junkies in our poor communities? What if both parties search for a strategy to address the issues at the heart of reparation, repatriation and redistribution? What if we looked outside the capitalist box to find a new way forward on the issues? What if we go back to the motherland and see Africa through the lens of our ancestors rather than through the western cultural ones?

Chapter 75

DICTATORSHIP

Partisanship- Lobbyists-Class affiliation -Liberalism-Conservatism-Socialism-Communism- totalitarianism- autocracy-monocracy-despotism- Nationalism-Patriotism

According to Wikipedia, dictatorship is `a form of government in which absolute power is concentrated in a dictator or a small clique. Dictatorship therefore implies absolute power or control of a political situation, a country and the world. The problem for the western cultural thinker is that the rhetoric here is difficult to separate from the reality of what western democracies really are. If partisanship is replaced by the label under discussion, the problem becomes more conspicuous or to put it how the French writers would, the signifier and the signified do not correspond. Using the politically correct language, western leaders operate a system of democracy where the people determine who leads them. Correct. There is no dictatorship by the media, by the existing government, by lobbyists, class affiliates or interest groups. Correct? As you can see, the operational definition of democracy and that of dictatorship is quite difficult to separate conceptually, epistemologically and philosophically; that in itself compounds the problem.

Each political party dictates the terms of its followers and any leader or faction in the party who attempts to free him or herself from the party policies will find themselves in room 101. Put simply, the western cultural politician has to tow the party line; has to be controlled by the absolute doctrines of the political party that s/ he joins. Democracy does not apply as the leader will be accused of taking the party either too far to the left or too far to the right. In such dictatorships, there is no centre ground or rather centre ground is not meant to be part of such dictatorships. Effective western leaders are those who resonate with the dictatorship stance celebrated by the majority which leads to another dimension of the problem. The majority opinion has now become age-related, gender related and culturally related; this is problematic historically, socially and politically. The 2016 American elections and EU referendum elections both illustrate this point perfectly as the party faithful, particularly on the conservative and republican sides were struggling to believe in the merits of democracy itself. Within the English labour party the battle between the Blairites and the Corbynites raged on with the same ferocity and neither side realising the need to fight for the centre ground.

Persuading the public is not only problematic but virtually impossible as many have lost faith in the party rhetoric, the party line and the party leaders and other issues are now dictating the decisions at the polls. The issue for voters is that the reality of their situation is not corresponding to the rhetoric that politicians offer; the issue of poverty denial and deficit denial and of course the issue of immigration. How can the western thinker solve the problems dictated by the plethora of problems in their own societies? Should the language change first to redefine political correctness? Should politicians think of a new way of operating democratically? Should there be a complete change of thinking about the system of government itself? Should the western cultural thinker refrain from using rhetoric in this context and explore different ways of communicating the reality of this dystopian world?

Black perspective

Dictatorship in our community has resulted from being dictated too for far too long and our black male leaders masquerade as democratic but we all know that they suffer from the effects of years of being dictated to. The problem with many black leaders stems from the repressed interrelated problems of one authority, one way of thinking and one way of believing. For the black political leader, he conflates his personal argument with his position of power so that if his argument is challenged, he takes it personally. He tends to see someone with a different perspective as someone who is making a personal attack on him and this is problematic in many ways because it leads to personal hurt, nepotism (favouritism for those who do not criticise) and disunity as those with opposing views are pushed out or opt to jump. Unless there is a separation of focus of ideas from speaker or an independent way to assess the merits of the argument, then black leaders in democratic countries will forever be accused of being dictators.

This issue of dictatorship has deep roots in the legacy of slavery as years of blind obedience, oppression, psychological and emotional abuse have taken their toll. Our forefathers operated like Pavlov's dogs and this conditioning manifests itself in different ways in the home, in the workplace, in society and in the world. We are simply obeying authority figures without assessing what we are being told and this has created a culture of dependency that must be addressed systematically and comprehensively from the top down rather than bottom up. Every aspect of the culture from leadership down to young children seem to be affected in different ways and the problem must be tackled on all levels. Think about it. In Africa and the diaspora, we have all experienced times when we criticise the speech and the speaker who then take it as a personal criticism. More formally, there is no separation or disassociation of the object from the subject – from what is being said from who is saying it. Within the culture, there is a belief that the speaker and the speech cannot be divorced and problems are then compounded as people are more focused on personality than on rationality. This way of thinking is what prevents black leaders from seeking compromise with others to reach a goal. Google what Amos Wilson and Chancellor Williams say about this and find out how the drive to seek compromise is hampered by the feeling that his personal position is going to be perceived as weak. To be a strong black leader, traditionally has been about having all the ideas for others to listen to. However, this tradition was borne out of the slave way of thinking and we have to find the courage to disassociate ourselves from it. Effective political governments must include an element of compromise in order for the party to move forward. Great minds in the same political party means that there will be great differences of opinion and differences of political opinion within a democracy, in the true sense of the word, means meeting each other on some kind of centre ground. However, this is problematic as a major change in collective cultural thinking must precede change in politics and change. How can we elevate ourselves from this cultural miseducation? How can we develop leaders who are willing to listen and learn from each other? How can we forward a new political agenda for our politicians everywhere without western cultural dependency? What if we have a comprehensive plan of action to change both the ideology and systems that perpetuate this problem?

Chapter 76

RULE OF LAW

Federal law – Constitutional law- State law- Business or corporate law- Civil litigation law-Employment or labour law-Estate planning law- Divorce law – Finance and security law – mergers and acquisition law-intellectual property law – Family law- Tax law- Criminal defence law- Traffic law- personal injury law- Bankruptcy law-Digital media law- entertainment law- immigration law

For the Western cultural thinker, the rule of law is one of the bastions of the concept of civilisation as all the people must be clear of the order by which society is governed. Everyone is expected to follow the laws or the rules no matter their station in life and failure to obey the rules results in punishment. Traditionally, this state of society has been in place as the vast majority of population respected the rule of law as the symbol of authority. The huge problem now is that there is no longer respect for this form of authority as the masses are no longer ignorant of what the rule of law is really about: allowing the privileged to maintain their rule over the majority. Rule of law takes place on many levels. Firstly, it functions as rhetoric by insisting that no person or government is above the law overlooking the fact that the context has changed as the masses are no longer ignorant of the truth. Secondly, it restricts the arbitrary exercise of power to established laws which function to shroud exploitation, enforce unfairness and hinder equality. Thirdly, the misleading use of the language that all people and institutions are subject to and accountable to law that is fairly applied and enforced is simply not true because the law is not about justice: it is about securing money and power for the privileged class of lawyers, celebrities, policemen, educators and of course politicians.

The cancellation of legal aid, the proliferation of paperwork and the time-wasting tactics by those at the top serve to undermine the fundamental rights of citizens who fight for freedoms rooted in natural, spiritual and moral laws. Absolute dominance in the conceptualisation, declaration and implementation of the laws of the land lead people to believe that the powerful are simply exerting power over the powerless. Lately, these laws are imposed with the military precision of dictators and totalitarians and those who even think of opposing these law-makers are banished into political oblivion. One cannot forget that the law is as complex and intricate as the human body with lawyers focusing on different areas of the body, not like doctors treating different types of ailments and diseases but rather like parasites obtaining power and protection for the privileged while offering no benefit to those who need to benefit from real justice. These enforcers of the law and their accomplices have led to a breakdown of law and order in society and advocate must find a way to transform this culture called western civilisation. As shown in 'Lord of the Flies', there must be another way forward other than clutching this conch. Perhaps, Jack and the hunters really do have the answers to this problem if one cares to reinterpret this classic novel. Should the western cultural thinker change the rules of the game or change the rules which govern the playing of these games? Should the western cultural scientist invent an entirely different game preferably one that does not use or abuse balls of any kind? Should the western cultural politician simply leave the law-making to an absolute or divine authority and quietly quit playing God?

Rule of law

For many of our people living by the rule of law is like being ruled by the law without reflecting on who made the laws and in whose interests. The law is about domination, the law is about security, the law is about control but the law is not about justice, fairness or equality. What slavery and colonisation did was condition our minds to obey the authority figure and this is where religion, using western operational definition here, worked wonders for the West. We were culturally indoctrinated to believe the authority figure without question, without critical assessment of the object. This enabled blind obedience and the continuation of respect, faith and belief in authority figures. Western culture cleverly and consistently associate the rule of law with God and the absolute, universal and just shrouding it in the rhetoric of Christian ethic. What we must understand is that the concept of 'the rule of law' is not western in origin nor is it unique to 'western civilisation' even though that is the case that is forwarded. As Ani points out, the law is based on 'the ideology of imperialism' which makes the western cultural thinker actually believe that it is his or her duty to control people of African heritage. Unconsciously and subconsciously, they feel that it is their moral or Christian duty to help us, to save us and to guide us. It is this false assumption of help that is causing further alienation, further exploitation and further conflict. Their help is counter-productive because it rests on the false premise that as people of African heritage, we have no cultural ideology that allows us to progress.

This is at the heart of the problem of the rule of law coupled with the over-centralisation of power in the hands of the elite and the way that top-down structures of security, politics, economics, education and health impose the same ideology of unfairness on our people. Statistics are not needed to prove the unfairness at every level of the oxymoronic criminal justice system, facts do are not needed to prove the economic inequalities, exclusion figures are not going to prove the miseducation of our people nor is the health service going to give any kind of independent evidence of the psychological damage the rule of law has systematically inflicted on our people. Politicians have all tried to implement cosmetic changes but they cannot even begin to address the issues. They are operating like a surgeon with a rotten scalpel trying desperately to get to the heart of the matter only to cause fatal injuries in the process. But the process must be assessed by both parties. It seems like we are conditioned not to question these surgeons before they inject us with the anaesthetic. Essentially, we need to open our African ancestral eyes to see the rule of law for what it is: a euphemism for the slave whip - the continuation of the legacy of slavery. We need to re-educate ourselves to realise that our ancestors obey natural, spiritual and intuitive laws and these must be the ones that we follow. Learning to see ourselves as a collective rather than as individuals is the first rule of law that we must obey and this is the most difficult to uphold in western societies. How can we pressure politicians to change the power structure by which laws are made? How can we help ourselves to unite for this fight? How can we work together with western cultural thinkers to agree new laws by which to live? How can we change the system and the ideology that informs the rule of law?

Chapter 77

WELFARE

Poverty- Dependency- Low paid work– Hopelessness- Depression-
Benefits- Handouts- Charity- social immobility –cycle of
underachievement-lack of privilege to progress-radical social
change – Aging population demographic –regulate parenthood

The Welfare State is a system that was established with excellent
intentions to eradicate the five giant evils of want, disease,
ignorance, squalor and idleness but instead it is eroding the five
godly goods of contentment, well-being, achievement, ambition and
entrepreneurship. Laid by the Beverage Report of 1942, Clement
Attlee implemented a National Health Service, a National system
of benefits to provide 'social security' with economic policies and
financial support by means of grants, pensions and other benefits
to address all social need. Crucially, this social system promoted
the belief that the State would take primary responsibility for the
individual and the social welfare of its citizens. Since its inception,
individuals slowly swallowed this beverage that inadvertently
removes individual and community responsibility; this thinking,
this reliance and this doctrine has diminished dignity, innovation
and skills. Seeds of dependency were sown and now the western
cultural thinker is reaping the effects of a poisoned tree with the
root being most toxic. Many politicians, both friends and foes have
different songs of experience but still seem happy to sing from the
same hymn sheet, watering their fears and sunning their anger with

smiles. Whether the welfare tree has friends or foes is not really the biggest part of the problem today but rather the fact that its fate will be determined by pythons.

This state of affairs secures power for the State whilst ensuring powerlessness for the masses. Rather than a safety net, it has now become a magnet for migrants, a pawn in the political game and a replacement for personal responsibility. The system saps the mental energy out of poor people in society and with the plethora of changes for austerity it will undoubtedly sap the psychological well-being of others. The challenges faced by governments revolve around finding a way to totally uproot this enormous tree without people really noticing. Austerity is clipping the branches and the leaves but the trunk still stands with everyone fighting to conserve the tree rather than uproot it. Junior doctors continue to challenge the spin doctors whose chants would bewitch Beverage himself bringing to bare his binary lens of socialist principles. These doctors are trying to spin for a reformed system that is simply unsustainable, simply unappealing and simply toxic on many levels.

The big problems then become matters of conscience. How can a system that is so entrenched within the psyche of the western cultural thinker ever be reformed? Can the system ever be reformed within the current societal parameters? Is it possible to change people's lives without changing their thinking about their responsibilities to survive? How can politicians promote collective responsibility rather than collective dependency? How can citizens be taught to bite the hand of the state to prevent its continual feeding of people? How can the Welfare state be saved from itself? Should people vote to lay the pythons outstretched beneath the poisoned tree? How can the western cultural thinker save the fallen State of mankind?

Black cultural

The state of being extremely poor is poverty and the system whereby the state maintains this condition for our people is welfare. Cornel West may describe the effects of welfare more accurately but suffice it to say that we are not living but dying off the welfare: dying of stress, dying of disease, dying of hunger and dying from the cultural indoctrination that makes us believe that we are better off living in western countries. The toxic dependence on the State has been infused into the psyche of our people to believe that we cannot bite the hand that is feeding us. Though well intentioned, this helping hand has mired our people into a cycle of underachievement where we learn to devalue our culture, devalue our ancestral connections and devalue ourselves. The hand has caused stagnation, shackles of poverty and hopelessness; most of all it has been instrumental in destroying the dreams of our men whose dreams are constantly broken by a system that continues to fail them. However, some of our own people who fail to understand the intricate nature and effect of welfare misdiagnose the complexity of this problem on the lives of the black family, the black community and the black individual.

The Welfare state inadvertently mirrors the ideology and culture which hinders equality. The omniscient state controls what needs to be controlled and what it perceives needs to obey an authority figure. The Welfare state operates like the plantation overseer treating us as if we are livestock to be fed and clothed to accept our lot in life; at the heart of this thinking is the ideological obsession of control which conditions us like Pavlov and Skinner did. After all, property owners being compensated for loss of property was one of the terms of the emancipation act. Feel free to google for the exact numbers here. Since then property ownership thinking appears under different labels:

experts, policy makers, liberalism, conservatism and socialism all of which fail to acknowledge the connection between economic and cultural problems. The failure to address these interrelated problems has led to a plethora of further problems that shackles us to the lack of economic progress as a people.

Many black politicians, notably Malcolm X called for a different politics to address the issues at source: a more militant, a more radical or a more nationalistic stance to reject the entire system that creates the problems at source. Whereas the civil rights movement believed in changes to the system to ensure equality, Malcolm insisted that the problem was with the system itself. Like many African leaders, like the Rastafari movement, the belief then and for many converts now, real change cannot occur without a different system. Many who still believe in the miracle of reforming the system admit that they need to pray for a miracle of some magnitude: the kind of miracles that happened in biblical times. What they have to acknowledge is the simple stubborn truth that the system cannot be saved from itself. How do we work to abolish the welfare system? Does a change to this system necessitate a change of ideology? Is there any possible way forward within a capitalist system which thrives on inequality? How can we lead on the changes that are necessary for our people to progress, prosper and find peace?

Chapter 78

EVIDENCE

Statistics – Expert- facts- figures- lobbyists- independent – Subjective- Objective –creative – made-up data – barrage of statistics- polls- surveys- political correctness –scientific basis- analysis of research –findings- examples – economic – uncertainty- opinionated – Bias

The Western cultural thinker works on the precedent of an obsessive rationalism that denies, detaches and devalues the human emotion from intellectual discourse. It is true that scientific evidence has created the materialistic world in which we live and it is also true that rational thinking has created a patriarchal world. It is a world where subjectivity is inferior to objectivity, a world where Science is superior to creative arts, a world where quantitative data is superior to qualitative data and a world where facts, figures and reason must reign supreme over emotions, opinions and intuitions. In the Western world, independent inquiry is invaluable yet totally dependent on evidence. This evidence must be in the form of statistics from thorough analysis of data that has been furnished by an expert from an established academic field and presented in a politically correct format. Western cultural thinkers then invest time gathering a barrage of statistics for the evidence to be heavily reliant on interpretation of figures. The aim here is for technical precision that intrinsically provides the recipient of the evidence with theoretical complexities that create the impression that it is indeed truthful data. Let us not forget that truth here is Orwellian and functions in the interest of the ministry.

The slogan 'ignorance is strength' is crucial here as many western cultural thinkers do not understand how the ministry works. Truth is manufactured, created, produced to control, influence or rather manipulate the masses. Everyone seems to believe that evidence could actually be objective and the EU referendum debate served to highlight the fact that all evidence is subjective. Each side simply acknowledged the subjectivity of the Other's expert whose credibility is stretched to reveal bias, subjectivity and opinion. No human being can be totally objective as bias exists within the DNA of the speaker as the campaigners conspicuously pointed out when President Obama took the stage. The world is a stage both in the Shakespearian and Orwellian sense and all evidence suggests that people are players or being played. Insistence on finding evidence is all part of the game masterminded by Big Brother or those playing at being Big Brother. Ignorance is Strength. War is Peace. Freedom is slavery. No further evidence required. The questions remain on how to progress beyond evidence and without it.

How can the Western cultural thinker reason without the rationalistic aesthetic? How can the scientist separate subjectivity from objectivity? What if evidence was redefined, reconceptualised and revalued to provide access for all people in society? What if experts acknowledge their subjectivity rather than insist that they are being truthful? What if politicians find different kinds of evidence in different cultures and apply to the solving of the problems that are faced in the Western world? What if politicians focus on finding a new vision for the country rather than occupying themselves with the tedious task of regurgitating rhetoric, stating statistics and dancing with data? What if the western cultural thinker finds evidence of the need to overthrow Big Brother and replace with the party of Brotherhood?

Black cultural perspective

Science has promoted the view that everything must be proved to be true in order to obtain truth but we have a different kind of truth as we operate on different philosophical premises. Our truth connects rather than denies the power of our emotions or rather our human spirit so according to Ani, the emotional-spiritual and the rational-material are inextricably bound together. She insists that it is a human being's spirituality that defines us as human and this is so evident in black cultural practices: audience participation, call-response, communal participation and question answer. It is a shame that some of us living in the West have been indoctrinated to believe that our African wisdom is folly when in essence it makes more sense than the western construct. Think about it.

We feel an authentic emotional sensitivity that informs our creativity and intelligence as 'it is the sensually immediate and not the intellectually mediated that gives pleasure that evokes and emotional response.' Put simply our intelligence is intuitive rather than artificial. What this means in terms of evidence, is like God, materialistic evidence cannot prove our truth because our truth is ancestral, spiritual and mysterious. There is a trinity of body, soul and mind that western pursuit of ocular proof that simply cannot be comprehended. We must not let their very different philosophical premise cloud our understanding of ourselves as a people with ancestral connections that empower us through our DNA to be strong, resilient and resistant to any form of oppression. Our culture's wisdom is another culture's folly mainly because of total ignorance of the ideology which informs it. We do not need to seek desperate data or to fiddle figures to achieve the pretence of fairness or objectivity; all we need to rely on is intuition as faith and reason are compatible in our culture. If we look at ourselves through the lens of western culture, we will be depicted as poor, destitute and ignorant but if we see ourselves through the lens of our African ancestral essence, we will see kings, queens and spiritually wealthy people as spiritual wealth includes all kinds of intelligences. We will all see ourselves as elite rather than bowing down to other elite; we will understand equality and not allow others to diminish our dignity. We do not need evidence from Hollywood, Harvard or our Highness to prove our worth because western wealth givers cannot afford to pay us our worth in gold.

Finding evidence that they require for reparation and repatriation is simply an exercise in futility. What we need is a barter with the West so that the minds of our children living here can have freed minds to see the evidence of our great wealth of knowledge. Ngugi Wa Thiongo, Marcus Garvey, Martin Luther King, Chinua Achebe and many others have paved the way and now we must build a legacy that shows evidence of our ability to change the world for all people living in it. After all, Africa is the motherland of all civilisations and what she has to offer can change the world forever. Shall we provide the world with a comprehensive ideology or philosophy of African cultural consciousness? What if we believe in ourselves to educate ourselves, our community and the world from whom our philosophy of life has been hidden? How can we gather evidence that does not conform to the Western constructs of data and truth? How do we find the courage to provide evidence for structural change in the system itself?

Chapter 79

EVIDENCE

Political Violence – Atomic bombing of Japan- the Vietnam war-Algerian revolution-Apartheid South Africa-World War 1-World War II- The Crimean War – The Iraq War – Syrian War- Nazi holocaust -Rwandan genocide-Bosnian war- Ukraine- Cold War

Political violence is a broad term used to describe violence perpetuated either by persons or governments to achieve political goals. It includes collective political struggle, which includes such things as revolutions, civil war, riots and strikes. Some insist that peaceful protest can also be a form of political violence. Psychological, physical and emotional violence has to be traced at source to fully understand how aggression has become a way of life for the western cultural thinker. Rooted in the infrastructure of the ideology of power and control, the young cultural thinker learns to be aggressive and competitive in cultural socialisation. Toys for boys include water guns, computer games and machines; aggression and competitiveness are further developed in sport, games and violent narratives –books and films. Boys are then encouraged to choose the Science subjects and learn to invent ways of seeking to destroy other things, other people and the other self- the emotional self which they are taught to control. Girls are now being socialised in a similar way and achieving similar effects as many are becoming as aggressive as their counterparts.

Political violence is not difficult for those who have been culturally indoctrinated. Forget game of thrones, western politicians are preoccupied playing games of drones. They are sleepwalking back into their childhoods thinking that war is some kind of computer game with foreign people as the baddies to be destroyed. This glorified global 'Hunger Games' has glamorised violence within the self and within societies everywhere; the world has descended into chaos with people scurrying as a result of their reaping. Poor districts applaud their heroes but this dystopian world is actually reality, a big brother reality show with everyone being proud of their fifteen minutes of fame. Politicians, aided by the media, are effective at ginning up hate and violence but no one seems to consider peace instead of war. Owen, Hardy and all the war poets would turn in their graves as all their writing about the futility of war has landed on deaf ears. Brutality seems to be the new brew and everyone is drinking it hot and cold; in the cold countries war seems more welcome as it warms the cold spirits; the brew is poured hot in warmer countries as it seems that it was made for their measure. Surely, Orwell rolls in his grave as he did not mean for his slogan to be employed as a manifesto pledge.

War is not peace: it is terrorism, it is hostility and it is a crime against humanity. Other people's lives are not collateral damage as each life is meant to be a journey of sacred pilgrimage. Life is more than a roller coaster, more than a game of chess and much more than this horrible blood sport played out on the world stage. Death is meant to be a destination when all seven acts have been played not when politicians choose to act. How can the western cultural thinker refrain from promoting war as peace? Should NATO vote to veto this dystopian cause or are they more concerned about a self-inflicting wound? Why isn't war condemned by those who preach condemnation? Should there be some kind of change to the ideology that causes never-ending war within the self, within society and most importantly within the world?

Black cultural Perspective

War is waged against our people in on all fronts: there is psychological war, emotional war, domestic war, spiritual war and economic war. Yet we rise. The pressure exerted from the drones of austerity, drones of oppression, drones of unfairness are operated by economic terrorists, security soldiers and political power brokers. Yet we rise. On the insistence of Christian Ethic, doctors, teachers and social workers are allowed in the war zones to work on the wounded but they operate like the missionaries did. Yet we rise. Our people may not have cuts and bruises to show our deep emotional and psychological wounds but the internal injuries are often fatal or have brain damaging effects. The systematic cruelty, exploitation and brutality of an oppressive system that continually terrorises our people must be stopped. This never-ending war that began with physical shackles has transformed into austerity that threatens to carpet bomb the poor out of existence and the bitter irony is that our politicians have signed up for this kind of attack. The torturous application forms, the telephone call terrorists, the money grabbing landlords, the eviction squad and the debt collectors all close rank to protect the warlords.

Victims of this sustained violence then become violent themselves as violent crimes symptomize the effects of mental conditions produced by repressed pain. Daily torture triggered by many different kinds of situations may cause reactions that are totally out of character for us and we all know that it does. For some of us, reactions are shown through a wide range of behaviours that are manifested physically, emotionally or sexually and many of us are either victims of abuse or perpetrators. We do not like to use the word 'abuse' to describe the harsh lashing of children, the increased volume on the voice when verbally reprimanding them, the acid tongued interactions with our partners that caused painful feelings, the early sexualisation of our young princesses, the blind eye turned when the older men date them. Many of us turn blind eyes but we have to collectively seek a way to stop the violent war on the community and within it.

Many dispute that the violent episodes of human history from the Haitian revolution to the US civil rights movement are carried in our DNA. Resistance is in our marrow as we continue to fight for justice. This multi-generational trauma, outlined by our sister warrior in her book, Post Traumatic Slave Syndrome, outlines exactly how the condition is undiagnosed and untreated and it is an enduring injury. It still lingers because the war continues undiagnosed and unstopped because many who inflict the wounds actually think that they are healing them. Many telephone terrorists begin by insisting that they are calling to help with our situation without realising that they are doing the opposite and inflicting more pain. They assure us that failure to pay would lead to legal proceedings. In other words, they threaten with the law, sending bombs through the letter box and when these do not blow us away they insist on sending foot soldiers (debt collectors) to finish the job; these helpers fail to offer a viable way to avoid the drone attacks. They honestly think that world war is peace. How do we break this cycle of violence, sold as peace to our politicians who refuse to be pacified? How can we insist that the established Church be more like the Good Samaritan in addressing the plight of our people rather than simply working on the other side?

Chapter 80

SECURITY

Security - Xenophobia – Intelligence-, immigration weapons/tools, War is peace – NATO –Ministry of Fear-defence spending – securing borders, securing property, securing jobs, securing funds for family, securing the self – security for MPs -MI5- MI6 –Cyber security

Security is a top priority for the western cultural thinker and the billions spent on defence and national security budgets provide ample evidence of this. Intelligence services provide governments with strategies for keeping the country and its people safe as laws are passed for enforcement by the police who are entrusted to protect the public from anyone or anything that threatens to hurt them. To understand the root of the problem, one must examine the implications of fear, unease and even paranoia. Fear creates the impression that there is something, someone, some force that ignites fear. Fear breeds hatred and hatred breeds aggression. Many western cultural outsiders and even insiders equate this fear with xenophobia which may unconsciously lead to negative feelings about immigrants and their motives. Others associate xenophobic feelings with nationalism and patriotism contrasting the success of western culturalism with different cultures. Other interpretations of this fear is evidenced symbolically in red which suggests that fear may be instinctual, biological and genetic. This fear of the unknown could almost develop into repressed hate and if these toxic feelings are allowed to fester, they may even cause mental unease and in extreme cases lead to paranoia.

What is evident here is that fear and unease about others seem to exist first in the western mind which has been programmed for centuries to think negatively about others; to mistrust strangers or see them as enemies. If there is any truth in this assertion, then one needs to examine in what ways this fear can be justified. Why would other cultural thinkers want to harm the western cultural thinker or what has the western cultural thinker done to alienate different cultural thinkers? Western cultural thinkers have invented atomic bombs, nuclear weapons, drones and all kinds of defence weapons to maintain security so why is there a need to feel unsafe, unprotected and insecure? What if the western cultural fear is all in the mind and all of these security measures are totally unwarranted as people from other cultures are simply here on earth to express love and friendship? Is the fear the tip of the iceberg of feelings associated with how the wealth was accumulated, how it is maintained and what it represents? Is it fear of losing reputation or fear of losing the purse? The latter is trash so no one will steal it.

Having the reputation of excellent intelligence, nuclear protection, security cameras, cyber security, police protection, security services and all other types of security measures surely deters anyone who even thinks of breaching this impenetrable fortress of security. Should the western cultural thinker seek to fortify the mind from the fear that haunts it? What if different kinds of intelligence services are employed, the ones that win hearts and minds? What if western cultural thinkers invest in safety and protection of mind rather than safety and protection of property? What if politicians prioritise securing an end to war and aggression rather than securing hatred that does not have a creed or religion? Should the real priority be to believe in a better world and fight the fear and hatred that is destroying it?

Black cultural perspective

There is an increase in war everywhere as the world is in a bad state. Western countries are like besieged cities but we need to fight for freedom of mind to think of ways to secure better futures for our people. Securing our freedom of mind to access and utilise our ancestral wealth must be our priority as this intelligence service must precede the protection of our dignity as a people. Capitalising on our cultural knowledge of interconnectedness, intuitive intelligence and love for each other will secure a better future for our children. We cannot continue to be conquered in our minds with western cultural indoctrination. Inner strength multiplied by intuitive intelligence to the power of principled politics can secure a better formula for our children. Fighting for fairness is futile in a capitalist power structure but fighting for freedom from the structure will ensure our security. It is going to be a long fight but we must be determined to secure a future for all people to believe in whilst fighting for us.

Securing a strategy to elevate the King's dream of civil rights to a vision of civil heights for all people must be the starting point. The impact of the civil rights movement gave psychological impetus to the need for justice for our people but the organisation of progress was not secured through policy making. Policies to educate rather than culturally indoctrinate were not secured and crucially there was no national security for the protection of our young men who needed to be occupied developing economic empowerment. To elevate ourselves, the strategic vision must be thorough, it must be comprehensive and it must be inclusive. There must be a detailed account and acknowledgement of the problems that exist within our community and those that are external and we must find the courage to work with others to find solutions which can be agreed upon. A comprehensive timeframe of action points must follow which include strategies for education, entrepreneurship and entertainment to appeal to people everywhere and for every stage of their journey through life.

The struggle for our dignity as a people must continue but not using the paradigms or philosophies of the past because all evidence shows that these are counterproductive. We have to progress beyond the principles of liberalism and socialism to find an African inspired philosophy of fairness and inclusion that would benefit all people. In other words, it should be democratic in the African sense of the word to secure the freedom to realise all human potential from the cradle to the grave or from the womb to the tomb. How do we begin to secure a future that everyone can really believe in? Should we form cross party think tanks to address the issues that are causing the problems on both sides? Should we insist that western cultural thinkers try to take just one step back and be driven for a while? Should we embrace difference rather than devalue it? Should we work on a much more profound vision of creation yet unknown? Should we secure the political will to fulfil Ayi Kwei Armah's proposal to ` direct our energies towards the recreation of cultural alternatives informed by ancestral visions of a future that celebrates our Africaness and encourages the best of the human spirit – by reclaiming our own image which lies in our ancientness an connectedness; not in a romanticised glorification of past... but tap the energy of the collective conscious will of our people'?

Thank you God for showing me that I am working from home for you and that I am your child and that the book is 100 percent positive in showing me that you are within me and not to feel afraid of the distance because you are with me and you will be with me every step of the way. I am just to enjoy my life and not get weiary of reading my book and reminding myself of my everyday walk with God. Where do I want to go this minute. I am going to sell God and sell metaphysics. God is still with me and has promised never to leave me so I could either clean up the house or teach Kenton more school work or simply be his mother. Home is where the heart is. Home is where you belong. Home is where you have your dreams and visions.

Chapter 81

POLITICAL SOLIDARITY

Nationalism-Patriotism-Socialism-Conservatism-   Liberalism-humanism-Multiculturalism-Assimilation-Inclusion- Integration-Diversity-Equality-Individualism-collectivism- Power- Control-Sovereignty

The western cultural thinker needs power to survive on an individual, societal and universal level and this power begins in the mind. Plato has shaped the mind to believe that control of the inner self, control of others in society and ultimately control of the world is a universal truth; one that is made credible through rationality. This truth has been propagated by the media, the government agencies and academia so that from the cradle to the grave thinkers are taught that power/control of the self and others is not only ethical but also a moral duty. The rest of the world is indoctrinated to think according to these western cultural rules of law which are internalised and communicated as shared practice or universal values. Plato must be honoured here for laying the foundations of this establishment of rationality that dictates this control of others through influential systems or institutions of education, economics, religion, law, politics and entertainment. Ideologically, this obsession strengthens all political affiliations.

Political solidarity can be operationally defined in this western cultural context as control or more euphemistically as political aggression. The western cultural ego seeks success through power over others and on this basis political partisanship does not matter as every western cultural thinker is consciously, subconsciously or unconsciously ideologically obsessed with power. Confrontation or keenness to wage war with others comes from this driving force, this energy to destroy the self and others. The western cultural self-image becomes one of being the subject while everyone else is the object; the self is seen as being intrinsically positive while consciously and unconsciously negating others in the quest to see the collective self as powerful and others as powerless. This way of thinking that fails to understand that genuine political solidarity must acknowledge the contribution of others or those who are different in ideology will always create a plethora of interconnected problems for any political movement that is really routing for genuine political change.

Liberalism has tried but has fallen by the wayside because it does not acknowledge that the unfairness endemic within the system needs to be addressed first. Unless liberalist thinkers tackle the persistent injustices at the heart of the system in which they operate, all equality discourses, all civil campaigns and all grievance claims will be futile. Unless the western cultural thinker learns to empathize with people who are different and acknowledge that injustice, inequality and institutionalised practice automatically widens the gap in political solidarity, problems would not be solved. The big questions: With western cultural countries now being so diverse, can genuine solidarity ever be a reality? Does any new political movement need to be made in China or at least employ Chinese resources? How can western cultural thinkers see diversity as being a contributory to solidarity? Can political solidarity really occur without a fundamental change in ideology?

Black Cultural perspective

Western cultural solidarity revolves around power and control but African ancestral interconnectedness binds us all together in unity. The problem is we do not know our own mental strength, our own spiritual power and our own African identity. We naturally have a shared collective consciousness, a shared collective spirit and a shared pain of continuing injustice. However, since slavery and colonisation our minds have been systematically tortured by western propaganda that has destroyed our capacity to envision ourselves as the strong collective force that we are. We do not need the visual register of Western cultural thinkers to dictate who we are as our African ancestral interconnectedness ensure that we instinctively we connect to truth; we do not see each other with our eyes but with our hearts or with our spirits. Unlike the western cultural thinker we do not need experts to guide our understanding of the world as each one of us has a strong intuitive spirit that tells us what the truth is about the world and how it was created. African centred lens, help us to develop these spiritual modes and perceptual mechanisms that allow us to connect with genuine spirits hidden in the physical body. It is like we have a sixth sense to perceive whether people have genuine spirits or not and that is why we can see humanity beyond embodied cultural and ethnic differences.

The problem is that our people are still ignorant of our true ancestral, cultural and spiritual identity; this problem is compounded by our children growing up being culturally indoctrinated by western ideology rather than being educated to understand their true identity through African philosophies and perspectives on life. If we examine the historical underpinnings of the perceived disunity among African descendants we may be able to comprehend the complexity of the problem and how it is interconnected with other problems. Historically, slavery and colonisation destroyed our collective cultural self with shared common values of genuine love for each other. We had our own languages, our own cultural practices and our own civilisation which were destroyed by western cultural imperialism in all its forms. This toxic imposition of practices that were alien to our African collective consciousness immediately caused gross misunderstanding, gross mistrust and gross misplacement of loyalty. Increased loyalty to and dependence on masters for survival rather than reliance on our collective self was one of the most successful strategies used to divide us. Misplaced loyalty to those whose hands appear to feed us rather than to the field hands that work arduously to liberate us. Clever tactics by our masters with strategies designed to sell the propaganda of black disunity from generation to generation have been entrenched on the world stage. The tactic of division through colourism or the thinking that lighter skin was better than darker skin was a prominent one. Higher status given to those whose skin tone is lighter were allowed to work in the house to those while those with darker skin tone remained in the fields. Dividing us by the false essence of this outer racial appearance had far-reaching implications and continue to affect unity amongst us. Essentially, the slave condition perpetuated the idea of disunity and ever since no comprehensive plan has been put in place to alleviate it. The blessings of African unity have been systematically replaced by the propaganda that there is a curse of disunity. Put simply, the western cultural value system was and still is incompatible with our African ancestral identity. Therefore, any attempt to embrace western cultural values wholesale will continue to cause the multidimensional problem of disunity amongst African descendants worldwide. The civil rights movement tried to campaign about the problem by using race as the basis for the movement but since then the strategy has been hijacked by other movements. We now need to move beyond issues of civil rights to strategies to elevate our people to civil heights.

Let us look at the reasons that cause tension and see where there is common ground. There is common ground in the fact that we all experience some form of oppression. Yet we rise. There is common ground in the fact that we all had to struggle against obstacles at some point in our lives. Yet we rise. There is common ground in the fact of our shared history has both positive and negative elements. Yet we rise. There is common ground in our quest for a better future for our children. Yet we rise. There is a common ground in our continued fight for justice. Yet we rise. Any disunity comes from the lack of power to orchestrate the solutions to the many problems within our community and we must fight for more power. This power has political, intellectual, economic, spiritual and cultural dimensions as power cannot and does not deny the significance of race but rather aims to show that race in and of itself denies the significance of power. Case in point: President Obama's position. Western culture saw Mr Obama as the first black president but the system aimed to disempower him rather than elevate him like Othello's power in the Shakespearian context. By contrast, many in Black culture saw Mr Obama's position of power as the symbol of ultimate success for our people within the system. However, the system of western power is a collective force that empowers individuals in different positions. The system empowers the individual but the individual cannot overpower the system. President Obama could not make structural changes because the system would never allow him to do so.

Unless this astronomical problem is addressed at source, our people will continue to see themselves through western cultural lens that teach us to see ourselves negatively. This negativity begins with the false ideology that everything black is negative beginning with night and day. Night is associated with darkness, evil, danger, criminal activity and evil deeds. What if there was an African centred interpretation of the darkness of the night that saw the darkness as covering the natural world in order to force us all to evoke the spiritual world? What if there was no darkness to remind us that this is a time to sleep and rest from a day's work? What if there was no darkness over the earth and we just lived in the light of the day – every day? Does not the darkness or difference to daylight have natural scientific, spiritual and intellectual value? Is not all difference a classification or taxonomy rather than a hierarchy? Should we call for a thorough reinterpretation of Platonic ideology so that difference is accepted as complementary rather as hierarchical? Should we insist on a distinction between spiritual seeing of others (inner seeing beyond the physical) and mere visual seeing of others (mere observation with the natural eye)? Should we have comprehensive strategies to achieve genuine integration? Should we all work together for political solidarity as a people as Nelson Mandela admonished?

Chapter 82

FAMILY

Nuclear family – Single parent family- Gay or lesbian families – Adoptive families –Extended families –Cohabitation –Kin-Monogamy-Polygamy – dysfunctional families

Successful societies strive for successful family units and everyone would agree that there is a need to restore the moral integrity of the family unit. The plethora of problems associated with achieving this goal begins with the problem of definition. This is closely connected to clarification of purpose, function or importance of family as a unit. Other dimensions of the problem are legal, cultural and social in origin. Understanding and defining family is problematic in itself as it has been transformed from its traditional form to something virtually beyond recognition. All families provide a home for love and people to attempt a relationship. Love may take several forms but suffice it to say that it is sought after in child-raising, in communication, in friendship and in fun, members of a family attempt to coexist along the spectrum of closeness from a physical proximity to an intimate unity. Tensions arise from the traditionalist thinkers who at the far right of the spectrum insist on what the ideal family unit should be to those who argue that reality dictates a different essence. Attitudes to the family unit reflect generational, cultural and gender biases.

To avoid disunity and conflict, the western cultural thinker must be clear about the main purposes of the family legally, culturally and socially: to procreate, to educate about the values of love and community or to simply be a place for financial security and stability. Is work outside the home going to take priority over work inside the home and if it is, who is going to provide the values that the home does not have time to cultivate? If the answer is the school, then shared values must exist between the home and the school to ensure consistency and continuity. If the government agrees to take the responsibility of parenting from the parents, then it must be done effectively. Unemployment pressures now add another dimension here as even if agreed by the State, individual circumstances cause additional problems. Not only that but anti- religious pressure groups like gay rights, traditional male-dominated family units and some women's rights groups further complicate the matter of unity of purpose.

How does western cultural society promote unity of family purpose without being accused of prejudice or bias against other forms of social organisation? How do western cultural thinkers agree on the functions of the family without being accused of denying human rights to choose? Is feminism in part responsible for the breakdown of the family as a unit? Is there a need for smaller government favours for families? Should laws that allow schools to give out condoms and birth control pills without parental consent be repealed? Should excessive emphasis on the value of work or economics be reduced in order to raise the profile and status of work at home? Should there be a reduction in the hidden agenda to get together with someone with the same earning capacity or rather for financial security reasons? Should the individual, the society and the government all be singing from the same hymn sheet rather than singing the song of absolute freedom of choice?

Black cultural perspective

In modern times, without God and the Black Church, without culturally liberating education, without jobs and without a clear moral direction, our young people have descended into a laissez-faire YOLO mentality. Do any job that pays. Take drugs. Drink alcohol. Sing tunes. Play music. Dance recklessly. Eat excessively. Have a child. Have another one. Have as many as possible. For the younger generation, the issue of the family unit needs to be comprehensively addressed for the problems related to it are reaching astronomical heights with interconnected dimensions that threaten to destroy the dignity and reputation of our people: past, present and future. The huge problem begins with a lack of strategic vision to provide opportunity for young people to aspire and realise their dreams. Without dreams, life is a broken-winged bird that cannot fly but we are expecting our children to be Westlife and fly without wings. No rites of passage cultural education. No entrepreneurial opportunities. No role models. Essentially, there is a need for collective responsibility in creating an educational, entrepreneurial and entertainment core that cultivates family values.

Issues of early sexualisation, too much responsibility for siblings at a young age and attitudes of our young boys to sexual activity cannot be divorced from the problems stemming from the cycle of poor family structures within our community. Early parenthood and the pressures on both young people who have not even gotten unto the employment ladder morphs into additional problems. These may be economic, psychological, educational or social but all affect the nature of the family. The multidimensional nature of familial disunity suggests that collectively we have to teach our children how to plan, how to be responsible and how to be smart but most of all we have to show them a holistic and sustainable way forward that educates them for each milestone on their rights of passage journey. Nation of Islam and all complete cultural educational programs in the African diaspora insist on building strong family foundations for the betterment of our people. This cannot be achieved without comprehensive educational provision to address the issues that are hindering our progress.

During slavery times, slaves were purchased for profit which implies the intention of the owners: to use their property for reproductive purposes by maintaining a massive work force, for entertainment purposes, for leisure and pleasure and for educational purposes of maintaining ideological power and dominance. The perceived role of slaves and their children still seems to linger in both the minds of the descendants of slaves and their masters. The aim of the owners of property viewed familial purpose solely as supplying a work force. If we fast forward to the 1960s, with the Welfare State, the feminist movement and the Civil rights movement all inadvertently changed the dynamics of the Black Family in different ways. Whereas our grandparents stayed married for life, times have changed as our children no longer share the desire to trust in the Lord or wait patiently for Him. Is it time for us to have a long term strategic and sustainable plan of action to guide our young people away from the immoral transformation of society that is threatening rather than addressing the multiple challenges of the black family situation?

Chapter 83

EDUCATIONAL SOLIDARITY

Private-Public- Grammar - Boarding-Secular- Faith schools-Single sex-Comprehensive-Secondary- State school –Metaphysical – Epistemological – Ontology –empiricism- scientific inquiry- intuition – reasoning and logic -Cosmology –deductive-inductive reasoning-idealism-realism - perennialism- essentialism reconstructionism-progressivism- transformative learning

Educational division is underpinned by the ideological obsession of western cultural thinkers and the failure to unite what should be taught, why it should be taught and how it should be taught: curriculum, rationale and pedagogy. The nature of learning in diverse western societies has added to the plethora of problems created by lack of consensus in selecting educational provision for all. The variety of views often reflects a variety of cultures, a variety of needs and a variety of aspirational ambitions. However, the educational system always reflects the values and the needs of a self-serving elite with a total disregard for the interests of those from the lower classes who clearly have different needs to those at the top. Education provision is therefore made as if the context is unambiguous, as if everyone has the same needs and the same interests. Schooling decisions seem to be made to ensure that generations of domination and elitism carry on like business as usual. All the parliamentary political posturing fail to get to the details of what needs to be done other than make an ideological attack on state education without offering a clear vision on how to level the playing field for those in Dickensian states of hopelessness.

The problem of the painful legacy of class stratification in the west is that there seems to be a priority to protect the established order rather than improving access to the system of reform to ensure progress for all. This problem is compounded by the fact that all changes to education are ideologically obsessed with maintaining the status quo or rather further embedding inequality, unfairness and injustice for the lower classes. Of course, this fact is shrouded in politically correct language of giving all students the same curriculum to ensure equality and a yardstick of standard measures to fairly assess the progress of students regardless of class, gender and other variables. This kind of universal standard fundamentally fails to enhance life chances for all, fails to acknowledge individual differences by all and fails to test the hypothesis that the system is rigged in favour of the privileged. Schooling systems reflect the divisions in wider society; division by religion, division by gender and of course division by class. State education is bog standard and private education is gob standard where the elite are trained to regurgitate rhetoric without even fully understanding it. Graduates leave these institutions unable to think outside the paradigms of propaganda and actually believe that their role on this Truman show reflects reality. How can western cultural thinkers transform education so that it appeals to all classes at the same time? What if there was unity of educational purpose to lead to a moral transformation of society? What if the western cultural thinker researches education systems outside the single frame of western cultural reference? How can the western cultural thinker design a curriculum for fairness, for equality and for justice for all without re-examining the ideological obsession which prevents it?

Glynis Glasgow-Kelly

Black cultural perspective

Education for us must begin with the transformative learning as pioneered by Bell Hooks rather than the transmission of western cultural values in the current system of learning. Many of our people recognise the need to change the educational provision for our children but making small contributions without proposing a comprehensive curriculum plan will leave us where we have started. Creativity has always been at the heart of African centred civilisations where children learn to create their own journey through rites of passage and communicate our common humanity but this needs to morph into innovation so that job creation can be a real prospect for all people. The fact that our motherland is the continent that has the largest number of different languages confirms that we create our own system of communicating across boundaries rather than fully embrace languages and cultures that are imposed. Of all the other cultures, we have a closer relationship with nature as creators of our own life journeys and this ought to be celebrated in a comprehensive education for our children and for all humanity. This commitment to the challenge of cultivating creativity, recognising differences and transforming the whole child will undoubtedly lead to cultural esteem building and ultimately happiness.

The problem with implementation comes from the complexities involved in negotiating with those in power in whose interests this curriculum knowledge will not serve. Further problems arise as both parties lack consensus on approaches to this kind of educational policy and its practicality for the capitalist world. Innovative approaches need inspirational leadership and leadership here needs moral integrity. The latter cannot thrive within the infrastructure of the capitalistic system which breeds individualistic rather than collectivist and creative values. Problems are further compounded by the needs of the power brokers to protect the class system and the status quo with regards to education and other influential systems that operate to promote elitism and domination.

Educating our children ourselves will always be problematic unless we find a way to persuade the power brokers that our creative, intuitive and transformative model of education is fit for all humanity. Our hidden cultural essence is indeed universal and fit for freedom of thought, freedom of conscience and freedom of the body. A new model of education ought to liberate all young people rather than enslave them in western cultural paradigms of thought. A new model ought to also acknowledge the contributions of the spiritual, natural and material worlds without exclusivity and in this way we can all have unity of purpose rather than disunity over purpose. The key questions: How do we begin to negotiate with the West without causing additional tension? How do we incorporate the diversity of voices in the African diaspora? How do we explore and maintain our African collective principles without antagonising those who have spent generations concealing them? How can modern technological advancement boost our creativity? How can we address positive and negative dimensions of our cultural education whilst promoting all three world views?

Chapter 84

FEMINISM

Working mums – Yummy mums- Stay-at-home mums- Independent women- Married women- Unmarried women- Women's rights- Women's issues –Equality- womanhood- Wonder Woman- Superwoman- D H Lawrence

Western cultural thinkers admit that the material world, which was created by men for their benefit is indeed a patriarchal world. Male dominated ideology, male dominated political, intellectual, familial, recreational, social, spiritual and economic structures prove that the material world was made by men for men. Men will always succeed or progress from a privileged position of power because the world is patriarchal and has been designed to exclude women.

The challenge for feminism is not to simply follow in men's footsteps under the guise of seeking equality but rather to examine the ideology that empowers men in a patriarchal world in an effort to create a different essence, a different ideology and a different world. Not only that but feminists ought to be clear on what constitutes a female identity: is it work, is it motherhood, is it perceptions of beauty or do biological aspects, emotional aspects or women's ability to forge relationships with others? Western cultural women seem to reduce issues of equality to the workplace rather than stress a holistic identity: the problem becomes one of conceptualisation, one of ontology and one of existentialism. If one begins with the denotation of feminism as the theory of economic, political and social equality for the sexes then one sees straight away that such a dictionary definition rests on false assumptions about the nature of the sexes, the nature of economic reality and the nature of political and social reality. Case in point: attitude to the sex act.

Many western feminists argue that sex is just an act and women are free to have casual sex as this empowers women. Surely, women ought to move beyond copycat thinking and define a separate identity rather than adopting perceived male promiscuity and attitude to the sex act as being meaningless. Though there is some truth in gender differences and attitudes to the sex act, does not mean that women should try to follow suit because men traditionally got away with it. Even feminists must acknowledge albeit privately that sex affects the female head, the female heart and the female's health. This may be due to the fact that we have three openings to the inner self whereas men have two. In Lady Macbeth's words, that female opening is 'the passage to remorse' which feminists are trying to unsex and this has led feminists to pursue their own self-destructive witch hunt. In Freudian terms, feminists have penis envy which may cause emotional and psychological damage by their use or rather abuse of that rite of passage which they cite as a human right. Western cultural women are now drinking themselves to death, working themselves to death and sexing themselves to death in the name of equality to men.

The gears of the feminist drive has changed from suffrage to issues almost exclusively related to the pursuit of capital; the push for profits seems tantamount to women's desire to outmanoeuvre men at their own sport. Feminism is now the driver at the wheel of a vehicle that is spiralling rapidly out of control; it has rammed itself into homes, into churches, mosques and synagogues. It has wreaked havoc in schools, in hospitals and in houses of parliament and now the vehicle has been globalised creating mass destruction everywhere. What everyone seems to forget is that this vehicle was not designed to achieve equality but rather to hijack the movement of those who originally fought for equality. The engine was then faulty from the start because it was built with the wrong materials, the wrong tools and the wrong mechanical system. To propel this vehicle forward, there must be an acknowledgement of the false essence that created it and there must be a willingness to embrace taxonomy of women's rights rather than place the emphasis on hierarchy of such rights.

Feminism, like Frankenstein, has created a monster that is now out of control and has turned violently on its creator. Women are now fighting against each other on major issues like beauty ideals, religion and the role of women, women's work, sexual freedom, relationships, abortion, single womanhood, paternal rights and parenting. The key contention must be addressed that taking the women out of the home to work with the men leaves a vacuum that needs to be filled and unless that lack of love, lack of care, lack of empathy, lack of values and lack of morality is tackled, the feminist movement will never ever get all women on board. For the western cultural thinker, there must be a way to fill the monstrous hole left in the family home by both parents being preoccupied with work. Surely, someone should be there for the children to guide them on their journey through life. Money should not be valued above everything: quality time with children, human warmth, human compassion, human empathy, human relationships, emotional attachment and morality.

The key questions for the western cultural thinker then become: how can feminists resolve their huge identity crisis? How can western cultural women define the quintessential core of feminism without offending women of different cultures? How can feminism as a movement promote the essence of womanhood in a diverse cultural context? How can feminism deal with alleviating women's double work: domestic duties and pressures of workload at the workplace? How can feminists promote beauty without being idealistic? How can feminists learn to work collaboratively with men to make the world a better place rather than a world of relationships characterised by conflict and hostility? How can feminists refrain from their preoccupation with equality at work and focus more on valuing traditional empathetic roles of caring, sharing and loving others?

Black Cultural Perspective

Black feminism was born out of the perceived sexism of the Civil Rights movement and the blatant failure of the western feminist movement to acknowledge striking differences that afflict women of different cultures. It has grown out of a different position within societal power structures from western cultural feminism and rightfully insist on intersectionality, a way that sexism, racism and class oppression relate to each other inextricably. However, religion and other aspects of culture must also be included as women are defined within cultural customs, beliefs and practices. Theoretical groundings for black feminist thought are explored by Angela Davis, bell Bell hooks, Kimberle Williams Crenshaw and Patricia Hill Collins. Decades later, second wave feminism emphasising black nationalism, gay liberation moved black feminism on. Now, thanks to Alice Walker, we are now embracing womanism as another form of black women's liberation. Celebrities like Beyonce and her sister are now adding to the black feminist discourse. However, one may argue that feminism in black culture is one of those consumptions of western cultural thinking that complicates matters more for our culture than actually liberating it.

Case in point: it seems like some of our women have not fully understood the difference between single womanhood, independent womanhood, single motherhood, married womanhood and black womanhood and more importantly which hood to aspire to. If our young women feel like it is accepted within our culture to have a career and single motherhood rather than a career and married womanhood, our children will suffer. Should our young women aspire to career womanhood like Oprah Winfrey or lean towards a career and married womanhood like Michelle Obama? Black feminists should aim to have clarity of emphasis on the position for the betterment of the black family because it is the feeling within the culture that certain interpretations of feminism are among the issues that have inadvertently contributed to the demise of the black family unit.

As black women we have been oppressed in more ways than we wish to admit but yet we rise. We rise because of our enormous inner strength that has been tried and tested many times. We rise against the enormous pain that we experience from the weight of the oppression pressing down on us from all directions. We rise as women because our African ancestral strength is extracted during adversity like the; strength of tea-bag put into hot water. In order to retain our strength of will and character, we must address the issues within the culture that add to our continued oppression: economic access, attitudes of our men to women, the way we speak to each other, the way we speak to and discipline our children and the internalization of western standards of beauty that haunt our men and ourselves.

Black feminism cannot be tackled in isolation as it is part of the interwoven problems associated with what our sisters termed as intersectionality. Role integration is key here and so too is a comprehensive education system that teaches values to help build our community rather than values that serve capitalism. Everything that is toxic for our women and our culture is great for capitalism and we must now systematically address the plethora of problems that devalue, degrade and diminish our dignity as black women. Unlike western feminism, we must seek to abandon attempts to compete with men in favor of complementing their unique essence. We are women from the motherland and we have enormous strength which must be transferred into our capacity to love but years of oppression and psychological violence has turned it into pain.

How do we begin to address the issues of intersectionality? Do we insist on a separate system designed to forward our agenda? Should we propose to work with western women and request a new set of female definitions? Do we extrapolate ideas about Islamic teachings and combine with our African Ancestral interconnectedness to forge a completely new cultural identity? Is there a need to encourage more mainstream discussion of black feminism as Beyonce has proposed? Does freedom of black women entail liberation for all people, since it would require the end of every aspect of intersectionality? Is there an urgent need to recognize that the problems created from sexism and classicism cannot be divorced from black cultural issues as they are all interlocking?

Chapter 85

CORPORATE OR ECONOMIC SOLIDARITY

Corporate crime – white collar crime- organised crime-State-corporate crime- Administrative corruption-Bribery –embezzlement-corporate accountability-corporate class funds- corporate banking -globalisation – state-endorsed corruption

The problems of the corporate class are not based on the need to prosper but rather greed to prosper, placing profits over people and corruption over cooperation. The corporate class has effectively closed rank to block the progression of the middle class by dominating every major market: food market, clothing markets and housing markets denying access to economic success for many small businesses. This dominance by the corporate class has widened the equality gap to such an extent that many western cultural thinkers, mostly the middle classes are now rebelling against the fact that they no longer have clear access to wealth or a real future to believe in. The greed of the corporate world has divided societies everywhere as traditional loyalties have been eroded leaving instead a widening gap of rather chasm of unfairness, injustice and inequality.

Essentially, the corporate class enjoys the blessings of corporate unity as they merge, globalise and rule the market place while those who lie beneath are cursed with disunity as their small businesses are purged rather than merged, mobilised rather than globalised and fooled rather than ruled in the marketplace. Big business owners wallow in their political privilege to avoid taxes, manipulate the masses and raid pension funds, bringing the issue closer to home. Stores are closed around the western world as corporate firms operate as if they are playing computer games destroying ordinary lives without any remorse. They wipe out small shop owners, the traditional traders with big superstores causing alienation and extreme problems for those whose minds can no longer be occupied with work. Meanwhile their accomplices in government work arduously on strategies to prevent the spread of corporate power of another kind. Such surveillance should be applied to both corporate worlds so that there is genuine equality for all. Through the lens of morality, the western world may be able to transform a system that is no longer sustainable for those at the top, those in the middle and those at the bottom of society. Big corporations need to be privy to a different form of intelligence to help them to see themselves in the mirror and force them to reflect on what they have done to the world in their relentless pursuit of capital. There is no acceptable face to this kind of capitalism or any way to avoid the glare of corporate greed. Yet many take pride in applauding it as the bastion of capitalist shining glory.

How can the western cultural thinker devise a way to morally transform the structures and ideology of a corporate system of greed that is simply unsustainable? What if big businesses find a way to work in collaboration with selected small businesses? How can the corporate world improve their policy or record on environmental pollution? What if the western cultural thinker finds ways to work in collaboration with others to tackle inequality at source? How can the gap between job making and job taking be bridged? How can western cultural thinkers find different political landscapes to address morally reprehensible methods of achieving fairness for all in modern societies?

Glynis Glasgow-Kelly

Black perspective

The West enjoys the blessings of unity in business whilst selling the curse of disunity under the euphemistic term of small business enterprise and we have swallowed it hook, line and sinker. Have you ever wondered why black businesses never seem to grow into global enterprises? We have always had brilliant ideas but we never seem to be able to convince our own people to support us in developing from small to corporate. Yes, there are obstacles. Yes, there is a lack of funding. Yes, there is lack of expertise in operating in a western world. However, there is a clear misunderstanding of the root causes of the problems here which stem from the miseducation of our people about ourselves, about our culture and our leaders' understanding of leadership and moral integrity. All black leaders in Africa and the diaspora who have tried to implement policies that have not been approved by western leaders have been sanctioned spitefully and maliciously; our people tend to focus on the effects of the sanctions rather than the causes or reasons why sanctions were imposed. If western leaders feel threatened they will close rank and retaliate with both psychological and emotional violence. Cases in point: Haiti, Cuba, Zimbabwe. This same principle can also be applied to other black groups and organisations within the diaspora: Rastafari movement, Nation of Islam, Black Panthers, Black Wall Street and now Black Lives Matter.

If we come back to business, any financial initiative that serves to improve the economic well-being of our people collectively will face huge obstacles as western society thrives on the negation of our people. The latest ploy is to encourage all of us to start a small business, knowing that global success can only be achieved with corporate endeavours. We are now experiencing a situation of disunity designed to cause further disunity which is described vividly by Chancellor Williams:

> *The picture of several thousand Black organizations, each independent and vying for leadership, is substantially the same picture of fragmentation and disunity in Africa that led to the downfall of the entire race. We have often seen that even in earlier times very often all that was involved was that somebody wanted to be the "head," was not getting there fast enough, and therefore, organized his own little state. Most of them perished, picked off one by one. The same thing will happen to any Black organizations, standing alone, that disturb the white mind.*

What is highlighted here is our thinking that has been dominated by western ideology so much so that we tend to believe in pursuing success for individual reasons rather than for the collective good of the majority. Though individual success is encouraged, collective success is cultural as it is quintessentially access to our African ancestral interconnectedness. Herein lies the root of the problem of disunity: it is not the absence of money but the presence of misunderstanding of ourselves. We need to understand our true cultural essence, we need to understand the root causes of our problems and we need to understand how western ideology has affected our relationship with each other as first world people. We have to educate ourselves first before we can be successful in any business venture because if we mistrust each other we cannot do business. Unless we free ourselves from mental slavery, unless we decolonise our minds, unless we are prepared for a long, long, long walk to freedom of mind to think differently, we cannot do business with each other.

Looking back to the historical underpinnings of the black cultural disunity discourse, slavery and colonisation planted the seeds of disunity, mistrust and misinterpretation of our African ancestral civilisation. Genuine understanding of the first world order would show that unity existed in all African civilisations. Let us not forget that all collectivist political movements from communism to Marxism to socialism to liberalism all stem from an African cultural emphasis or mantra that `it takes a village to bring up a child'. Let us not forget that it was not only the valuable material resources that were stolen from Africa, valuable knowledge was stolen too. However, many western cultural thinkers who argue that if we were united, then we could not be divided easily fail to understand the complexity of the ideology that informed slave trade agreements. If our African leaders recognised what the real terms of the trade entailed, they would not have sold our own people initially. What began as a trade turned into spiteful political aggression, manipulation and extreme violence. However, the big question here still haunts us all - do we need to take some responsibility for our own conquest?

In the context of slavery, psychological damage was inflicted through the hegemonic use of religion, miseducation, economic dishonesty achieved through colonisation and imperialism. Chancellor Williams also writes about what he calls racial reclassification or interbreeding which helped to disrupt our African cultural integrity and identity and still lingers today. Through Pavlov style conditioning, our people have learnt how to respond to the cultivation of selfishness on every level. Food was thrown to the slaves in the streets and everyone was expected to grab for their share and their survival. This grabbing for oneself is still one of the lingering effects of that legacy. Our whole existence since slavery revolved around grabbing for ourselves in order to merely survive. Consequently, our thinking has become focused only on the present, denying us access to past thoughts and future improvement. Since slavery, we have been conditioned to think, live and enjoy the present gratification and this affects every aspect of our lives especially our planning for the business of the family, the business of economic care and the business of entertainment. We have not learnt to unite and rule because the conditioning of slavery has divided us so that we can be ruled.

We are now being encouraged to do our own small entrepreneurial business to scatter our limited resources, our limited time and our limited support in so many different directions. We can never be effective in this way while western cultural organisations are merging for global dominance. Mergers mean strength. Unity means power. Why do we give our leaders a pass when it comes to accountability and transparency in business? How do we avoid the dynamic of fragmentation and disunity that has led to our conquest in the past, lingers on in our present conquest and haunts our dreams of avoiding future conquest? How can we create a comprehensive schooling programme that teaches entrepreneurship, cultural education in an entertaining way? How can individuals build business ideas without being worried about someone else promoting a similar or rather, identical idea? How can we cultivate leaders who are not driven by a selfish desire to be in charge? How do we forward agendas of unity without disuniting with those who would have serious ideological disagreement?

Chapter 86

MALE/FEMALE RELATIONSHIP DISUNITY

Marriage and relationships for the western cultural thinker has become a beautiful game with fifty shades of deception. The rules that govern the playing of the games are forever changing in range on the spectrum that spans from `I will always love you' by Dolly Parton to `Oops, I did it again, I played with your heart, got lost in the game' to `We will never ever ever get back together' by Taylor Swift. Status is also one of the main rules of the game with marriage merely an exercise in power broking with prenuptial contracts and divorce settlements serving to seal business deals. Couples in the West are falling in love with the figures, financial and otherwise to gain shares before and after the knot is tied. These ties that bind them all together are blessed with Christian love so their hearts and minds are always in the right place. Class affiliation does not matter because these are purely business mergers made for interest and maintenance of power, however, it is defined. Think of all the power couples globally to find evidence to substantiate this claim or simply go to google. The problem then becomes an existential one, an ideological obsession with power and control that inadvertently flaws the purpose and philosophy of relationships.

If the value system of relationships can be reduced to western capitalist values then who is going to provide the traditional function of a marriage as an institution built on genuine love for another human being, vowing to love them for better, for worse, for richer or should poorer be emphasised in this context. If children are seen as a mere commodity, sent off to boarding school because everything in these elite worlds are simply paid for, then how can young people every learn to show empathy to human beings in a diverse world? If the relationship is initiated, sustained and ended on the basis of capitalist principles and the whole infrastructure of values associated with western philosophy then relationships are doomed from the start. Young people are learning to fall in love with figures, singing material girl songs and others encouraged to believe in life after this sort of love by those who are well experienced to give advice on these matters. Honestly, love has become as superficial as the day and gifts dedicated to its celebration but perhaps western cultural thinkers could take advice from Scottish poet Carol Ann Duffy and give onions on this day instead; just being honest and truthful about love and relationships here. Love is not a cute card or something superficial but rather a key virtue that has multiple layers of meaning, value and purpose that the western cultural thinker ought to examine more deeply.

The problem of this attitude to love and relationships is that the same thinking is applied in different institutions, different settings and towards different people who hold different values to those propagated by the western cultural thinkers. Is it time for western cultural thinkers to acknowledge the underlying ideology that informs male and female relationships? Will such relationships always be strained when money walks instead of talks? Put more formally, should there be a different value system to fall back on when changes to financial situations take effect? Should partners value inner qualities first rather than capital gains? Does this explain why financial loss may lead to partners committing suicide? How can this genuine love be cultivated?

Black cultural perspective

In black culture in the African diaspora because of colonisation, slavery and imperialism we have adopted the system of judging our men on the basis of the amount of money they possess or western standards of good looks. In other words, we have come to present ourselves as private dancers who dance only for money and any old music will do. Unfortunately, the majority of our brothers do not have the financial power to woe women in the same way that men of different cultures have. Put simply, our men are broke. When brothers get the money and the power they see many of our sisters as trying to get shares of it or others feel obliged to partner with women who share their values. Some of our sisters try to do likewise by getting involved with the brothers with money whether they are married or not, just to ensure that their children are financially taken care of. Do not shoot the messenger here. The hip hop generation led by Kanye would express the relationship in more colourful terms arguing that the woman is nothing but a gold digger and she does not want a brokes ....(word that rhymes needed here). The sisters would respond and write about the man who sits on the passenger's side of his best friend's drive trying to hallo at the sisters who do not want those brothers. Many sisters who are financially able themselves, only want the father's financial involvement in the upbringing of the child not any other involvement and this has led to a series of other problems. Some brothers are even prepared to do the role reversal and be gold diggers themselves by dating women who take care of them financially or who love them mainly for mythical reasons. There is nothing wrong with that. Equality matters. In other relationships, women and men look past the sex of the breadwinner and just get on with life under the circumstances presented.

Nowadays, problems generated by pressures of being in and out of work have led to many relationship problems including lack of money, self-esteem issues, employment issues, marriage issues, child care issues, mental health issues, and the list goes on. If relationships are formed out of greed and not need more problems are created in the absence of personal discipline and spirituality. Slavery and colonisation had a detrimental effect on our people in Africa and the Diaspora and there is a need to heal the mind conditioning that destroyed our African ancestral love and respect for each other. Our ancient African civilisation cultivated respect for men and woman and treated us all as kings and queens. Western mind programming has destroyed our love for ourselves, for each other and for our community but we must fight to regain our cultural heritage. What is needed here, must be a way to cultivate job opportunities that build the self-esteem of our people whilst gaining financial power at the same time. We need to create a workplace that allows both men and women need to be happy meeting each other and then happiness will shine through at home and at social gatherings. If both men and women are stressed at work, stressed at home and stressed at leisure time, then we would not be able to make positive contributions to society. How can we defeat the ideology that dominates our thinking? How can we learn to address social, spiritual and material poverty to improve our living conditions? How do we work together in love to build strong relationships and secure the black family unit? Where do we begin on this long walk to our freedom?

Chapter 87

CHURCH DISUNITY

Brotherly Love- Humility- Cooperation-Peace-Unity of God's people-
One church-Unselfishness-Love Fellow Christians-Agreement
among Christians

All Christian churches preach about the blessings of unity but seem to
deviate from practicing what they preach. Western cultural established
churches present a unified front but behind the closed doors priests
and ministers insist on the silence of the lambs. Members with
different views or sombre secrets are unified in their purpose to let
the sleeping dogmas lie quietly in the closet. Some secrets are historic,
others are divisive but all are confidential and thus curtailed from the
current climate of exposure. What is indeed exposed is the worldly
pleasures of materialism, individualism and consumerism that have
crept quietly into the church and taken a front seat. This divorce from
the traditional principles has led to a series of problems resulting in
further denominations or further divisions on an individual, social
and national level. Like Jesus, the Church has modelled a tradition of
one person being in charge as the figure of authority but many leaders
of the tradition of the established church are simply not modelling
moral integrity. Not only that but explicitly and implicitly, religious
leaders are modelled by politicians, executives and experts and by
association misjudged as being symbols of divine authority.

Elitism is another by product of this way of thinking as the upper
classes are seen as the powerful and the good when the elite are

often strangers to the truth. Surely, Christ and his mission was all about inclusiveness, fairness and justice for all but the elite get their position by cultivating the opposite. Many have forgotten about the unity of the Holy Trinity of Father, Son and Holy Spirit as three in one epitomising unity not division. Yet Christians are proud of their divided identities: Roman Catholics, Anglicans, Evangelicals and so forth. Some Christians would not even take communion with others who do not subscribe to their beliefs. Does this partisanship belong in the church? The Apostle Paul would have a field day if he saw what is happening today.

With war and conflict on the global stage, surely the Church should be more vocal about the atrocities rather than being almost complicit with the perpetrators in this dystopian world. Without being pacifist, is not war a crime against humanity akin to crimes like slavery, colonialization and capitalism? Is corporate domination of the global market contributing to economic, social and spiritual poverty which Christ preached against? Why is the Church seemingly silent on the issues that are causing divisions? Is it that Christians seem focused more on their divided identities: Roman Catholics, Anglicans, Evangelicals rather than waging war against sin? Is it true that some Christians would not even take communion with others who do not subscribe to their beliefs? Does this partisanship really belong in the church? Would the Apostle Paul have a field day if he saw what is happening today? Is it impossible for churches to work together in unity or does God need to work a miracle of some magnitude to heal the divisions? Is there going to be separate heavens for separate denominations or should churches focus on preaching the message of the common good? How can the established Church unify itself, the society and the world?

Glynis Glasgow-Kelly

Black cultural perspective

It seems like our black churches are characterised by disunity but sometimes things are more complex than appearances. What seems to be the issue is that every time there is a major disagreement about aspects of church policy, members decide to leave rather than find ways to settle differences. This relates to a flaw in thinking, a miseducation about how to resolve differences rather than walking away to cause disunity. Case in point: Name 10 denominations which come under the umbrella of Black Church. You may begin with Baptist, then Pentecostal. Keep going. Keep going. We will be going for a very long time. Sometimes one has to wonder if the church has forgotten what the Lord hath said seven times, yes seven times about unity among believers? Google Philippians 2:2, Romans 12: 16, Romans 14:19, Acts 4:32, 1 Peter 3:8, Phillipians 1: 27 and Ephesians 4: 3.Has the church forgotten what the Bible said about the Holy Trinity? Has the church forgotten the scriptures that insist those who are without sin casting the first stone? Does the church spend too much time fighting inward? Why do members spend so much time talking positively and negatively about each other? Why do pastors take time to preach against hypocrisy rather than exhort members to be holy? Why do both hypocrites and saints in the congregation shout 'Amen' to the force of the casting: the stonier the words cast at members from the pulpit, the louder the Amen to sanctify the casting?

The historical underpinnings of the role of language in colonisation of the mind are evident in the tone, diction, economy of detail and volume of the sermons spewed from the pulpit. Preachers modelled the commands of the masters and of the Master and this spelt double trouble for language learning. Emphasis on Ephesians Chapter 6 v

5: Slaves be obedient to your masters serves as a painful reminder of the legacy of mental slavery. This biblical literacy rooted problems of critical unconsciousness and miscommunication on every level and many minds still suffer from the belief that learning is simply about obeying the authority figure without questioning the speaker or the speech. This problem also morphs into challenges in cognition as language use and thinking are closely related and closely connected; the effects of one dimensional, inflexible points of view has definitely caused deep misunderstandings of people, of reality and of our cultural essence.

Surely, if the church spends as much time on real evangelism as it does on inward fighting, the churches would be full of new sheep. What .. churches fail to realise is that we have all sinned; no one is perfect so no one should be casting stones. No one should be rejoicing when someone's faults are pointed out, in other words. No one should be praying for individual blessings when the collective curse of `disunity' seems to abound. Should pastors think of ways to pour healing oil on the wounds rather than letting the wounded soldiers die? Should churches lead on mediation rather than solely focus on meditation? Should churches simply practice what they preach or rather be Christian in words and deeds – in principle and practice? Should pastors refrain from being emperors who are mainly concerned about the expenses and state of their empires or rather be servants of God making the sacrifice of selflessness?

Chapter 88

LOVE/ DISUNITY ISSUES

Eros- Agape-Pragma-Philautia-Narcissism-Philia-Storge-Ludus-Sexual union

The world needs to be spreading love to everyone as agape seems to be in dangerous decline. The greatest gift of all has many layers and complex tapestry woven differently by different people with different threads. The art of love also conjures different images in the mind and is not just an affair of the heart. Children are meant to be educated about self-love, puppy love, friendship, love for everyone, romantic love, long standing love and family love. The problem for the western cultural thinker is that only romantic love is encouraged through chance meetings with potential partners. Without a system of educating about love, without a system of observation good role models and without a system of relationship building, love is self-taught via the internet. If all major religions describe love as being sacred, valuable and divine, the greatest gift of God to humankind then more should be done to teach how to love. With so many different kinds of love to experience the young generation are left to navigate through life without learning collectively how to manage the development of the virtues necessary to sustain a lasting relationship. Many fall in love but many very rarely stand tall and commit for the long term. Without learning how to forgive, how to resist other temptations, without adequate love guidance, many are left with the traditional DIY self-help kit.

Western culture's wholesale failure to address the problem of the glorified gallery of porn on the internet has led to a series of interconnected problems that leave young people confusing what should be friendship with sexual activity or adventurism. Not only that but self-love and self-esteem are often used interchangeably and popularised as the greatest love of all with philautia being replaced by self-gratification and love between friends (philia) that aimed to show loyalty and sacrificing for them and showing emotions has been replaced by rather pretentious relationships of friends in greed rather than supporting friends in need. Western cultural appetite for voyeurism also presents interrelated problems and so too does the thinking that love can be bought and maintained. Another challenge is definitely the thinking that everything and everyone is replaceable; nothing is sacred any more. With the decline of even the Christian ethic from the western cultural psyche learning about the highest form of Christian love, Agape will pose further complications for the young cultural thinker. The lack of love is glaring in modern society as love for everyone regardless of culture, gender or class is becoming an unreachable dream where the world seems content to be divided and ruled by hate.

The big questions for the western cultural thinker become: how can seven different types of love be cultivated in a diverse society? How can love possibly grow when the pressures of life escalate out of control? How can the western cultural thinker learn to empathise with others without having a value system that promotes genuine love for others? How can love ever be possible within this dystopian war torn world of hate in which we live? How can love possibly grow without solid familial, spiritual and cultural roots? How can love be nurtured without trust, patience and commitment to support it?

Glynis Glasgow-Kelly

Black cultural perspective

The heart is more than just a symbol of love; it is the greatest gift of all that comes from the heart of the mother and the motherland. Her physical body provides three passages for the water of love to flow through contours on the safari of love. The natural curves carved to perfection for her rites of passage through the seven ages of life. The inner self sees the heart circulating love around her body which fills the vessels with a spectrum of emotions from passion to anger to death. This powerful force can fuel passion, anger, revenge and hate or it may be just be that the force of hate is love or should that be love's hate. The mother knows that love may be fiery, deadly and dangerous and that is why it must be nurtured from the cradle to the grave. Its conception and development lies within her, she knows that she is the heart of the home, the heart of our community and the heart of the world. Everyone's first love experience, the first kiss and the first touch comes from the mother; she is the primary provider of a sense of belonging, a sense of place and a sense of a home. Our children also need an environment that is warm and welcoming like the motherland. However, this ideal does not always work in our women's worlds as our world outside Africa is not really our home.

The huge problem with giving love for those of us in the African diaspora is that western influences, western beauty ideals and western feminism have undermined the stability of motherhood in our community changing attitudes to parenthood and women's role particularly attitudes towards the notion of staying together for the sake of the children. The stability of the home has been shaken and the force of the earthquake has virtually destroyed the home as we now believe that working outside the home is much more important that duties of dedication keeping the home. Prioritising work over partners, over children, over housework and over relationships (particularly with the child's other parent) has left a huge vacuum that is threatening the very existence of the black community itself. Yes, some of our men are hard work and a leopard never changes its spots nor does a cheetah but we have to try to make relationships work. The younger generation are running out of role models in their communities and we must invest time in forming and maintaining relationships. We ought to provide forums where our young people can learn to love as friends, learn to love fellow brothers and sisters differently, learn from those whose love is long-lasting and very importantly learning to love themselves for self-esteem without being self-gratifying.

How do we begin to teach the next generation about this deeply important human virtue? How do we distinguish between self-love, self- confidence and self-esteem? How do we cultivate love under the strain of the pain of oppression, unfairness and inequality? How can we foster relationships when many of our men have not learnt how to commit, how to be partners and crucially how to love? How do we prevent the declining sense of community at such a crucial time with huge childcare costs spiralling out of control? How do we refrain from judging our men using western standards of attractiveness, western standards of relationship codes and western values of love? How do we begin to cultivate love for ourselves, love for our community and love for the world from our position of political powerlessness?

Chapter 89

SPORT

Tennis- Golf-Athletics-polo- boxing-Individual sports- Team sports-football-basketball-cricket-rugby-ice hockey-volleyball-netball-

All the world's a stage and men's games were designed specifically for the patriarchal players. For western cultural men, life is a competitive sport, a computer game and a game of balls. Such sport is more than a phallic symbol, more than entertainment, it is effectively a way of life for the western cultural male. Their attitude to sport can be extrapolated to business, relationships and the recreation of war or rather competition; it is all a game. These players assemble at pubs, unite for sporting events, play for profits, enjoy music and drone warfare with equal political pleasure. Let's set the Shakespearean stage to for the entrance of these players: sporting superstars, the banking boyhood, the music moguls, the virtuous veterans and the pally politicians all united in purpose. Yes, disagreements occur, but there are referees, regulators and reasonable resolutions. What unites them is a combination of purpose, participation and power dynamics. The purpose of being competitive, having control and participating in domination drives men to heights of enjoyment and power that justifies the ludicrous amounts of money paid to simply play or watch these games being played. Men concede that all men are not created equal and pay for the privilege of being spectators, commentators and most importantly, to pay for sport to be profitable. For men, every aspect of life seems to be operated on the game principle and even the singers support this view "Life is a rollercoaster, you've got to ride it".

What many sportsmen realise is that the game has to be won in the mind first and the idea that this pastime is worth such vast amounts of money defies morality. Yet men, women and children all support this means of wealth creation without even realising that these games can only be won by a select few. No one seems to think of the problems that are created when professional sport could only be profitable for less than one percent of the population. No one seems to question the unfairness of players in team sports earning unequal pay for playing the same game. No one seems to question the need for performance related pay particularly for national teams. Sport effectively helps to cultivate acceptance of unfairness endemic within the thinking behind the system itself. The rules that govern the playing of these games are the same rules embedded in the wider infrastructure of the patriarchal system of globalisation. Sporting superstars enjoy being on the global stage earning huge wealth while women argue for their equal share. What western cultural women seem to forget is that this world was not designed with them in mind and trying to beat men at their own game will prove futile just like their numerous efforts women have made to learn the offside rule. The big questions for lovers of sport: How can sport be made to benefit participants, spectators and investors in equal measure? How can male sporting superstars work collaboratively to change the rules that govern the playing of the games – all games? How can comrades change the traditional rule that all sportsmen are created equal but some are more equal than others? What if sportsmen think of a different sport that embraces different talent with appeal to different audiences with entirely different rules to apply fairness and equality for all people?

Glynis Glasgow-Kelly

Black cultural perspective

The stereotypes abound about black men and domination in sport but we need to think critically here. It is not that black sportsmen simply have natural athleticism but rather than our men have been culturally indoctrinated to believe that they only have physical skill just as western cultural thinkers have been programmed to believe that they are more academic. Having African DNA means that we have interconnectedness of physical, mental and spiritual power but sadly we have not been educated to channel the power in the three different directions: heart, head and body. We have been made to believe that our enormous strength is purely physical when the strength can be redirected to the brain, to the spiritual and to the body simultaneously. Black men's power is not restricted to the physical realm but has enormous capacity for intellectual and spiritual exploration that just needs to be harnessed. If we consider the fact that our evolved nature in Africa and the diaspora is mediated by environment and culture we will see the case in point. Kenyan runners excel at long distant running because the culture and environment demanded that they have endurance. However, their cultural endurance is not confined to athletics as culturally Kenyan academics have called for African languages to replace the language of colonisation. For this to be realised, there needs to be endurance of having the audacity to hope and to cope.

Similarly, Jamaicans are known for sprinting excellence and there exists a 'get rich as quick as you can' in Jamaican culture that is unparalleled in other Caribbean islands. African-American men in basketball and other sport show that cultural conditioning amplifies beliefs and affects performance. It is not that certain men can't jump but rather that certain men have not been programmed to believe that they can jump just as some black men have not been conditioned to believe that they can read defences or read full stop. Our men have not been taught how to read but what to read. Instead, our fabulous male superstars have created their own rap literacy and excelled in that sport too. Their wisdom to use this sport to search for answers to the tough life provides clear insight into the complexity of our reality in this world.

The reality has been created by those who have the power to control the perception of our people and mislead hearts and minds about our true identity. If we return to the historical underpinnings, our men were always seen mistakenly for physical purposes only and sadly our men have been indoctrinated to think in these terms. If we look at the successful slave revolts and the current resistance in certain countries like Cuba and Zimbabwe, we have to concede that battles are won in hearts and minds first. Sporting success operates on the same principle and that is why superstars like Serena can dominate her sport by simply strengthening her mind, her body and her heart to win twenty three grand slam titles. Michael Jordan, Usain Bolt, John Ngugi all show enormous discipline of mind, body and spirit, our African ancestral interconnectedness. The problem is we do not fully understand our own collective strength and we need to educate ourselves differently. How do we begin to change the misguided understanding of our self, our community and our world? How do we channel the energy within to show the world that we have the strength of mind, of body and soul to make all forms of sport successful and accessible to all?

Chapter 90

PHYSICAL DISCONNECTION

Separate locations - Geographical disconnection- class disconnection –familial disconnection-alienation- spiritual disconnection- radicalisation

According to Professor Mike Savage in his book, *Social Class in the 21ˢᵗ Century*, the traditional three-class analysis of social stratification is out of date. Savage sees seven rigid distinctions between social classes in certain locations of western culture: the Elite, the Established middle class, Technical middle class, new affluent workers, traditional working class, emergent service workers and the Precariat. The privileged class sitting pretty at the top may think of these like the seven commandments whereas the precariat or rather the poorest and most deprived social group may regard these as the seven deadly sins of society. This physical dislocation is parallel to the dislocation in education, in profession and in thinking. However, there is a unifying cultural perspective as everyone seems to be looking upwards with the view to relocate in a position above, like going to heaven. Relocation serves a unifying purpose as cultural thinkers tend to move upwards or mobilise to areas closer to the scene of the positions of privilege. Not only that but these elite areas were designed to justify separating one class of people from others as commanded by Plato but to the precariat these sins are as deadly as the ones entrenched in the system of another location, far away from the minds of western cultural thinkers, a place called South Africa.

From a very early age, young people have been taught that they are entitled to these privileged positions which those at the top had secured for themselves from finances secured and passed down from generation to generation. In England, for instance 46,000 slave owners received compensation for loss of their slaves in the biggest financial payout in the English government's history. This money was used for inheritance purposes to secure location of generations and generations. Google for evidence here from all official records of what happened to compensate the slave owners after the abolition of the slave trade. Confirm officially that the only other big financial bailout made by the British government was made in 2008 to bail out the banks who secure another form of location or position for the collective.

Essentially, the class system with its emphasis on social mobility encourages geographical relocation or disconnection from the class beneath. This is a necessity for personal advancement and upward mobility. Different areas or locations distinguish the middle class from the upper class and both classes from the lower class. The ideology of the capitalist system values people by their possessions and this value system of financial success, disconnects them from the holistic self, from holistic society and from the holistic world. The astronomical problem is that for many different reasons, the system is no longer sustainable for the middle and lower middle classes whose route to elevation has been blocked by the greed of the upper corporate class. Money becomes the huge price the western cultural thinker is prepared to pay for the privilege of platonic power. The huge question for all seven strata of society to address: how can hearts and minds be changed to embrace a new ideology that gives thinkers of different generations, different classes and different locations in the world a fair future location for everyone to believe in?

Black culture

The full force of the unjust, unfair and oppressive system is killing our people and we are crying out because we can no longer breathe. Generations and generations of us believed in the system of education as the route to success for everyone living in Africa and the African diaspora but the truth about the design of the system is clear for everyone to see. The education system exists to keep us in our place at the bottom of the social ladder by indoctrinating rather than grammar school educating the masses. To be well educated means that there must be a systematic and analytical understanding of grammar to ground knowledge of language and all systems work. Without that foundation, reasoning and logic operates top down; it is like building a house from the ceiling rather than solidifying the foundation. Many of our brothers particularly have a triple treble miseducation by class, by gender and by culture multiplied by age, location and ideology especially of the composition of self. This lack of self-esteem, cultural esteem and locational esteem has led to the situation in the black underclass or more formally the black precariat which may be interpreted: 'living in a state before the cars were even invented pre- car – I – at meaning that I am in a behavioural location that dates back before the car was even invented. To clarify, the precariat refers to our people from the ghetto who react to their environment like the Skinner rat, the urban rat, the field rat or the hood rat, simply scurrying or rather hustling to survive in the system that has dislocated them in major western cities. Seriously, the state of the global black underclass is no laughing matter and we have to trace the legacy to its source.

Different locations can be traced back to the legacy of imperialism, slavery and colonisation where slaves and masters were disconnected from their families, their continent, their locations both rural and urban and the self. The transatlantic slavery disconnected all involved in the trade in Europe, in Africa, in the Caribbean and the Americas. Geographical disunity or disconnection continued after the abolition of the slave trade, after colonisation and during immigration as the wind rushed many from their beautiful homes in the Caribbean to work in England only to realise that 'England is a pleasant place for those who are rich and high but England is a cruel place for such poor folk as I' are personal reflections of the past. Our people have been disconnected, discredited and disrespected by the system that continues to sustain unequal access to progress.

We are starting protests only to end up like Animal Farm because we are blaming leaders rather than the system that dislocates them from family and friends, from their own culture and from the self. If everyone had equal access to progress then we would all progress, if there were jobs for everyone to realise their dreams then there would be elevation for all people. We cannot forget that the system was originally designed to secure power for those at the top not to provide access to the top. It is a system of security for those at the top to keep them safe by imprisoning those who threaten their secure position. The system was not designed for justice, equality or fairness for our people because the whole system of education, religious ethic, justice, employment and politics all serve to negate black, to negate Africa and to negate our earthly spirit. Still we rise.

We must now rise from the dust of the earth and fight for the freedom of all people who are oppressed in different locations around the world. We must not aspire to create further divisions by class but to negate the ideology that creates the slavery to the mentality of class. Those who move to middle class areas thinking that they have escaped the system only soon realise that the people there wish that we would simply go back where we came from. The point is whether the crab is in or out of the barrel, the system soon shows that relocation does not make you different to the crab in the barrel.

Social mobility also involves socially distancing oneself from the community and this in turn leads to an inadvertent disconnection from the community; this process of social and emotional distancing from the urban underclass leads to greater divisions. One Kittitian calypsonian refers to it as 'the brain drain' where the question is asked why do we take our best talents and put them on a plane? In the West, our best talents are put on the train of economic migration, the train to the City, the train to upward mobility. Relocation is a brain drain that has destroyed the social and moral fabric of our communities. When those who have left, finally return to the ghetto it is not to improve the plight of the poor or to offer a hand up but rather to offer a hand out of western culture to impose similar standards on the underclass – a process that is akin to mental gentrification.

The urban underclass or rather the precariat can no longer be ignored with social media reminding the world that giving the powerless instrumental power to share their community values will be counterproductive for those who insist on maintaining the status quo. If black leaders and followers continue to impose gentrified initiatives on the lower classes, they will not work. If black communities fail to thoroughly understand that we are interconnected as a people with African ancestral truthfulness in our DNA, then any attempt to deny that would be futile. If we fail to acknowledge the legacy of universal improvement and uplift by Marcus Garvey then our living will be meaningless. If we fail to acknowledge Nelson Mandela's legacy of forgiveness and reconciliation, then we cannot progress as a people.

If we fail to acknowledge our collective hurt, our collective pain and our collective human spirit then we will never free ourselves from mental slavery. If we fail to understand Mugabe's legacy of resistance, Obama's legacy of highlighting the limitations, the restrictions and the frustrations of being in the system, we will never progress as a people. President Obama, like Othello proves that no matter how high we ascend in the house, aptly named, it will forever imprison us as a people. Finally, if we fail to learn the lesson that we are members of one body, one nation and one world then all areas, all locations and all people capitalised by ignorance, lawlessness and mindlessness will burn at the stake and those who come around with buckets of fuel or the Eloi arsonists who come around with buckets of water, we will all be consumed by the strength of its flames. How can we begin to climb this Mount Everest? Should we take a long walk back to Africa, the motherland and study our culture with different eyes? Should we begin by understanding the pain of the past, then ponder the present to find a future to believe in? Should we begin with a process of healing the hurt? Should we ask the Creator to help us design a different model for the progress of man and womankind?

Chapter 91

RACIAL (HUMAN) DISUNITY

African-European-Muslim-   Chinese-Japanese-Caribbean-
American-Communist-Socialist- Collectivist -Conservative-Liberal
democratic- Labour-Islam- Christianity- Judaism-Buddhism-
Hinduism-Sikhism –Scientism

All racial groups are members of one body, the human race
which operates exactly like the physical body. The physical body
is comprised of an amalgamation of different internal systems;
the heart, the brain and the circulatory systems. Together the
internal organs exhibit complexity, uniformity and symmetry in
the functioning of the human body. Similarly, each racial body,
before large scale migration, provided an internal cultural system
which centred on valuing certain organs of the internal system
over others. Hence, the first world of Africa promoted systems that
focused culture on values of the heart, promoting love, harmony
and collectivism that valued all people equally through rites of
passage. The second world created by the Middle East promoted
cultural systems that revolved around religion and operated as the
internal circulatory system for the human race. The emergence
of the third world that centred culture on the use of the brain to
build a materialist world required the movement of people, the
movement of resources and movements in ideology. The shift to
capitalist ideology meant that the first and second world essences
had to be undermined in order for materialism to flourish: human

harmony, equality and spirituality had to be dismantled, degraded and devalued in order for the empires to be built.

The problem now for the western cultural thinker is to find ways for all the vital organs of the human body to work in tandem with the brain without focusing on the external features of the human body. At present disease and environmental factors are causing problems for the heart of the human race but the mystery of it all is that it still continues to beat. It beats with the help of the circulatory system, the life blood of the human body and the marvellous machine of the brain. For the complex human organism that exhibits symmetry and order to survive, all parts of the body need to be valued, need to be respected and need to be acknowledged. The dynamic internal and external frameworks of the individual and collective human body are fascinating: the individual has a unique physical structure that houses a beautifully designed and intricate inner self: one entity of the self can be seen and the other entity remains unseen. Similarly, the collective first world essence can be seen in communist China, in socialist France and in liberally democratic America. The legacy of Moses, Jesus and Muhammad that collectively spread peace and good will to all still circulates in the system of many. All separate but equal entities work with the brain to allow the entire human body to feel the spectrum of human emotions in an earth designed for our existence with natural resources ensuring our contentment through life.

The problems for the western cultural thinker then become: how can the mind begin to look beyond the physical appearance of people when it has been conditioned to judge on appearances? How can the western world learn to acknowledge the positive contributions of the first and second world people? Does the western world need to adopt an entirely new ideological approach to the two worlds that preceded it or is sharing power too big a price to pay?

Black cultural perspective

As the motherland, Africa is the heart of all civilization, the giver of life and the heart of darkness. Conrad misinterpreted the physical darkness as negativity because our outer darkness was designed to conceal our inner beauty of strength to rise, of power to enlighten and of love to share. Like the heart, we pump blood around the body with our blood type being overwhelmingly universal. The power of our blood pumps spirituality, emotion and joy despite diabetes and other diseases that cause our collective body problems. The strength of our blood is parallel to the strength of our physical bodies and our brains are even stronger. After systematic attempts to destroy our mind through slavery, through colonisation and through capitalism, we still rise. The ribs protect our heart but many efforts to cage our hearts have failed because we find ways to protect our spirits. Nelson Mandela did. Robert Mugabe did. Malcolm x did. Barrack Obama did. Numerous brothers imprisoned still rise. Numerous sisters and brothers imprisoned in various institutions still rise because the African heart of strength, sustainability and spirituality will always rise in us. In essence, how our heart is protected by the ribs and how the vessels are able to navigate around the bones is simply amazing, the handiwork of an omnipotent being whose intelligent design of the human body mirrors the complex design of the collective body. Awesome!

The heart of the problem amongst Africans in Africa and the diaspora relates to shades of skin colour commonly referred to as colourism.

This breeds shades of disunity and squabbles about one's racial identity which was originally designed to disrupt cultural integrity. According to Chancellor Williams, historian and sociologist, in 'The Destruction of Black Civilisation' 1977 insists that racial amalgamation (interbreeding and racial reclassification served this purpose and if examined in its historical context, this is accurate and explanatory of the different attitudes to skin tone differences which still remain prevalent today. Light skinned people are viewed differently to darker skinned people both internally in black cultural circles and externally in western cultural circles. The legacy of slavery and colonisation still have lingering effects on our collective consciousness and unless we find ways to completely free our minds this thinking will continue to cause collective heart disease. Essentially, this disease has spread around the rest of the body as everyone becomes obsessed with judging people on outer appearance only. Failure to focus on the inner self, the inner reality and the inner spirit is causing problems for the outer body individually and collectively. Unless there is a monumental shift in thinking and valuing the inner self, the world will continue to plunge into the abyss.

The big questions then become: how do we begin to change our collective thinking about colourism? How do we change an entrenched ideology that colour matters more than spirit? How do we convince young people to be attracted to inner beauty rather than outer beauty? How do we cultivate values that lay the foundation for a different ideology that takes us beyond race in the human race? Does the physical distance between black and white bodies mirror the distance between our ability to perceive inner and outer beauty?

Chapter 92

ENGLISH RHETORIC

Ideology- Philosophy – political correctness- convoluted -polite rhetoric-moderate rhetoric -inflammatory-divisive-vile-toned – neutral –empty

English Language of all the languages in the world, functions on the same logic of the floors in the Tower of Babel, the higher the level, the more the need to translate for the masses on the lower floors all left divided and ruled because they are simply lost in translation. Rhetoric is the level occupied almost exclusively by politicians who wallow in the privilege afforded them to use language to conceal the truth rather than to express it. The grand state of the art parliamentary stage house the players who use their cleverly worded one-liners to antagonise those who forget their correct political lines. Charges of being inflammatory, vile and divisive in their use of rhetoric merely serve to maintain the pride of political power whilst navigating around the truth about rhetoric itself. The rhetorical ethic becomes gripping viewing and audiences everywhere are compelled to watch these players being economical with the truth on this grand stage. The dramatic irony of it all is that this moral ethic plays out against a fierce reality in audiences everywhere that threatens the very existence of the stage itself. The problem is Orwellian as the audience is no longer lost in translation, as ignorance is no longer a strength for politicians and crucially key members of the audience understand that the rhetoric simply functions for performance purposes or rather to maintain the power of the players. Audiences now have knowledge of dramatic irony, foreshadowing and language for the stage.

This stage was built by Plato, whose logic of metaphor begins with the charioteer in control of the self. To be a western cultural rhetorical user, one has to manage to control emotions whilst speaking the Queen's English. Received pronunciation implies an ideological commitment to the use of rhetoric that creates impression on many different levels: to imply the class and expertise of the speaker, to perpetuate the cultural heritage view of the tradition of language and to function as a medium of communication. Young players learn the traditions of the language from the day they enter the stage and are forced to spend their lives completing their seven stages. After years of experience of rhetoric, the western cultural thinker hopefully has a second childishness learning to redefine, rediscover and revalue how meaning is really made: through a reinterpretation of Plato. To change the false premises of language and rhetoric requires new formulaic assumptions about the world and about the global majority. How can the western cultural thinker begin to reinterpret the ideology about which they are obsessed? How can the western cultural thinker learn to deny cosmic, intuitive knowledge that seems to resonate with global majority cultures? How can western cultural thinkers learn to replace rhetoric with the reality of the human experience, the human instinct and most importantly the human spirit? How can the western cultural thinker clearly and distinctly perceive the triumph of reason rather than the triumph of rhetoric? How can the western cultural thinker realise that rhetoric can no longer be a western cultural Trump card? Does the billion dollar question become: how can democracy survive without the tower of rhetoric that made it great or more importantly does the Tower of Babel need a new kind of rhetoric to make democracy great again?

Glynis Glasgow-Kelly

Black cultural language

We have an entirely different value system and philosophy that does not encourage us to maintain any myth of righteousness or rhetoric. Language for us comes from a genuine proposition about the nature of reality and does not function to mislead, manipulate or manufacture truths about experience. As Ayi Kwei Armah insists "dishonest words are the food of rotten spirits" and our ancestral interconnectedness embraces the release of the human spirit so much so that we relate intimately with other cosmic beings. According to Ani, "knowledge of the universe comes through our relationship with it and through perception of spirit in matter. The universe is one; spheres are joined because of a single unifying force that pervades all being and meaningful reality issues from this force." Our interpretation of the universe is reasonable in the spiritual rather than the Platonic sense of logic of metaphor and complex symbolism. We do not need to use deceiving superficialities or facades of power but we do need to use language that distinguishes black language and literature from Western cultural discourses.

Black use of western cultural language in the African diaspora should be distinguished from the intended use of language by the producers of the language. Colonisation meant that we had to consume a language that was not intended for our use and that continues to cause us real problems of identity. We had our own languages in Africa before slavery and we were forced to learn the language of our former masters which has 'paralysed' our thinking, our culture and our perceptions of ourselves. The absence of a formal black language in the Diaspora particularly ensures that the process of mind colonisation continues. This process of learning a language that was not designed to elevate our people has amplified the divisions among our people akin to the one created by the tower of Babel. Constant misinterpretation and poor translation has led us to misunderstand each other and mistrust each other as eloquently outlined by Amos Wilson and Chancellor Williams. Loss of our language and our African ancestral connectedness has caused a lot of pain and Kenyan academic Ngugi Wa Thiongo refers to this loss when he wrote about our mother land 'the burial of African languages by Africans themselves ensured that the assimilation process into colonial culture was complete.' He insists that "Africans have not fully acknowledged their loss like a trauma victim who resorts to drugs to kill the pain".

Since slavery and colonisation, we have not collectively filtered the language before consuming it. Instead we continue to consume it without understanding the philosophy or ideology which underpins it and our children continue being part of a system of miseducation with language functioning to communicate the rhetoric rather than criticise it. How can we deconstruct the rhetoric that has been designed to deceive us rather than elevate us? How can we reconcile with those who seem incapable of separating the rhetoric from the reality? How can we reclaim our identity without rejecting the tool of rhetoric that served to create and sustain the crisis? How can we repossess, reconstruct and redefine rhetoric for our reality? How can we find another way of reducing rhetoric, without resorting to the use of the Trump card?

Chapter 93

LANGUAGE IN CULTURE – CULTURE IN LANGUAGE

The English language is a medium of communication and an academic discipline. The former is used by many around the world as a medium to express ideas about culture, traditions and customs but it must not be confused with the academic discipline of English which encapsulates the cultural heritage, history and traditions of the English people. The canon English writers –Dickens, Conrad, Orwell, Austen, Hardy, Doyle and the like were influential in upholding the conventions of writing, Cecil Rhodes, Queen Victoria, Winston Churchill and Beverage are key historical figures and English cultural values being the rule of law and democracy. These are hailed as precious English cultural customs. The English language as a medium of communication is the dominant language of the world second only to Chinese. It functioned as a tool of enslavement, cultural indoctrination and colonisation of people around the world; the ragbag of words and phrases from around the world is evidence of its culture of collecting without clearly acknowledging the contributors. The problem of the cultural indoctrination exists in the term and now this brainwashing has become counterproductive. If people are occupied and denied access to their own cultural capital, they cannot become independent of those in power. When those in power no longer have solutions, the problem is highlighted when the occupied are so dependent that they have no way of helping themselves. These occupied peoples (immigrants, non-Europeans, foreigners) are viewed as parasites, a burden to the State and worthy only of being imprisoned.

Language and History are inextricably linked. The history of the English language is the history of empire, imperialism, classicism all rooted in the tradition of inequality. Positions of privilege which lie at the heart of social stratification has been problematic in the past, continues to problematic now and will continue to create even more problems in the future if not tackled at source. The traditions in the use of English language (as opposed to the western cultural languages of French, German or Spanish) to persuade and argue inadvertently serve to maintain a culture of dominance, a culture of ignorance is strength. Culture is conveyed through the intertwining of language and its connection to the history of Empire.

Language profoundly affects the way the world is perceived, expressed and experienced. It shapes the way that people think as without consciously knowing it, language dictates what is thought, what is felt and how to express both of these. The problem of western cultural language revolves around its purpose to dominate, to control and to mislead others not only in expressing constructions of reality but also in shaping people's perceptions of that reality. How can the western cultural thinker right the wrongs of the language that has done as much harm as good? How can the producers of language heal the world of the divisions that it has created albeit unintentionally? How can the western cultural thinker rid its language of the history of oppression that it continues to perpetuate? How can the culture and history of language rid itself of the negative elements whilst retaining the positive aspects of the language and its cultural capital?

Glynis Glasgow-Kelly

Black cultural perspective

Language defines a community's way of life and our culture is paralysed because our language is that of the coloniser. Kenyan academic, Ngugi Wa Thiong'o wrote of linguicide being committed when Africans adopt foreign languages lock, stock and barrel. The absence of a black language in the Diaspora particularly ensures the process of mind colonisation continues. Ngugi refers to a similar loss when he wrote that "the burial of African languages by Africans themselves ensured that the assimilation process into colonial culture was complete". He insists that "Africans have not fully acknowledged their loss like a trauma victim who resorts to drugs to kill the pain". Black cultural language is more individual, the mother tongue or voice and identity of the speaker. By contrast, Western cultural language is about necessity and power which requires certain codes for different settings. In different terms, it is about character and voice with the voice being one's real black perspective tucked away in the western cultural envelope with the label of appeal to the mainstream. In other words, we are forced to use western cultural language but we still reflect our individuality that lies beneath the power structures that dictate that we work for `equality' rather than to recognise our different cultural essence. Franz Fanon insists that our identity is not a fixed essence but that we are operating as "individuals without an anchor, without horizon, odourless, stateless, rootless".

As a collective, we share the experience of a profound disconnection from our homeland, our languages, our original History, our identity. We share the experience of struggle, of pain, of anger with transportation, colonisation, and migration from Africa. That pain is communicated in the tone, volume and expression of the words that we utter and we are wrongfully accused of being R.A.D: rude, aggressive or defiant. Black women especially have been accused of being all three but our R.A.D tempts us to reply that we are resistant (to oppression), aggrieved (by sanctions) and determined (to stand up for justice). We must resist learning language that continues to colonise the mind, culturally indoctrinate and subjugate rather than educate us for liberation. Let us not forget that western cultural language was originally taught by missionaries so we learnt this language in a biblical context designed for clever conflation of the two authorities so we learnt to be obedient, to listen to the authority figures and to essentially consume everything without filtering it first. Western cultural language was not designed to teach us how to think critically but rather what to think and refusal to obey the authority figures on earth meant that we were being rebellious, resistant and refusing to simply do 'as we are told' and deserved punishment.

Consuming language means consuming culture. Consuming culture means consuming history. Consuming history means consuming identity. How do we even begin to refrain from this colossal consumption of language and culture? How do we even begin to educate our children for liberation? Should we campaign for black language and literature be taught as a separate subject on the mainstream curriculum? Should we study language in its social and historical context in an attempt to filter the negatives? Do we need an examination of our collective use of western cultural language?

Chapter 94

HISTORY IN LANGUAGE – LANGUAGE IN HISTORY

British Empire – Imperialism- Slavery –Colonisation -Science-Rationality - Absolute truth- Official language –Commonly spoken language- Leading language -Old English-Middle English-Modern English- Idiolect-Sociolect

Historical revisionism or the function of language in the Orwellian ministry of truth is as intricate to the English Language as the tradition of class stratification yet many western cultural thinkers seem to be unaware of the deep rooted problems that this creates for all who speak it. Language was instrumental in the establishment of the British Empire and is now the means by which it is maintained. It includes all major aspects of British traditions, British economy, the legal, political and justice systems and therefore functions as an imposition which serves to smother the truth about its role in sustaining power. Language becomes more than rhetoric as it functions as propaganda, in the same way as History and the Media, misleading both the speaker and the listener inadvertently discrediting the discourse.

The problem for the western cultural thinker is deep rooted, multifaceted and Orwellian in every sense as it causes problems for freedom as slavery, for war as peace and for ignorance as strength. In its social, historical and cultural context, language shapes each person's views, knowledge and interpretation of the world and all theorists: Chomsky, Saussure and Piaget write of its influences from the cradle to the grave. Culturally, all practices are governed by language use – legal system, justice system, educational system, sport and entertainment and of course the political system. Making language more transparent would lay the foundations for a moral transformation of the individual, western society and the world. Think about it. All laws would change. All policies would be revised. The education system would be transformed to change the life chances for all. The truth about history would be told to empower the powerless and help the powerful to fully understand how their wealth was acquired, how it is maintained and how it should be shared.

The implications of language being completely entwined in history, for language teaching and language policy are far reaching. Yet some western cultural educationalists fail to explore language in its historical and cultural context, fail to use appropriate pedagogy and fail to examine historically based linguistic differences to promote understanding instead of misconceptions or prejudices. Until the truth about language and history is told by the ministry of truth, the younger generation would grow up in a dystopian world where ignorance would be slavery rather than freedom. How can the western cultural thinker begin to tackle language and history? Should they instruct young people on the historical background and roots of language usage so that they are not learning meaningless symbols? Should educationalists insist on changing language learning policies so that awareness and understanding of historical cultural differences are being taught? Should language be taught from different cultural perspectives so that children's learning is transformed rather than transmitted? Should political, legal and everyday use of language be expressed to convey the truth about history rather than conceal it?

Glynis Glasgow-Kelly

Black cultural perspective

To understand black culture, language and identity is to understand our history of oppression, struggle, pain, anger, injustice and poverty. It is not that we cannot use Western Cultural language in its Standard form to conceal the truth about our true African History but rather our spirits naturally resist the use of language to hide rather than express the truth about our history.

In 'telling it like it is' rather than being polite (a euphemism for gentle deception), we are telling the truth about the injustices that we continue to endure, about the pain of not having access to positions of privilege in society and our frustration of being disconnected from our true African history and our culture. To understand our black cultural language is to understand the roots of the culture that gave birth to it and the ancestral interconnectedness that still shapes it. We are simply ignorant of the power of our cultural heritage and have allowed western cultural thinkers to persuade us that our history began with slavery and colonisation. Empires and civilisations existed in Africa prior to European descent on the continent and we need to be better educated about our hidden history. Kenyan academic, Ngugi Wa Thiongo described language as the means of spiritual subjugation as western philosophy thrives on the denial of the human spirit. In his book, 'Decolonising the Mind' he writes at length about this whole process and how to move forward as a people.

This process needs to be made manifest in manoeuvring language as a vehicle for our new culture in the African diaspora. Our traditional use of language and literacy has limitations, limitations that come from this history of biblical literacy. From these biblical roots, stems the oral tradition, charisma and language of protest politics. This is evident in the sermons of black preachers, black teachers and black politicians. What we need is to progress beyond protest politics by being proactive about a literacy-based collective that is separate from the biblical tradition. A literacy-based cultural initiative that harmonises cultural interests from church values to Hip hop, an initiative that allows people to express different thoughts whilst being focused on a common good. One does not or cannot deny that the language of music–the blues, rap, hip hop all have the same historical underpinnings and modes of expression but we need a congregation of people to comment on different ways of seeing, interpreting and understanding things outside the traditional realms. Rappers and other singers grew out of the oral language tradition but if we continue to live in Western countries, we ought to develop literary based cultural events. We need to be proactive rather than reactive.

Through the years, over the generations, black cultural education has not addressed this deficiency in our development of literacy. That needs to happen to prevent our children from growing up not knowing how to separate western cultural language from our own. It is like trying to speak two languages simultaneously but being totally unaware of the fact that you are bilingual. Our first language is interfering with our understanding of English language in its quintessential form. Yes, it is true that we have tried to use certain words and phrases that we claim as 'black' but the structural changes required to repair the damage to our collective literacy still need to be addressed. How do we build a whole new learning of language and history?

Chapter 95

LANGUAGE AND CULTURAL IDENTITY

Gender-Social Class-Political correctness- Rhetoric -Politeness-Christian ethics -Antics-Tone- Objectivity-Ethnicity-Idiolect- Sociolect

Language identity (idiolect and sociolect) is simply the feeling of belonging to a group and is related to nationality, ethnicity, religion, social class, generation, locality or any kind of social group that has a distinct culture. Culture shapes identity which is intricately linked to language. In this way, language identity is not simply characteristic of the individual's affiliation but also of the culturally identical group of members sharing the same cultural identity. In this context, it is difficult to separate language and cultural identity from what is referred to as identity politics. Consciously or unconsciously, language is used to forge or strengthen identity. The problem then becomes salient when the western cultural thinker describes him or herself in terms of multiple identities through which complex navigation has to occur. Without a satellite system, the western cultural thinker is lost in a world of forgeries and falsifications of identity. Passports take the form of cultural misappropriation or put poetically `passports of personas' with code-switching and linguistic versatility being stamps of approval. Other problems which result from the use of certain passports include sowing seeds of divisiveness, cosmopolitanism and false tolerance under the umbrella labels of multiculturalism, assimilation and diversity. The western cultural thinker is left with a huge dilemma of trying to fight the pain of societal fragmentation in order to gain societal coherence. The culturally inappropriate word for the state of western cultural society is one of chaos.

This state of affairs is evident in homes, schools and virtually every institution where cultural identity possesses this false essence. At home, children are overwhelming placed in childcare while parents focus on the priority and main value of work. Raising children has now become a financial burden to many western cultural parents and children no longer grow up experiencing the blessings of traditional language life. Essentially, schools, whether academy, state, private, faith or grammar experience the same species of challenges which are compounded by the fact that teachers have a plethora of problems with identity themselves. In fact, all western institutions seem to suffer from the effects of French cultural identity encapsulated in their term `laissez-faire'. If western cultural thinkers, live and let live or allow freedom to operate `sans frontiers' society will become the dystopia that Orwell predicted. In fact, it has. Freedom is slavery. War is Peace. Ignorance, of the impact of language and cultural identity, is strength.

The key questions then become: how does the western cultural thinker begin to disentangle the intricacies of cultural identity from the language which functions to create it? How can language be used to convey the truth about the problems caused by identity politics rather than conceal it? How can the western cultural thinker learn to use language to construct a cultural identity that cultivates cultural cohesion rather than cultural division? How can language be used as a tool for education rather than a weapon of its mass destruction? How can language be used to create a utopian world?

Glynis Glasgow-Kelly

Black Cultural Perspective

Cultural identity has traditionally been looked at as one shared cultural and historical reservoir passed down from generation to generation with shared ancestry, shared collective self and a shared pride of being part of that culture, that people. Though there may be superficial differences, the essence of cultural identity is one of collectivity in beliefs and unity of purpose. The problem is that this definition is problematic for us in Africa and the diaspora because it fails to take into account the many interactions, influences and impositions of different cultures. If we upgrade the definition of cultural identity to include this definition by cultural theorist, Stuart Hall we can get a clearer picture. He insists that cultural identity is a matter of `becoming' as well as `being'. It belongs to the future as much as to the past. It is not something which already exists, transcending place, time, history and culture. Cultural identities come from somewhere, have histories. But like everything that is historical, they undergo constant transformation far from being eternally fixed in some essential past they are subject to continuous play of history, culture and power.

The problem for us lies in the fact that those who control the power of language are the ones who manipulate the perception of ourselves and that is why Ngugi Wa Thiongo insists that language has paralyzed our culture. Our language identities highlight the different ways we are positioned by and we position ourselves within the narratives of the past. Case in point is outlined by Cesaire (French Caribbean writer), the Caribbean has three presences that influence culture – The African presence, the European presence and the American presence. Essentially, these influences all add to the complexity of Caribbean identity and language use. However, the most repressed influence is undoubtedly that of our African heritage as it exists within our DNA; those in power aimed to silence this powerful influence by using slavery and colonization but still we rise.

Our cultural use of language reflects our history of the pain of continued unfairness, continued injustice and continued inequality. It also represents our personal experiences of present pain and how our character uses mechanisms to resist the oppression of the system. Our cultural voice echoes the pain but is often misrepresented as aggressiveness or rudeness as the sharpness or harshness of the tone is parallel to the force and impact of the inner pain the continued sense of injustice inflicts. With commands to use less imperatives, more modal verbs, more variety in use of vocabulary, greater organization and structure, more imaginative ideas, do we need grammar schooling? Is it really possible to change the way we speak in terms of tone, volume and content without changing the underlying pain that continues to sustain it?

Chapter 96

LANGUAGE AS POWER

Rules- Regulations – Policies –Treaties –Laws –Codes of Conduct –Pledges -Agreements – Settlements –Documentation – Curriculum-Imperialism–Class stratification-Imposition–Executive-Influential – Instrumental power

Language has a strong relationship with power and this power is three dimensional: executive, influential and instrumental. Politics, advertising and media are referred to as influential power agencies whereas agencies with explicit power imposed by the state, legal, educational and conventional business organisations are termed as instrumental power agencies. The power brokers all use language as a political tool to ensure the status quo or maintain power so in this regard language is used for expedience rather than integrity. The political power brokers cleverly use language in laws, taxation policies and bureaucratic systems to influence our day to day lives and win the battles of hearts and minds. The ability of politicians particularly to use executive power to influence our lives is remarkable but the bitter irony is that our collective power through the democratic process ensures that we give them the power to do it. What a paradox!

The problem created by language and power is monumental because the masses are no longer listening to the power brokers. In fact they are committing a crime of high treason but refuse to be imprisoned. Instead, they rally around the leaders who use language that gives them a future to believe in. They have replaced the official influential agencies with social media. They are not listening because government policies have not taught them how to listen, how to reason or how to gain power. Some with extreme opposition to the power brokers even burn themselves at the stake. Whether one wishes to accept responsibility for the demise of society or not, the fact remains that language has lost its power to persuade people to engage in the political process mainly because ignorance is no longer a strength especially among the jobless younger generation. The roots are being spread rapidly because in every area of life, power is being exercised through language: during conversations, in relationships, at the workplace through power dynamics and through all forms of spoken and written language. The list can easily extend to consider political speeches and all other forms of interaction that are underpinned by theoretical approaches to structural features of speech, use of rhetoric and register.

How can the western cultural thinker solve the problem of power in language use? Should a pragmatic approach to politics be considered in this context? Should there be a greater emphasis on lexis and semantics (forms and meanings), forms that include or exclude (insiders or outsiders) and other structures (at phrase, clause and discourse level) which may be used to exercise power? How can the western cultural thinker show how rhetorical devices are used to mislead rather than persuade people? How can the western cultural thinker adapt conversational maxims to encourage fairness? How can those with power find a way to use language without the corruption implicit in their intended use? How can influential power agencies like advertisers persuade rather than impose cultural influence?

Black Cultural Perspective

Western cultural language functions as imposition, as a cultural medium of power, as "a footnote to Plato" to conceal the truth that the success of their culture relies on our cultural negation. We use language to express the truth about our reality, about our resistance and about our religious beliefs. Ngugi Wa Thiong'o has always encouraged us to resist the use of colonial labels and Christian doctrine and has warned against the adoption of `foreign languages lock, stock and barrel'. Essentially, Ngugi accused Africans of committing a `linguicide' which destroyed the history, culture and memories of African society. He continued ` the burial of African languages by Africans themselves ensured that the assimilation process into colonial culture was complete. This phenomenon was referred to by Ngugi as a `death wish' that occurs when memories are erased during assimilation and people have not fully acknowledged their loss – like a trauma victim who resorts to drugs to kill the pain. Ngugi objected to the exclusive use of western languages as this was ensuring the `psychic suicide' of Africans who regard their own native languages as `shameful', `inelegant', `incapable of expressing scientific or intellectual thought' and too crude to be exported to other lands.

What Ngugi is emphasizing is the need to have different ways of dealing with the world – different perspectives, different interpretations, different languages. As African governments discouraged children from speaking in their mother tongues, Ngugi insists that this has resulted in `a linguistic famine in African societies'. The use of language is therefore not only a tool for expression of thought but is also a weapon in the battle for the survival of our culture, our history, our collective memories – our souls. The huge challenge is finding the courage to fight for our souls. Historically, language was used during enslavement and colonisation as both a weapon and a tool: it was a weapon in the battle for dominance and a tool to ensure the mental subjugation of our people. What is evident is the inseparability of culture and language as our culture has been disempowered, devalued and degraded.

Colonisation had political implications and the hidden agenda for language was to indoctrinate, program and control the minds of the colonised. Mental slavery which Marcus Garvey and other thinkers refer to continues to happen through official language which is used as a political tool to ensure the status quo. The questions now become: How do we disentangle the implicit bias and negation in the imposed language that provides the only medium of communication for many? How can we free our minds without having a separate language for liberation? How can we negotiate a settlement for the future use of language within the confines of the language itself?

Chapter 97

LANGUAGE AND LOGIC

Philosophy- Rationality- Critical Thinking- Objectivity- Factual-
Expert- Abstract- Interpretation- Meaning-Inference- Implication-
Paradigms- empiricist

Language cannot be divorced from the logic of the ideology which
underpins it. The western cultural thinker operates on the logic that
science is socially, culturally and spiritually independent; that reliability
and validity in objectifying language is through scientific knowledge.
Another key assumption based on the rational model of the universe
is that scientific knowledge and intelligence automatically detaches
emotion, passion and religion from its thinkers. Quintessentially,
western cultural thinkers believe in the words of Ani 'that the
scientific method leads systematically and progressively toward the
truth and that the function of science becomes that of establishing
an invulnerable source of authority that cannot be challenged'. The
problem for the western cultural thinker who tends to believe that this
is the absolute or divine truth and most importantly, the only form of
rationality has led to a series of interrelated problems with the biggest
one being virtual misunderstanding of the ideologies of other cultures.
This complete ignorance of other forms of rationality that provide
equal validity, equal reliability and equal access to truth has added to
the complexity of the problem.

There is definitely a need to examine the nature of meaning, language
use, language cognition, and the relationship between language and

reality. If the western cultural thinker is serious about examining the root causes of the problem their ideology presents then they have to prioritize their inquiry on the *nature* of meaning. They have to explore semantics to explain what it means to "mean" something. If there is a fundamental misunderstanding of what speakers and listeners do with language in communication then the problem cannot be fully addressed. Crucially, language and the logic of learning and how it relates to the minds of both the speaker and the listener will also have far-reaching implications for how language and meaning relate to truth about reality. There must be a focus on what kinds of meanings can be proved to be true and engage in truth oriented philosophy of language. The huge problem is that language constructs reality as it operates on the same principles as 'The Truman Show' as language drives understanding, conceptualization and interpretation of the world. Media mobilizes metaphors for meaning. Reality is created through words. Words create reality. False appearances create a false reality. Miseducation creates misunderstanding

The big questions about language and logic then become: How can the western cultural thinker divorce the language from the philosophy which underpins it? How can truth be constructed when historically, socially and culturally, language functions to systematically distort it? How can truth be constructed when the absolute truth about the self operates on the same false principles of the language which functions to conceal it? How can language be divorced from influential, instrumental and executive power agents whose ideology and professional integrity are judged by their strategic misuse of language for the sustainability of the logic that has established and maintained the global ministry of truth?

Glynis Glasgow-Kelly

Black cultural perspective

The problems we have with language and philosophy is the fact that we are using western languages since slavery and colonization that explicitly and implicitly represent black negatively. Ngugi Wa Thiongo is absolutely right in insisting that using the language of the colonizer, the oppressor, the dominant power has paralyzed our culture. The philosophy of the English language itself depicts us, devalues us and degrades us and implies that our cultures are inferior to theirs. Let's examine some of the uses of language: blacklist, blackmail, black sheep, black gold, black Friday, black culture. In western paradigms of reasoning and logic, black cannot be seen in a positive light by virtue of the fact that the logic of western culture needs the negation of blackness for its existence and success. Herein lies the magnitude of our problem with using languages that were not designed for our education, improvement or cultural progress but rather for the maintenance of our continued oppression.

Semantically and pragmatically, language and western logic negates black by claiming their philosophy is based on biblical metaphor but when examined one finds that it is based on biblical misinterpretation, cultural bias and historical revisionism. It is based on misinterpretation of nature by clever manipulation of associations with natural metaphors: blood with love and danger, green with grass and innocence, white with clouds and daylight and black with night and dirt. If we take a different interpretation of night and day here, if the dichotomy of day and night function only for only as classification rather than hierarchy, we will see the contrast through different lens. We can see night representing the overshadowing of the world so that we are forced to think of spiritual things or to see the inner world. If we change the word 'dirt' to 'earth', a different image, a different feeling or a different emotion is conjured immediately. Cleverly associating color imagery with religion has also been used to validate the negation of our people but we must now rise above it. How do we work to change the relation between language and the nature of reference, representation and our truth? How do we begin to understand that language is a matter of knowing what truth or falsehood implicit in the very use of language itself? Do we need to fully understand the connection between western cultural truth, western cultural language use and our African ancestral truth and the language we use to express it?

Chapter 98

LANGUAGE AND RELIGION

Symbolism-Metaphor-Performance-Metaphysics-Diction-
Politics -Control

Language and religion seem to share a structural connection that have the same impact on the mind of children who are easily converted to learning both. Both systems are even linked in terms of a sacred connection: Hebrew is the sacred language for Judaism, Sanskrit for Hinduism and Arabic for Islam. Religion and language acquisition, both require a certain cognition that involves distinct diction, syntax, speech patterns which have a psychological effect on the speaker and the learner. Religious ideology controls perception of the natural world and the words are used symbolically with different operational meanings and values. Mother tongue language acquisition is very easy for young children and so too is their conversion to religion; the younger they learn it, the more fluent or converted in will be in later life. Parallels may be made here to imprinting in birds during a critical period and it may be that religion infused early in life has a different degree of commitment to those who converted later on in life. The problem then for the western cultural thinker is how to prevent the perception that language and religion are mind parasites rather than mind builders or how to accepting the huge political, imperative and performative function of these parallel systems.

Viewing religion simply as a narrative, a school of thought and a cultural ethic that is mediated through language has not contributed to understanding religious experience. The words, the pictures painted with words all express or convey religious tenets but the relationship of religion to language is much more intimate, almost instinctual, almost inbuilt. All societies, all cultures, all peoples seem to have some form of religion so much so that it can be described as a universal phenomenon. Many theorists, notably Chomsky have insisted that children have an innate linguistic ability to master the complexity of language in a very short period. The competence in understanding the structural system of language then boosts their performance of the language. Other modern western cultural theorists trace linguistic learning to evolution of human languages rather than to the evolution of the species. The western cultural thinker could be tempted to argue that this line of reasoning can be applied to religion as early access to religious language can affect their thinking about spirituality later. Religious learning then functions as a mother tongue or first language that is successful by virtue of the fact that it was inculcated in early childhood and therefore rooted in the mind.

As Terrence Deacon states in his book` The Symbolic Species': Languages are not static but evolve over time; they behave in fact like living organisms. The same is true of religions. Deacon writes: "As a language passes from generation to generation, the vocabulary and syntactical rules tend to get modified by transmission errors, by the active creativity of its users, and by influences from other languages... Eventually words, phraseology and syntax will diverge so radically that people will find it impossible to mix elements of both without confusion. By analogy to biological evolution, different lineages of a common ancestral language will diverge so far from each other as to become reproductively incompatible." The big question then becomes: How can the western cultural thinker create compatibility

Glynis Glasgow-Kelly

for the second language and the mother tongue or for religion and language?

Black cultural perspective

Language and religion have been used, misused and abused to colonise and enslave the minds of our people worldwide. In Africa, language and religion or rather spirituality cannot be divorced from our DNA of interconnectedness, strength and truthfulness. However, years of slavery and colonisation has cursed our culture with the false spirituality of disbelief in our unity. For this reason, many of us in Africa and the diaspora tend to term the false essence as disunity and wonder 'why black people cannot unite'. To unite we need unity of purpose, unity of politics and unity of language because the language of the oppressor is symbolic to the system of the oppressor and on that basis western use of language and religion cannot be divorced from the intended purpose of slavery and colonisation. The dual use of language and religion has paralysed our culture and we need to create a different system, a different language and a different religion for all people who have descended from the Motherland. The motherland must work with the fatherland and the young free spirits must be allowed to soar to reach for their dreams. Everyone dreams and if we find a language that encourages everyone to value life and to capitalise on cultural values, civil rights and civil dignity, then together we can build a marketplace.

The colossal problem is that language and organised religion have colonised the mind to see ourselves negatively and any fight for freedom of mind has to acknowledge the huge psychological damage left by this dual legacy. Language and religion are so deeply interfused

460

in our psyche that it is difficult to escape that sense of helplessness, hopelessness and haplessness. Put another way, the duality of language and religion has operated as mind parasites or viruses to such a degree that many of our people have permanent injuries. Decolonizing the mind will call for a comprehensive education for reparation program for the next generation, a new strategic vision, a new strategic direction like that proposed by Marcus Garvey. Unless we embrace a shared language and religion for universal improvement to provide a future that brings out the best in everyone; by giving everyone a future to believe in, our collective condition will continue to suffer and society will continue its freefall into fanaticism, fundamentalism and far right and left extremism. Unless society ceases to create conflict by using language to delude, deceive and destroy communities then the future of the world will cease to exist.

How do we use language and religion to save ourselves, our community and the future of humankind from this colossal wreck? Should we list all the virtues of religion: the seven types of love, happiness, peace, honesty, caring, sharing, freedom, commitment, trust, respect, empathy, patience, wisdom, use of time, discipline, faith, belief and contentment and try to materialise these concepts? Should we replace from spiritual subjugation with spiritual uplift? Should we focus on the language of mental wellbeing rather than mental slavery? Should we commit to a long walk to psychological freedom rather than use language and religion for psychological colonization? The trillion dollar question becomes: if language and religion are so important, so interconnected, so intertwined like fatherland and motherland, like hearts and minds, like rich and poor, good and evil is it possible that both originated and evolve together and that and future to believe in must involve both systems?

Chapter 99

LANGUAGE AND THE BLACK BOX

The Brain- Television-The Media- Politicians –Lawyers –Intelligence services-Educators-History -Love- Hate-Honesty -Peace-Truth-Freedom-Wisdom- Patience-Good-Evil- Patience- Law-War-Ignorance-Fear-Anxiety- Power- Psychology-Rhetoric-Wordplay-Allusion-Parallelism- Political correctness- Persuasive techniques-Mixed metaphor-Ideology—rationality –myth-Truth

The mind is a sophisticated recording storage device and its full programming capacity remains a mystery to all in the field cognition: neuroscientists, psycholinguists, psychotherapists, psychiatrists, linguistics and social psychologists. The power of the mind over the body is clearly demonstrated in all cultures from birth as whatever is planted in the subconscious mind, and nourished with repetition and emotion will one day become reality. The beliefs about power, the beliefs about fear of other people that have been sown by traditional western cultural thinkers are now being reaped in abundance. Through the use of the traditional black box of television, the psyche of the western cultural thinker has been misled, misguided and manipulated to believe that the world is indeed The Truman Show and that truth is one-dimensional. This thinking has had a profound impact on the black box of individuals and major cultures who have embraced western influences. However, with the emergence of social media, the traditional executive, instrumental and influential power brokers are now faced with a plethora of problems all interconnected, interrelated and intertwined with the problems created by different power sources. Different kinds of knowledge now cultivates different kinds of power with social media being instrumental in globalising different perspectives on learning, intelligence and understanding one's own thoughts, one's own purposes and one's own inner conflict. The astronomical problem for the traditional power brokers is a loss of power, a loss of control and a loss of the bastion of language that enables western cultural success through communication.

This dystopia was predicted in 1984 by George Orwell as he, like Winston was tortured by guilt. The knowledge that the English language is the torture system of communication in a dystopian world which has manipulated the truth about history, about science and about the real big brother to create this Truman Show shows the enormous power of the human mind, the black box. The curious paradox for the western cultural thinker is that Trump disrupts the Truman Show by disrupting this Tower of Babel in Big Brotherland; even more curious is that Brexit happens at the same time in the Motherland. Corbyn clutches the conch of democracy, like Piggy in Lord of the Flies, while Jack's union of hunters are having all the fun. Surely Shakespeare will love to write this play for Lady M who looks like an innocent flower but the audience knows that being a serpent means being a serpent. The big problem for the western cultural thinkers then becomes one of reality creation: If war is no longer perceived as peace, if freedom is no longer slavery, if ignorance is no longer strength, how can reality by formed using the traditional method? If the eyes are no longer made a fool of the other senses, what next? Do western cultural thinkers trade in the Orwellian stage for a Shakespearian one?

Black cultural perspective

Did you realise that the English language use of the `black box` is the only intrinsically positive and valuable item described using the word `black`? The black box for us represents the brain of all humanity with enormous strength that lies in its ability to fuse knowledge of spirituality, rationality and intuition to achieve peace and reconciliation against all odds. Our people were physically enslaved, raped, oppressed, colonised, falsely accused, culturally indoctrinated, ridiculed, divided, disconnected, degraded, devalued but yet we rise. The power of our mind is enormous but we must engage on an intellectual adventure to understand its power. There must be something about the black box of first world people that points to the first cause and first reasons for existence. Why were humankind created? If Africans were created the first world or the metaphysical world, then the Middle East created the second world, the spiritual world, and finally Europe created the third world, the material world. The divine truth about what Plato represents then becomes clearer: he divided the world, using abstract thinking into extremes for the purpose of hierarchy not taxonomy: black and white, good and evil, rich and poor, male and female, old and young, scientific knowledge and religious knowledge.

Through clever use of the language of split narratives, Plato has managed to mislead, manipulate and control the world of humankind. Like Eve in the Garden of Eden, we have been tempted and deceived by what we see or rather perceive through cultural indoctrination from slavery to colonisation in this material world that Plato has created. The use of Platonic language has paralysed our thinking and our collective consciousness so much so that we see ourselves negatively by perceiving false essences, false values and false spirits.

Our black box has been damaged and we have lost our knowledge of our true history, our true ancestral interconnectedness and ourselves. We confuse the love for each other with hate because our brains have been programed to hate. We disrespect, devalue and degrade our cultural dignity and language because we don't fully understand our true essence. We have been systematically programmed with negativity about our collective culture and we must now be prepared for a long, long walk to real freedom of mind.

The big questions become: where do we begin to heal the damage done to our collective psyche? How do we begin to address the gulf between the thinking that conceives appearances as reality? How do we conceive rationally without implying the existence of the language that dictates our thoughts? How do we fully understand the black box (human mind) in this context when language and thinking are so closely related? Do we need an entirely different system of language teaching or a separate black language and literature course on the mainstream curriculum? Do we need to change our thinking about life and what we should really value by returning to Africa intellectually? Do we reject the value system of the material world and try to rebuild the first world language ideology? Do we insist on looking at our individual self, our society and Africa through different lens? How do we prioritise education for elevation to show the strength, resilience and mystery of the human mind and its power over the body? Does our collective black box need a thorough spiritual cleansing of this evil of appearance over our African ancestral reality?

Chapter 100

LANGUAGE AND LOCATION

Social location-Educational location-Sequential location -Physical location- Geographical location-Spiritual location- Political location-Philosophical location- Class location –Historical location – insiders -outsiders

Location is often seen as geographical but in this context it refers to what influences one's language learning journey from conception to the grave; their current sense of place, positioning, perspective and point of view on language and its importance as a vehicle on this journey through life. At conception, DNA provides the blueprint, then after birth, the social (familial), cultural, and geographical location begin to shape the child's development. Educational location then determines the child's spiritual, political and class journey. Parenting provides the satellite navigation system to direct the child to make decisions and rerouting or shifting geographical locations can affect the child's historical, sequential and cultural direction to his or her final destination. If decisions are made during the crucial years for language acquisition, then the child may become bilingual and the second language or second culture may interfere with the first language or mother tongue or mother culture. Time matters. History matters. Language acquisition periods matter. These are the matters that pose problems for the western cultural thinker who tends to encourage multiple relocations for social mobility.

Social mobility tends to be a term used euphemistically refers to place and positioning within a place but it can also imply navigation through the system within a place as an insider or as an outsider. In terms of language, insiders would refer to those who have a cultural heritage advantage as the mother tongue users and those who are second language users, as outsiders. In this context, language acquisition and use would imply that outsiders perceive language from a different perspective and therefore could be more critical of their second language. For the western cultural thinker, this poses a problem of being restricted in their ability to see things from a different perspective to their own. Evidence of this can be found if one researches the number of western cultural thinkers who speak a foreign (non-western) language. This cultivates the incapacity to see the world through the eyes of people from different cultures with different perspectives and with different forms of rationality, intelligence and philosophy. Essentially, this has far-reaching implications for integration, class stratification and gender equality. If the mind is not programmed to think that different languages, different cultures and different people exist, then true equality, true integration or true morality can never be clearly and distinctly perceived in the western cultural mind. If the mind cannot see (perceive) the gender unfairness endemic within the patriarchal capitalist system, if the mind cannot see that the system was designed to exclude rather than include outsiders, then such a mind has been severely injured, brain damaged or fatally wounded.

The big questions then become: how can the western cultural thinker find the motivation, the belief and the strength to learn different languages, different cultures, different rationalities and an entirely different ideology? Does the western cultural thinker need to work with different intelligence services of global majority cultures to devise the universal language of truth?

Black cultural perspective

Our culture, our people and our languages have been dismantled, dispersed and disconnected from the motherland so much so that Africa and the African diaspora is fragmented on every level. An honest historical perspective would show that this fragmentation was not by accident but by design to blueprint the success of western culture. Slavery and colonisation served to show the colossal misunderstanding of the use of multiple languages being spoken in our motherland. Multiple languages simply implies multiple ways of representing the same proposition of truth and this highlights our ideological obsession with unity, interconnectedness and truthfulness. Our first world cultural thinkers valued life, valued love and valued learning but the third world of materialism denies us access to our values. Through clever manipulation of language and instrumental power agents, the third world thinkers have managed to control the minds of many first and second world people but still we rise from the bitter, twisted lies. Like moons and like suns we show that genuine love can happen between feuding families, feuding nations and feuding worlds.

We have always worn our hearts on our sleeves and our music has always been the food of love. We have always consulted with spirits and many of us still question if those spirits can speak truth. We believe that the world is one stage and all men and all women are simply players and their rites of passage are the seven ages of man. We believe that history, tragedy and comedy are interwoven to create the majestic tapestry of life. We believe that our daily conscience battles are soliloquies that are misconstrued as mental ill health when all we are trying to do is decide to be good or not to be good, to fight the system or not to fight the system, to be strong or not to be. We believe that justice will always be served to those who play most foully for their success or for those who have our blood on their hands. We believe that we will always get our pound of flesh but we will never spill an ounce of human blood in order to get it. We believe that all our men in power in the African diaspora will have an experience like that of Othello and in the end show that we share affinity with those in Aleppo. We believe in divine retribution that will murder the sleep of those who murder others to maintain power. Above all, we believe that those who steal our purse steal trash but those who steal our reputation as a people who are now entering second childhood of learning truth about our history, truth about our culture and truth about our contribution to the world as the creators of first principles, first purposes and the first world.

The colossal questions then become: how do we change the ideology of those whose language gives them the power to create false perceptions? How do we help to liberate the language of the spirit, the language of the heart, our mother tongue? How do we prepare our people for this long, long walk to freedom for minds that have been tortured, brutalised and damaged in mental slavery and colonisation? How do we begin to rise from location to location in our communities, in our nations and in our own minds to support each other as we rise and move on from civil rights to civil heights, from protest to progress; from teaching to transmit knowledge to teaching to transform it and most crucially from valuing materialism to valuing morality?